CHAPTER OF GOVERNESSES

CHAPTER OF GOVERNESSES

A Study of the Governess in English Fiction 1800-1949

by

KATHARINE WEST

COHEN & WEST LTD
109 GREAT RUSSELL STREET, LONDON, W.C.1

FIRST PUBLISHED IN 1949

PRINTED IN GREAT BRITAIN AT
THE UNIVERSITY PRESS
ABERDEEN

TO

FLORENCE HOMER MOLE

(' MOLEY ')

A REAL-LIFE GOVERNESS

PREFACE

In *What Maisie Knew* Henry James says of his young heroine that she 'vaguely knew, somehow, that the future was still bigger than she, and that a part of what made it so was the number of governesses lurking in it and ready to dart out'. If for 'future' we substitute 'English fiction', Maisie's awestruck apprehension may be taken as aptly expressing my own feelings during the writing of this book. Governesses kept jumping out from unexpected novels, and I was forever rearranging my material to fit them in. And I had to make strong barricades round my subject to prevent irruption from certain demarcated areas.

In the first place, I excluded all true stories told as fiction, though by so doing I cut out Miss Rachel Field's *All This and Heaven Too*. Next I drew the line at costume pieces, except stories set in the period of their author's childhood and a few Victorian classics. This ruling unfortunately excluded Miss H. W. Chapman's *I Will be Good* and Mr. Patrick Hamilton's play, *The Governess,* which would have provided our only example of a governess who was criminally insane.

Yet such restrictions were very necessary. Even within my given period of 1800 to 1949 I had more than I could comfortably cope with. I was always having my attention drawn by memory, desultory reading or conversation, to governesses tucked away in unlikely corners. And sometimes a hunted governess would, fox-like, put up another who was lying low in covert.

Not, of course, that I make any claim to be exhaustive. Readers may have the satisfaction of finding me guilty of leaving out their favourite governesses. If I cannot disarm such criticism I can at least blunt its weapon's edge by disclaiming any pretence to have read every novel written since 1800. I am a slow reader and a forgetful one. Moreover, I have other things to do besides reading, and other books to read besides those suspected of harbouring governesses. I have only tried to make my survey representative and fair.

Before I let the reader loose in my portrait-gallery of governesses, I must meet in anticipation yet another criticism. All the time I was writing I had to ask myself how much knowledge the author of such a book as mine could assume his readers to possess. How allusive could I be? How much must I explain? The erudite reader welcomes allusiveness, since every allusion taken is a feather in his erudition's cap. On the other hand, someone less well read or more forgetful is merely irritated by references to unknown people and events. Worse than this, readers are selective. The Brontë addict, perhaps, never reads Dickens; the Compton-Burnett fan knows nothing of Angela Thirkell.

On the horns of this dilemma my guiding principle has been that anyone who reads no novels is unlikely even to begin my book; whereas those who (like myself) easily forget names and plots but remember atmosphere, will on the whole be flattered if I expect too much of them. I have therefore taken for granted that most people will (for instance) remember vaguely what Becky Sharp was like, even though the Crawley family-tree escapes their memory. While with a governess who plays a small part in a big book —like Ruth Pinch in *Martin Chuzzlewit*—it has sufficed to explain her tiny setting and ignore the rest. With more obscure and forgotten books, however, such as *The Good French Governess*, *The Governess* by Lady Blessington, *Amy Herbert* and *The Daisy Chain*, I have had to assume ignorance, and give an outline of the story. With the occasional odd result that the better a book is known, the less there is about it in my *Chapter of Governesses*.

I took my title out of the mouth of Miss Blanche Ingram

in *Jane Eyre,* who started the subject at Mr. Rochester's house-party. Before any reader goes further, let him be warned by the speed with which Miss Ingram tired of the topic. For just as the other guests were warming up to it she said, 'curling her lips sarcastically'—'I suppose now we shall have an abstract of all the governesses extant.' And so shall *we,* of all the governesses who have darted out on me from English fiction.

For their kindness in allowing me to quote from copyright works I tender my sincere thanks to the following: The Bodley Head Ltd., for quotations from *The Golden Age* by Kenneth Grahame, *The Complete Short Stories of Saki,* Stephen Leacock's *Nonsense Novels,* and Sir Max Beerbohm's *Works and More*; Jonathan Cape Ltd., for quotations from *No Promise in Summer* by Elizabeth Evelyn, *Mistress Masham's Repose* by T. H. White, and *The Way of All Flesh* by Samuel Butler; Chatto & Windus, for quotations from *The Governess* by Mrs. Alfred Hunt and Violet Hunt; William Collins, Sons & Co. Ltd., for quotations from *The Ballad and the Source* by Rosamond Lehmann, *Full House* by M. J. Farrell, and *The Wheel Spins* by Ethel Lina White; Constable & Co. Ltd. and the Hon. Harold Nicolson, for quotations from *Some People*: Peter Davies Ltd., for quotations from two novels by Elizabeth Taylor, *Palladian* and *A Wreath of Roses*; J. M. Dent & Sons Ltd., for quotations from Joseph Conrad's *Chance*; Gerald Duckworth & Co. Ltd., for quotations from Maurice Baring's *Lost Diaries*; John Farquharson on behalf of the Literary Executors of Henry James, for quotations from *The Turn of the Screw* and *What Maisie Knew*; Victor Gollancz Ltd., for quotations from two novels by I. Compton-Burnett, *Elders and Betters* and *Daughters and Sons*; Hamish Hamilton Ltd., for quotations from *Miss Bunting* by Angela Thirkell; Hodder & Stoughton Ltd., for quotations from F. Anstey's play *The Man from Blankley's*;

The Hogarth Press, for quotations from *The Edwardians* by V. Sackville-West; Hutchinson & Co. (Publishers) Ltd., for quotations from *Children, My Children!* by Peter de Polnay; Macmillan & Co. Ltd. and the Executors of Miss E. M. Delafield, for quotations from *The Diary of a Provincial Lady*; Macmillan & Co. Ltd. and the Executors of Sir Hugh Walpole, for quotations from *Jeremy*; and John Murray, for allowing me to quote from Sir Arthur Conan Doyle's novel *The Sign of Four* and his short story *The Copper Beeches*.

K. W.

CONTENTS

PAGE

I. Early Nineteenth Century 13

Introductory — Maria Edgeworth: *The Good French Governess, Practical Education* — Jane Austen: *Pride and Prejudice, Mansfield Park, Emma*—Mrs. Craik: *John Halifax, Gentleman*—Lady Blessington: *The Governess.*

II. Early Victorian 54

Elizabeth Sewell: *Amy Herbert*—Charles Dickens: *Martin Chuzzlewit*—W. M. Thackeray: *The Book of Snobs, Vanity Fair*—The Brontës and Governesses — Anne Brontë: *Agnes Grey* — Charlotte Brontë: *Jane Eyre.*

III. Mid-Victorian 87

W. M. Thackeray: *The Newcomes* — Charles Dickens: *Little Dorrit*—Charlotte M. Yonge: *The Daisy Chain, Womankind* — Mrs. Henry Wood: *East Lynne*—Wilkie Collins: *No Name*—Sheridan le Fanu: *Uncle Silas*—Mrs. Gaskell: *Wives and Daughters*—Jean Ingelow: *Dr. Deane's Governess*—George Eliot: *Scenes of Clerical Life, Middlemarch* — Schools versus Governesses — Anthony Trollope: *The Eustace Diamonds, Barchester Towers.*

IV. Late Victorian 148

Samuel Butler: *The Way of All Flesh*—Mrs. Alfred Hunt and Violet Hunt: *The Governess*—Sir Arthur Conan Doyle: *The Sign of Four, The Copper Beeches*—Joseph Conrad: *Chance*—Kenneth Grahame: *The Golden Age*—Hugh Walpole: *Jeremy*—Harold Nicolson: *Some People*—Henry

PAGE

James: *The Turn of the Screw, What Maisie Knew*—F. Anstey: *The Man from Blankley's.*

V. Edwardian 194

The Edwardian Age—V. Sackville-West: *The Edwardians*—Rosamond Lehmann: *The Ballad and the Source*—Elizabeth Evelyn: *No Promise in Summer*—Marion Crawford: *The Undesirable Governess*—Saki: *The Schartz-Metterclume Method*—Schools versus Governesses Again.

VI. The First World War 215

Peter de Polnay: *Children, My Children!*

VII. Between the Wars 218

E. M. Delafield: *The Diary of a Provincial Lady*—M. J. Farrell: *Full House*—Ethel Lina White: *The Wheel Spins.*

VIII. The Second World War 232

Angela Thirkell: *Miss Bunting.*

IX. Post-War 236

Post-War Speculations—Elizabeth Taylor: *Palladian, A Wreath of Roses*—I. Compton-Burnett: *Elders and Betters, Daughters and Sons.*

X. The Grotesques 251

Maurice Baring: *An English Governess in the French Revolution*—Stephen Leacock: *Gertrude the Governess*—Oscar Wilde: *The Importance of Being Earnest*—T. H. White: *Mistress Masham's Repose*—W. M. Thackeray: *The Rose and the Ring*—Charles Kingsley: *The Water Babies*—Lewis Carroll: *Through the Looking-Glass.*

CHAPTER I

EARLY NINETEENTH CENTURY

Introductory ; Maria Edgeworth, *The Good French Governess, Practical Education* ; Jane Austen, *Pride and Prejudice, Mansfield Park, Emma* ; Mrs. Craik, *John Halifax, Gentleman* ; Lady Blessington, *The Governess.*

MR. G. M. YOUNG, in his brilliant *Portrait of an Age,* has written slightingly of the nineteenth-century governess, as displayed in the novels of that period. 'The figure of the governess', he maintains, 'snubbed, bullied, loving and usually quite incompetent, is a stand-by of Victorian pathos. Lady Blessington first introduced it into literature, it reached its apotheosis in *East Lynne.*'

For once, Mr. Young's exhaustive erudition has failed him: he has allowed himself to jump to a conclusion without careful examination of his take-off. The downtrodden type of governess undoubtedly existed. But she was probably introduced into English nineteenth-century literature by Jane Austen in the much-canvassed case of Jane Fairfax; she was only one type among many; and she reached her apotheosis in *The Man from Blankley's,* and not in East Lynne, a house where (as we shall see) 'the governesses were regarded as gentlewomen'.

Although the downtrodden governess certainly existed both in fictional fact and in her own imagination, and indeed predominates in the examples which we shall presently review, she represents only one type among many. These we shall classify roughly under six heads, namely: *The Downtrodden,* the *Valued Friend,* the *Strict Instructress* (or *Dragon*), the *Self-Seeking Adventuress* (had Mr. Young forgotten Becky Sharp?), the *Villainess,* and the *Snob-Exhibit.* All these categories are amply illustrated in a number of books ranging chronologically from Maria Edgeworth to Henry James—and beyond him into the Atomic Age. Their stories often provide entertaining reading in themselves; and many of these governesses play important—indeed leading—parts in their employers' lives. Even when they are mere supers, a study of them throws an interesting light on social history.

Who were these women? What can we discover about their *venue,* their training, and their economic and social status? In other words, who were their parents, and what sort of schools turned them out, and to fit what standards of attainment? What salaries did they ask—and get? How much holiday were they allowed, and what (in the absence of National Insurance) became of them when they retired? How did they make contact with employers, and what references were required on either side? What rooms were allotted to them, and what clothes were considered seemly for them to wear? If we can discover when and with whom they ate; what were their relations with employers, pupils and domestic staff; and what position they occupied in the household, then we shall know a little more about the manners and customs of nineteenth-century society.

Before embarking on the nineteenth century proper, we must remember that when Miss Austen wrote the governess was already an established institution. She must, therefore, have been a commonplace in the eighteenth century. So, although I do not propose to ransack Georgian literature for examples, I cannot resist starting my study with Maria Edgeworth's story of *The Good French Governess.* Indeed, it really comes within our period, for though it is set in the seventeen-nineties, the volume of *Moral Tales* that includes it was not published until 1801.

Few of the social problems which loom so large in later stories of a governess's life arise in the case of Madame de Rosier. She is neither oppressor nor oppressed, exploited nor exploiter. Yet although her case is simple in this respect and her story is a short one, there is a great deal of interest to be said about her. For Maria Edgeworth was an educationist; and Madame de Rosier is less a woman than an embodiment of her creator's theory of Practical Education. This theory, derived by Richard Lovell Edgeworth from Rousseau, and applied by him with modifications and varying success to his twenty-odd children, was adopted enthusiastically by Maria, his eldest and most devoted child.

Not only did she collaborate with her father in a book called *Practical Education,* but all her stories and novels except *Castle Rackrent* were tracts designed to make it known and help parents to put it into effect. *Rosamund* and *Harry and Lucy* were written to be read aloud in the nursery; *The Parent's Assistant* (despite its repellent title) was deservedly beloved in generations of schoolrooms, while the *Moral Tales* were aimed at what we now call the teen-age group. In all of them children are stimulated to self-help, self-command and self-education; but in none, perhaps, are the principles so explicitly exemplified as in *The Good French Governess.* It was written for girls, but for girls who before long would have children of their own to rear; and it set before them all the advantages of employing a perfect governess.

Madame de Rosier was 'a lady of good family, excellent understanding and most amiable character', whose husband, son and property had all been engulfed in the French Revolution. She herself took refuge in London, where she had many friends. Too proud to accept charity, she 'easily secured recommendations as a preceptress', and obtained a situation with Mrs. Harcourt, a widow with four children. Though a fine lady, Mrs. Harcourt took an evening off from her social duties in order to introduce the new governess to her children, as 'a friend in whom she had entire confidence'. Except for religious instruction (Madame de Rosier was naturally a Papist), Mrs. Harcourt 'invested Madame de Rosier with full powers'. Most Victorian governesses would have welcomed the security and authority implied in such a *carte blanche*. Madame de Rosier, however, secretly deplored it as evidence of her employer's irresponsibility, while taking advantage of it for her pupils' sake.

These pupils were three girls and a boy. Isabella, aged fourteen, had a good memory. This she had been encouraged to use for the acquisition of information, which she paraded in society until she was regarded as a prodigy. Matilda, a year younger, could not compete with her sister in memorising; she had therefore been contrasted with her unfavourably, had become despairing and indolent, and had taken refuge in vanity. Herbert, aged eight, had been taught his letters by his mother's maid, and was a boorish little savage merely because he was always treated as one. Favoretta, the baby, was shown off at her mother's parties and pampered by everyone in the house. All four, it must be observed, had been spoiled by unwise treatment; all were good at heart and sound in brain. For it was one of Richard Lovell Edgeworth's tenets that nurture was all and nature nothing. All four, in their different misguided ways, were admirable material for Madame de Rosier's educational magic.

She began by trying to disencumber Isabella of her useless knowledge, and teaching her that facts are only useful as pabulum for reason. She even went so far (against Mr. Edgeworth's general principles) as to cultivate her imagination with selected passages from the poets. In Matilda she discovered a gift for mathematics, while assuring her that by exertion she could become anything she pleased. She made Herbert feel that reading was a tool rather than a task, and lured Favoretta gradually from the influence of the lady's maid.

I have said that Madame de Rosier worked magic. Like

other magicians she worked her spells through ritual paraphernalia. Although a foreigner, she had access to a fascinating institution called the Repository for Rational Toys, whose contents were based on the principle that ' children dislike useless, motionless playthings '. Thither she drove with her charges in the carriage. And there Isabella chose a silk balloon on which to draw a map of the world; Matilda, a loom and a perspective machine; Favoretta, a basket-weaving outfit; and Herbert, a dry printing-press and a packet of radish seed. Not that Madame de Rosier wished ' to purchase the love of her little pupils by presents; her object was to provide them with independent occupations; to create a taste for industry, without the dangerous excitation of continual variety '.

Henceforth, ' by interesting herself with unaffected good-nature in their amusements, she endeavoured to give them a taste for the sympathy of their superiors in knowledge '. (This is a hit at the servants' hall, the pantry and the stables, whose inmates Miss Edgeworth always regarded with vigilant distrust.) ' Children will necessarily delight in the company of those who make them happy. Madame de Rosier knew how to make her pupils contented by exciting them to employments in which they felt they were successful. She now and then suffered them to experience the misery of having nothing to do.'

It is all very well for us to laugh at the Edgeworths, to deplore their Utilitarianism and compare them with Mr. Gradgrind. But there is a great deal of truth in what they taught. They may have exalted usefulness at the expense of imagination, and sacrificed the play of the spirit to the work of the hands; yet they did treat children as reasonable human beings rather than dangerous animals. And as we go on into the nineteenth century, we may well wish that more mothers and more governesses had been brought up on their teaching. We shall find no other governess, for instance, taking a little boy to visit a carpenter, a coach-maker, a cooper, a turner, a cabinet-maker and a tinman's shop, as Madame de Rosier took the ecstatic Herbert as soon as he had learned not to meddle. For she held the sound belief that ' shop ' talked by an expert is the best of talk, and that workmen are the best practical educationists.

Madame was so successful in winning the children's hearts and their mother's confidence that she excited the jealousy of Mrs. Harcourt's maid. Such jealousy is a common source of discomfort and friction in Victorian households. As we shall see, many a maid, nurse or house-keeper rightly or wrongly resented the influence of the governess; and Mrs. Grace—in her admirable, racy idiom—foreshadowed all their arguments.

' I don't pretend to be a French governess, for my part ', she protested as she combed Herbert's hair; ' but I can read English as well as another; and it's strange if I could not teach my mother tongue better than an emigrant. She never takes much pains. Easy earning money for governesses nowadays. No tasks!—no, not she! Nothing all day long but play—play—play, and going to see all the shops and sights, and going out in the coach to bring home radishes and tongue-grass, to be sure—and everything in the house to be as she pleases, to be sure. I am sure my mistress is too good to her, only because she was born a lady, they say.' But Herbert stuck up for his new governess and her new system of education: ' She is my friend—and she taught me to read without bouncing me about, and shaking me, and Master Herbert*ing* me for ever.'

Mrs. Grace was seriously determined to oust her rival, either by making Mrs. Harcourt jealous of the children's love (in which she nearly succeeded), or else (in the last resort) by blackmail. For she knew the secrets of her mistress's toilet. ' We have a new French governess and new measures ', she confided to a crony. ' She is quite like my mistress. But no one can bear two mistresses. A lady who have never made a *rout* about governesses and *edication,* till lately, and now, perhaps, only for fashion's sake, would rather part with a French governess, when they are so many, than with a favourite maid who knows her ways.'

But Madame de Rosier dispelled Mrs. Harcourt's jealousy, and even beguiled her into spending more time with her children—and enjoying it. When it came to a show-down with the maid, Mrs. Harcourt said to Madame de Rosier 'with an expression of real kindness mixed with her habitual politeness: "In the slightest trifles, as well as in matters of consequence, I leave everything implicitly to your better judgment."' Turning to Mrs. Grace, she added severely: 'Madame de Rosier and I are always of one mind about the children; her orders are to be obeyed.' Mrs. Grace retreated for the time being with a flea in her ear: 'Madame de Rosier has bewitched 'em all; I think it's odd one can't find out her art.'

Madame de Rosier was treated by the Harcourts and their friends as a social equal to an extent never approached in any of our later examples. For instance, when the girls were given tickets for a very exclusive French reading party, Matilda gave hers to Madame, as 'she confines herself so much with us'. And on one occasion Madame was asked to go to a dinner in Mrs. Harcourt's place 'where she knew her company would be particularly acceptable'. This is something very different from going to the drawing-room to play country-dances, or making the fourteenth at a family party.

On the night in question, Mrs. Harcourt spent the evening quietly at home with the children and learned the truth that 'they who have only seen children in picturesque situations are not aware how much the endurance of this domestic happiness depends upon those who have the care of them'. She found some hours alone with her offspring still too great a trial, even after Madame de Rosier's reformation of the children and herself; and before the evening was over she carried off the two older girls to the opera. Favoretta, sent to bed, fell for the last time into Mrs. Grace's clutches, and met with an adventure which resulted in the unmasking and dismissal of that deceitful servant. At the same time any traces of jealousy lingering in the mother's mind were finally dispelled. 'Your children', Madame assured her, 'always show you affection by their own desire, never by mine: your penetration would certainly discover the difference between attentions prompted by a governess, and those which are shown by artless affection.' 'My dear Madame', replied Mrs. Harcourt, 'you are a real friend.'

Among the devices assiduously practised by Maria Edgeworth in the inculcation of right principles was that of contrast. In her stories the whiteness of good is intensified by the blackness of bad; the industrious apprentice outstrips the idle; a hoed garden produces more radishes than a neglected one. So, in this story, the products of rational education are contrasted with a Miss Fanshawe, the product of a fashionable, expensive school. Miss Fanshawe's mother, who 'treated the improvements of modern female education as dangerous innovations', had sent her to a school where she learned to behave like a Dutch doll in company and a vulgar rattle in private. The outcome of the comparison is, of course, entirely in favour of Isabella and Matilda, who talk with equal good sense before their elders and among themselves. Miss Fanshawe's girlish confidences when she gets them to herself are interesting as a comment on the schooling of the time; and she talks with a silliness indistinguishable from that of the younger Bennet girls in *Pride and Prejudice*.

'That's the best of going to school', she observes: 'It's over some time or other, and there's an end of it; but you that have a governess and masters at home, you go on for ever and ever, and have no holidays, either: and you have no out-of-school hours; you are kept *hard at it* from morning till night; now I should hate that of all things.' But to Isabella and Matilda, we need hardly say, 'it did not appear the most delightful of all things in the world to have their education finished'.

We need not follow the rather creaking machinery of Madame's discovery of her son—alive, and supporting himself in Soho. We may, however, observe in passing that he would never have been found had he not (like so many of Miss Edgeworth's young heroes) combined ingenuity with industry, and constructed a new line in netting-boxes. We cannot help feeling, moreover, that even then his mother would never have clasped him to her bosom had she been a Bad rather than a Good French Governess.

After he had told her the story of his escape to England and introduced her to his humble friends, Madame de Rosier said: 'I will introduce you to *my* friends tomorrow. *My* friends, I say proudly, for I have made friends since I came to England; and England, among other commodities excellent of their kind, produces incomparable friends.' It is clear from this that it was as a foreigner and not as a governess that Madame de Rosier considered herself well treated by the Harcourts. *Émigrées,* she thought, might be cold-shouldered by the pusillanimous. But that a lady should not be treated as such, merely because she was so poor that she was reduced to teaching—that had evidently not entered her head.

Back with the Harcourts she was wrapped round with loving consideration. 'Isabella brought her an excellent cup of coffee' (Was the making of this, part of a French governess's curriculum?). 'Mrs. Harcourt, with kind reproaches, asked why she had not brought her son *home* with her.' The carriage was forthwith sent to fetch him; and when he arrived 'the sympathy of all her joyful pupils, the animated kindness with which Mrs. Harcourt received her son, touched Madame de Rosier with the most exquisite pleasure. Mrs. Harcourt did not confine her attentions within the narrow limits of politeness—with generous eagerness she exerted herself to show her gratitude to the excellent governess of her children.'

Her exertions resulted in the discovery that the de Rosiers' sequestered property had been restored to them. So Madame had to return to her own land, leaving Mrs. Harcourt to carry on her ' plan of education '. And by now she could feel that her good work would not be wasted. 'A sensible mother, in whom the desire to educate her family has once been excited, and who turns the energy of her mind to this interesting subject, seizes upon every useful idea, every practical principle, with avidity, and she may trust securely to her own persevering cares. Whatever a mother learns for the sake of her children, she never forgets.'

The Good French Governess is only a short story, and a forgotten one at that. But it is one of the few tales that we have to consider in which a governess as such is the main character. Becky Sharp and Jane Eyre were governesses, but they were a great deal more. Above all, they were women; and their ' governess ' interest is merely incidental. Moreover, *The Good French Governess* is of especial interest as being the only study of a governess considered primarily as a teacher. Other governesses, as we shall see, made great play with their accomplishments and curricula; but few are seriously criticised for their educational methods.

It should be noted that Madame de Rosier's advanced ideas are not regarded as unique. Mrs. Harcourt says to her girls: ' My dears, you will all of you be much superior to your mother—but girls were educated, in my days, quite in a different style from what they are now.' While Mrs. Fanshawe—who is depicted as a lover of the old order in everything—is laughed at for regarding ' the improvements in modern female education ' as ' dangerous innovations '. Either Miss Edgeworth was using her assumption of this modern education as propaganda, in which case she was merely trying to persuade her fashionable young readers that practical education was the *dernier cri*; or else she was herself genuinely convinced of the existence of a movement for the better (if not higher) education of women. And well she may have been, for she had been brought up in a ferment of educational theory and enthusiasm, generated by her father and his friend, Thomas Day.

The interest from our point of view lies not so much in her making this assumption, as in the subsequent evidence that (throughout the coming century) nobody else took any notice of it whatsoever. Mrs. Harcourt was probably right in thinking that her own generation had been badly taught; she was certainly wrong in believing that the teaching of future generations would be any better. She herself had been at least as well equipped as the average middle-class woman throughout Victoria's reign and even later. We shall find satirists throwing scorn on governesses' pretensions and deriding employers' snobbishness, but we shall hear no more of modern methods. What was good enough for Miss Fanshawe will be good enough for the Bertram girls, for Blanche Ingram, Amelia Sedley, Ethel Newcome, Little Dorrit and the rest. *The Good French Governess* stands, a solitary landmark, in the history of educational theory as displayed by the governesses of English fiction.

Like all Miss Edgeworth's stories, it is the fictional embodiment of a theory. The theory itself is expounded in her *Practical Education*, where she sets out her plan for bettering ' the important office of governess '. In the choice of a governess, she maintained, ' fashionable accomplishments ' should be ' only secondary objects '. The prime considerations should rather be ' a sound, discriminating and enlarged understanding, a mind free from prejudice, steadiness of temperament' and integrity. Once engaged, the governess should be treated as worthy of her trust. Not only should she be shown 'perfect equality and kindness'; but her calling should be honoured as a profession and rewarded as such. Men who educated the future leaders of the country, she pointed out, were often rewarded with fat livings. For a woman engaged on a similar task, a salary of 'three hundred a year for twelve or fourteen years would be a suitable compensation'. It would put her in a position either to 'settle in a family of her own' or to be 'happily independent, secure from the temptation of marrying for money'. Miss Edgeworth hoped that a few influential families might, by adopting such a generous policy, raise to a higher level in every home the already improving status of governesses. She was an optimist, who believed that governesses and their employers were perfectible, along with the rest of mankind.

But although we may see a rise in salaries during the next hundred and fifty years, and find many individual employers who are considerate, we shall never find governesses in fiction treated according to Miss Edgeworth's dreams. She was, as we have seen, far in advance of contemporary thought about women's education; and her standards for women educators were equally doomed to neglect.

Coming now to Jane Austen's novels we abruptly leave Maria Edgeworth's educational enthusiasms behind us. Miss Austen was not concerned with theories. Governesses interested her not educationally but socially. And as we should expect from her delicate sense of social nuances, the position of a governess is regarded by her characters as a ticklish problem.

Of the five Bennet girls in *Pride and Prejudice* we are told specifically that they had no governess. Yet the two elder ones, Jane and Elizabeth, grew up intelligent and well-read under their father's influence. Mary, the third, was a prig who compiled collections of moral extracts and sang so relentlessly at parties that on one occasion she provoked her father into saying: 'That will do extremely well, child. You have delighted us long enough.' Mr. Bennet was an intelligent man; but he valued his own peace and quiet above the welfare of his daughters, unless they promised to be as gentle and sweet as Jane, or as amusing as his favourite, Elizabeth. When he realised that Kitty and Lydia, the two youngest, were shrill, empty-headed baggages, he retired to his study and left them to their mother's tender mercies. As she was a vulgarian who thought only of getting her girls married, it is small wonder that they grew up with no ideas beyond bonnets and bandboxes, balls and their attendant *beaux*. When Lydia finally eloped at the age of sixteen, her parents no doubt wished that she had had a schoolroom and been kept in it.

Long before this disastrous occurrence, Elizabeth Bennet had been warned in no uncertain terms about the dangers attending the lack of a governess. When Elizabeth went to stay with her old friend Charlotte Lucas, who had married the egregious Mr. Collins, she was taken to dine at Rosings with Mr. Collins's patroness, Lady Catherine de Bourgh. The party was received by Lady Catherine, her sickly daughter, and a Mrs. Jenkinson—who had been the young lady's governess and was now kept on to place her footstool and adjust the fire-screen. Lady Catherine was an ill-bred, managing, domineering dowager, whose word was law in her own circle, and who saw no reason why that circle should be small. Elizabeth, now drawn within its circumference, was immediately subjected to examination.

'Has your governess left you?' was among the first questions. 'We never had any governess', replied Elizabeth. 'No governess? How was that possible? Five daughters brought up at home without a governess? I never heard of such a thing. Your mother must have been quite a slave to your education.' Elizabeth, thinking of her mother's crass ignorance, 'could hardly help smiling, as she assured her that had not been the case'. 'Then who taught you?' continued Lady Catherine, 'who attended to you? Without a governess, you must have been neglected.' This time Elizabeth thought of her bookish father and tried to explain that those sisters who wished to learn had been 'encouraged to read, and had all the masters that were necessary'. Thinking of Kitty and Lydia, however, she had to add that 'those who chose to be idle, certainly might'.

'Aye, no doubt,' Lady Catherine pounced triumphantly. 'But that is what a governess will prevent, and if I had known your mother, I should have advised her most strenuously to engage one. It is wonderful how many families I have been the means of supplying in that way. I am always glad to get a young person well placed out. Four nieces of Mrs. Jenkinson are most delightfully situated through my means; and it was but the other day, that I recommended another young person, who was merely accidentally mentioned to me, and the family are quite delighted with her.' Turning to Charlotte, she added with pride: 'Mrs. Collins, did I tell you of Lady Metcalfe's calling yesterday to thank me? She finds Miss Pope a treasure. "Lady Catherine", said she, "you have given me a treasure".'

So imperious were Lady Catherine's demands upon her subjects, so limitless her self-conceit, that sycophantic applause was exacted even for her successes as an agency for governesses. Mrs. Jenkinson cannot have been very happy at Rosings; and I imagine that only advancing years and a broken spirit can have persuaded her to stay there after her pupil had grown up. Perhaps, too, her duty to her nieces kept her faithful to her strategic post.

Although the arrogant Lady Catherine, who professed surprise that Elizabeth's uncle should keep a manservant, was equally surprised at the Bennets' lack of a governess, there is evidence that a governess was considered something of a luxury. Miss de Bourgh had one, though all the best masters had been at her disposal and Mrs. Jenkinson's duties could probably have been equally well performed by a maid; whereas the five Bennet girls, in their humbler home, had been allowed to educate themselves with the aid of such masters as they themselves demanded. Catherine Morland, too, in *Northanger Abbey*—who grew up in the eighteenth century as one of a family of ten—had no governess. She was taught by a master to play the spinet; but 'writing and accounts she was taught by her father' and French by her mother. It was true that Mr. Morland was a clergyman with sons to send to school, who could not be expected to spend much on the education of his daughters. Yet one would have thought that in so large a family a governess at twenty-five or thirty pounds a year would have been a true economy. She could have taught the little boys their three Rs and the 'great girls' their accomplishments; and would have taken so much off Mrs. Morland's busy hands that she would have saved the wages of a maid. With Mrs. Morland, 'a woman of useful plain sense, with a good temper', a governess could have worked well; but I admit that Mrs. Bennet would have been almost impossible with her frivolous ideas and selfish temper.

Mansfield Park is less generally admired than Miss Austen's other books, though to me it is almost the favourite among them all. Little Fanny Price, the heroine, is probably responsible for its relative unpopularity: she lacks Elizabeth Bennet's wit, Emma's spirit, and Anne Elliot's gentle charm. She is, I must admit, rather a colourless little creature. But we must remember the poverty and squalor of her home in

Portsmouth—a home in which a governess would have been unthinkable—from which she was taken by her prosperous relatives, the Bertrams, to live with them at Mansfield Park, and the various new and dominating personalities which there surrounded her. Sir Thomas Bertram was kindly but severe, a heavy father and an alarming uncle. Lady Bertram was a good-natured mollusc, chronically bewildered by the goings-on of her high-spirited children, while to compensate for her inertia there lived next door her widowed sister, Mrs. Norris, who was always at hand to scold and criticise poor Fanny.

There was also a governess, Miss Lee, who is not a sharp-drawn figure. She let herself be put upon not only by Lady Bertram but also by Mrs. Norris, who (when Fanny arrived) assumed that it would be 'just the same to Miss Lee, whether she has three girls to teach, or only two'. Now Mrs. Norris was not only a snob of the deepest dye; she was also so heartless a bully that no social stigma necessarily attached to being badly treated by her. Had Miss Lee stuck up for herself, Sir Thomas at least would have seen fair play. He once insisted that Fanny should have a fire in the schoolroom, and would have done no less for the governess. Indeed, a bullied dependant would have detracted from his own importance as *paterfamilias*.

We must therefore reluctantly assume that Miss Lee was a poor creature with no more enterprise than was needed to wind Lady Bertram's wool, exercise pug, and teach the girls 'the Roman Emperors as low as Severus; besides a great deal of the Heathen Mythology, and all the Metals, Semi-metals, Planets and distinguished Philosophers'. But there is no evidence that she was despised even by the headstrong Bertram girls; and in Fanny Price, the poor relation, she found a useful understudy for the performance of a mass of drudgery.

Some years later Sir Thomas had to visit his estates in the

West Indies, and his children took the opportunity to organise amateur theatricals which they knew he could not approve. Their mother, as usual, was inert; and Mrs. Norris aided and abetted them from a desire to curry favour and an irresistible impulse to organise. Even the virtuous Edmund, Fanny's best loved cousin, took part on the specious pretext that he might keep within bounds the silliness of the rest. Only Fanny stood apart through shyness and an innate sense of what was right. But they needed Fanny to play a part in *Lovers' Vows*; and Mr. Yates, the mainspring of the whole idea, was cited in order to persuade her. He had recently assisted in abortive attempts to produce the play at another house-party; and to prove how 'trivial, paltry, and insignificant' was the rôle of Cottager's Wife, he adduced the fact that 'at Ecclesfield, the governess was to have done it'. From which we may deduce either that the governess at Ecclesfield had been as eager as Fanny to efface herself, or that her employers had wished to keep her in her place. The fact that she was asked at all merely shows that she was expected to take part in the family's festivities without making a fuss, but that this part was to be as small as her part in *Lovers' Vows*.

These governesses in *Mansfield Park* are thumbnail sketches scarcely clear enough to excite our curiosity. In *Emma* Miss Austen has made two portraits in the round, vivid with perspective, shading and colour. Here we find the two categories of Valued Friend and Downtrodden Martyr clearly exemplified in the cases of 'poor Miss Taylor' and Jane Fairfax. Jane never actually became a governess; she was saved from that fate by her marriage to Frank Churchill. But had she ever taken a situation, she would undoubtedly have found in it all the suffering that she anticipated.

As for 'poor Miss Taylor', no one but her employer,

Mr. Woodhouse, could have called her 'poor'. 'Sixteen years had Miss Taylor been in Mr. Woodhouse's family, less as a governess than a friend.' When Emma was a small girl she had been a mother to her, and as the child grew into a woman they had enjoyed 'the intimacy of sisters'. Emma remembered 'how she had taught and how she had played with her from five years old, and how nursed her through the various illnesses of childhood . . . the equal footing and perfect unreserve which had soon followed Isabella's marriage was yet a dearer, tenderer recollection'.

When Miss Taylor married Mr. Woodhouse's neighbour, Mr. Weston, no one but the hypochondriac Mr. Woodhouse pitied her; and he did so only because he thought any change must be for the worse. Moreover, no one thought she had married above her station. Even in the jealously guarded society of Highbury the older inhabitants thought her marriage to a gentleman the most natural thing imaginable. It is clear that a sensible woman, even if she were a governess, could establish herself comfortably without incurring criticism as a schemer.

The only person to question the marriage was a newcomer and an upstart. After Emma's scornful rejection of an offer of marriage from Mr. Elton, the Vicar, he had flung off in a pet to Bristol. And there, on the rebound, he had been caught by a Miss Hawkins who lived with her brother-in-law, Mr. Suckling, in a commodious residence called Maple Grove. Mrs. Elton was affected, pert, familiar and altogether outrageous. She took Highbury under her wing, and tried to teach it the manners of high life as practised at Maple Grove. And as it was difficult to patronise Miss Woodhouse herself, who had spurned Mrs. Elton's *caro sposo,* she did her best to take it out of Miss Woodhouse's sometime governess.

'And *she* appears so truly good', exclaimed Mrs. Elton to Emma, after making the acquaintance of the Westons:

'There is something so motherly and kind-hearted about her. She was your governess, I think. Having understood as much, I was rather astonished to find her so very lady-like. But she is really quite the gentlewoman.' Had Emma not been an arch-snob, all her loyalty would have flared up in defence of her old friend. Instead, she brooded inwardly on Mrs. Elton's slight to her own gentility. It was on behalf of herself rather than Mrs. Weston that Emma's feelings were outraged. 'A little upstart, vulgar being!' she said to herself of Mrs. Elton, after that lady had left the house. 'Astonished that the person who brought me up should be a gentlewoman!' We must love Emma (as Miss Austen did) in spite of her faults; but her taking of Mrs. Elton's slight as an injury to herself puts her for once on the same level of insensitiveness as the Vicar's wife.

Mrs. Elton did her best to proclaim her equality with the Woodhouses and Knightleys, and her superiority to everyone else in Highbury. But it was on pale, reserved Jane Fairfax that she poured all the spiteful vials of her patronage. Jane had recently left the friends who had brought her up as a daughter, and come to stay with Mrs. and Miss Bates (her grandmother and aunt) before setting out to earn her living as a governess. She shivered on the brink of this desperate plunge from day to day, hoping for something to happen which would enable her to marry Frank Churchill, to whom she was secretly engaged. Frank, it will be remembered, was Mr. Weston's son by his first wife. He had been adopted by his rich and tyrannical aunt, Mrs. Churchill, whose name he had taken and on whose whim his future hung. As Jane's prospects were so uncertain, and as a secret engagement was almost as reprehensible as an illicit *affaire*, it is small wonder that she shrank both from intimacies and from decisions.

Mrs. Elton, however, was determined to shake her out of her apathy and fix her in a job. 'You do not know', she cried, 'how many candidates there always are for the *first* situations. A cousin of the Sucklings, Mrs. Bragge, had such an infinity of applications; everybody was anxious to be in her family, for she moves in the first circle. Wax candles in the schoolroom! You may imagine how desirable!'

Hugging her secret, Jane was not to be rushed. She repelled Mrs. Elton's importunity by referring to employment agencies—institutions never again mentioned until we get to Conan Doyle's *The Copper Beeches,* published in 1891. 'There are places in town', Jane says, 'offices, where inquiry would soon produce something—offices for the sale, not quite of human flesh, but of human intellect.' 'Oh, my dear, human flesh! If you mean a fling at the slave trade, I assure you Mr. Suckling was always rather a friend of the abolition!' 'Governess-trade', Jane assured her, 'was all I had in view; widely different, certainly, as to the guilt of those who carry it on; but as to the greater misery of the victims, I do not know where it lies.'

Jane Fairfax had made up her mind that if she must be a governess she would be a miserable one. With her faculty for losing parents, keeping embarrassing aunts, receiving anonymous and expensive presents, exposing herself to unintentional slights and generally manoeuvring herself into false positions, she was indeed the very stuff from which downtrodden governesses are made. She even enjoyed a bilious constitution and had been threatened with a decline. She was sensitive to the point of morbidity and had an artistic temperament; not one essential ingredient was missing. Her artistic gifts, however, were regarded by Mrs. Elton rather as an asset than a handicap. 'Your musical knowledge alone would entitle you to name your own terms, have as many rooms as you like, and mix in the family as much as you chose; that is—I do not know, if you knew the harp, you might do all that, I am very sure; but you sing as well as play—yes, I really believe you might, even without the harp, stipulate for what you chose.'

It sounds as though a governess were sometimes regarded as a sort of *prima donna* on the hearth, and pampered accordingly. Jane, however, did not aspire to luxury. 'It would be no object with me', she protested, 'to be with the rich; my mortification, I think, would only be the greater; I should suffer more from comparison. A gentleman's family is all that I should condition for.' And such a family, as she knew, she would be unlikely to find through the kind offices of Mrs. Elton.

During Mr. Knightley's strawberry party at Donwell Abbey, Mrs. Elton (with her large bonnet and be-ribboned basket) returned to the charge. Emma, sitting indoors, heard her tell Jane that she had heard of another situation. 'It was not with Mrs. Suckling, it was not with Mrs. Bragge, but in felicity and splendour it fell short only of them. . . . Delightful, charming, superior, first circles, spheres, lines, ranks, everything.' Poor Jane, baited beyond endurance, broke away from this rhapsody and hurried home through the midsummer heat. But after the miseries of next day's exploration to Box Hill, when it could only be said that 'Mr. Frank Churchill and Miss Woodhouse flirted together excessively', poor Jane burned her boats and accepted the desirable situation.

'To look at her', her aunt Miss Bates confided to Emma in the course of a morning call, 'nobody would think how delighted and happy she is to have secured such a situation. To a Mrs. Smallridge—charming woman—most superior—to have the charge of her three little girls—delightful children. Impossible that any situation should be more replete with comfort. Jane will be only four miles from Maple Grove. Except the Sucklings and the Bragges, there is not such another nursery establishment, so liberal and elegant, in all Mrs. Elton's acquaintance. Jane will be treated with such regard and kindness! It will be nothing but pleasure, a life of pleasure. And her salary, I really cannot venture to name her salary to you, Miss Woodhouse. Even you, used as you are to great sums, would hardly believe that so much could be given to a young person like Jane.'

At this Emma sympathetically exclaimed: 'Ah, madam, if other children are at all like what I remember to have been myself, I should think five times the amount of what I have ever yet heard named as a salary on such occasions dearly earned.' Mr. Woodhouse's contribution to the discussion was highly characteristic of himself, though not, perhaps, of all employers: 'I hope it is a dry situation, and that her health will be taken good care of. It ought to be a first object, as I am sure poor Miss Taylor's always was with me.'

Miss Austen has confronted us fair and square with the basic factor controlling the relations of a governess with her employers—namely, the amalgam of their various characters. The treatment of a governess depended, in the first place, to a great extent upon her own personality. Jane Fairfax, sensitive, shrinking and reserved, was destined to bring out the worst in parents and children alike, and would have felt humiliated however much she was treated as a member of the family. Miss Taylor, on the other hand, had sufficient character to make herself loved and respected in almost any household. Even if a registry office had sent her to Maple Grove instead of Hartfield, she would surely have contrived either to reform the Sucklings or to find herself a more congenial situation.

The complementary element, however, the employers' character, was even more important in days when it was hard for any wage-earner to pick and choose, to chop and change. Unless a governess was experienced, armed with good references, possessed of some private means or a home to fly to—unless, above all, she was of exceptionally determined character—her employers had it in their power to make her life a hell of petty miseries and humiliations. If they were *nouveaux riches*, purse-proud and pompous, then their governess's refinement put them to shame, and her helplessness provoked their cruelty. Jane Fairfax was certainly wise in requiring gentility rather than wealth in a possible employer; for just as kind hearts are more than coronets, so are they more than wax candles in the schoolroom. Over and over again we shall find that employers are judged, socially as well as morally, by their behaviour to the governess. If this is proud and overbearing, it follows that they must be vulgar. If it is friendly and considerate, they are gentlefolk. And if, as sometimes happens, it is fawning and gushing, they are stamped as snobs who value their governess for her record of employment in houses grander than their own. As no man is a hero to his valet, so no woman is a heroine to her children's governess.

John Halifax, Gentleman, by Mrs. Craik, was a best-seller for many years after its publication in 1857; and the fact that it has recently been reprinted in at least two popular editions of the classics suggests that there is still a demand for it. I believe it has introduced many young people to the greater Victorian novels, but I fail to see what they find in it which is easier to read or more attractive than the stuff from which its betters are composed. It is as sentimental as the worst bits of *The Old Curiosity Shop*, and as informative about machine-wreckers as *Shirley*; yet it lacks Dickens's humour and Charlotte Brontë's dramatic power, and is crammed as full of preaching as a temperance tract.

To us, however, it commends itself by the presence of two governesses. The first of these need not concern us, as she finished her working life before the end of the eighteenth century and the beginning of the book. Even the second was functioning as long ago as 1826, the year of Mrs. Craik's own birth; for *John Halifax, Gentleman* is a costume piece. But as I have exempted a few Victorian classics from my general ban on historical novels, this one may be legitimately included in our survey.

By 1826, John Halifax—sometime orphan and tanner's boy—had become a prosperous and enlightened mill-owner; and had, through integrity and solid worth, established his position as a gentleman. With his wife Ursula, their three sons and a young daughter, he had recently moved into a large house near his Cotswold cloth-mills. There, too, there lived with them John's old friend Phineas Fletcher, whose father had given John his first steady job, and who is the narrator of the story. Maud, the Halifaxes' daughter, was a 'sprightly elf' of about fifteen, and her governess was 'the tall, grave, sad-looking, sad-clothed Miss Silver'. They all treated Miss Silver 'with entire respect', and would gladly have made her altogether one of the family 'had she not been so very reserved'. Ursula Halifax, who had never wished to employ a governess at all, found Miss Silver 'in her extreme and all but repellent quietness' especially difficult to get on with. Ursula was a warm-hearted woman, though occasionally quick tempered and imperious; and she admitted that the governess's 'impassable, self-contained demeanour' sometimes 'fidgeted' her. I sympathise with Mrs. Halifax; I am sure that at this stage I should have longed to shake Miss Silver, just as (in sympathy with Emma) I have always longed to shake Jane Fairfax. But John Halifax understood Miss Silver better. He had discovered her himself and persuaded his wife to engage her; moreover, like most fathers, he did not have the governess so constantly on top of him. 'Poor thing', he said of her one day to Phineas, 'she has evidently not been used to kindness. You should have seen how amazed she looked yesterday when we paid her a little more than her salary, and my wife gave her a pretty silk dress. I sincerely respect her, or of course she would not be here. I think people should be as particular over choosing their daughter's governess, as their son's wife; and having chosen, should show her almost equal honour.'

Like all John Halifax's sentiments, this is unimpeachable. How he would have disapproved of those many casual and arrogant employers with whom we shall become acquainted! But he spoke truer than he knew when he compared the choice of a daughter-in-law with that of a governess. At present, it is true, the boys said that 'she looked thirty at least'; and they laughed 'amazingly at her dowdy dress and her solemn, haughty ways'. Gradually, however, Miss Silver thawed out of her enveloping reserve. During the winter, the Halifaxes had a dance for their young people; and though Miss Silver had 'declined dancing' she appeared to great advantage that evening in her silk gown and chaplet of bay-leaves, and even her walk was 'statelier than usual'. That same day Guy, the eldest son, had strained his foot while skating with Maud and the governess; and during his convalescence Miss Silver 'showed him many little feminine kindnesses'. She was by now 'altogether much improved', and 'always made one of the "young people" who were generally grouped round Guy's sofa. Since she had learned to smile, it became more and more apparent how handsome Miss Silver was. And now that she evidently began to pay a little more attention to her dress and her looks, we found out that she was also young.' No wonder, then, that Guy on his sofa often gazed 'with a curious intentness at the young governess'; or that Edwin, the studious second son, 'persisted in taking Maud, and her governess also, long wintry walks' in order 'to study the cryptogamia'.

On Miss Silver's twenty-fifth birthday she made a

revelation. At Guy's instigation, she was presented with a handsome botany book; and when Guy was about to write her name in it she suddenly burst out at Ursula: 'I will not deceive you any longer. My right name is Louise Eugenie D'Argent.' She had, she confessed, concealed her half-French origin because she had heard of Mrs. Halifax's prejudice against French governesses. She had, moreover, renounced her father's name because it was worse than French. 'You knew him—everybody knew him—he was D'Argent the Jacobin—D'Argent the Bonnet Rouge.' With which defiant words our only governess of Terrorist parentage flung out of the room.

The boys, it appeared, already knew the secret; but little Maud had been listening 'with wide-open eyes' (as well she might) 'to all these revelations about her governess'. As for Mrs. Halifax, she thought it 'a dreadful discovery'; for if Ursula 'had a weak point, it was her prejudice against anything French or Jacobinical'. Imagine, then, her horror when Guy announced that he loved Louise and was determined to propose to her! Imagine—if it be possible—the consternation of the whole family when it was discovered that Louise could not marry Guy because she and his brother Edwin were already passionately in love with one another! 'Both my boys', exclaimed Ursula, 'both my two noble boys! to be made miserable for that girl's sake. Oh! that she had never darkened our doors.' John, though he reproached himself for 'want of parental caution, in throwing the young people continually together', judged more wisely than his wife, who would have forced Louise to marry Guy. He persuaded her that Edwin and Louise must marry, since they loved each other; and that Guy must make the best of a bad job. Guy, unfortunately, did nothing of the sort. He sobbed on his mother's neck, he threatened his brother, he insulted his future sister-in-law, and made his little sister cry; until Mrs. Halifax wisely arranged for Maud and Miss Silver to visit some neighbours until the storm was past. Phineas Fletcher noticed that 'in speaking of or to the girl who in a single day from merely the governess had become, and was sedulously treated as, our own, Mrs. Halifax invariably called her as heretofore "Miss Silver", or "my dear"; never by any chance "Louise" or "Mademoiselle D'Argent"'. For poor Mrs. Halifax now felt 'the mournful want of the natural sympathy due from one woman to another', and kept muttering to herself: 'If only she had made me love her.' But when at last Louise looked at her with swimming eyes and cried: 'Oh, be kind to me! Nobody was ever kind to me till I came here',— then, indeed, 'the good heart gave way; Mrs. Halifax opened her arms.'

The Halifaxes still had trials before them; for Guy, unable to live in the same house as his brother, went abroad and thence (temporarily) to the bad. And it was many years before he returned from America, still poor, but with his virtue re-established. It is good to know, however, that Louise made Edwin an exemplary wife, and thus atoned for all the havoc she had caused in his family. She certainly had need to be a good wife, for as a governess she had been unprecedentedly disconcerting. Not only was she half French, but also half Jacobin; not only did she marry a son of the house, but she made two sons fall in love with her. To deceit about her birth she had added deceit about her youth and beauty; and above all, she had hidden a passionate nature under an impassive, statuesque exterior. She had, in fact, come very near to being a thoroughly Bad French Governess.

There is no doubt at all that Clara Mordaunt, the heroine of Lady Blessington's romance, *The Governess*, (1839) belonged to the downtrodden category, but to the sufferings of a governess were added, in her case, those of a conventionally persecuted heroine. Just as Evelina, in Fanny Burney's novel of that name, was buffeted between the villainous Sir Clement Willoughby and the impeccable Lord Orville, so was Clara forever being compromised by the coarse addresses of a rake and misunderstood by an eligible prig. On both counts, as heroine and governess, she was abnormally oppressed, since rakes are apt to think a governess fair game, while employers consider that she should be above reproach. But while we must feel a double meed of pity for Clara's distress, we are privileged to rejoice doubly at her happy ending. For in the last pages the chrysalis that has languished in dark schoolrooms splits, and reveals a dazzling butterfly; the governess becomes an heiress in her own right and a peeress through her marriage with the prig.

Rather surprisingly, there are superficial resemblances between *The Governess* and the works of Maria Edgeworth. Both authoresses had the same background to their novels—a background which is Regency rather than Early Victorian—and a house in Grosvenor Square, with all its inmates, appears much the same to both. They have, moreover, many small conventions in common. Both are addicted to comic Irishmen, benevolent Quakers, and handsome creoles; both ridicule the fine ladies of their day; and both deplore the influence of ladies' maids on their employers. Above all, both are ardent crusaders on behalf of governesses.

One might imagine them to have been fellow-members of a Society for the Prevention of Cruelty to Governesses. But whereas Maria Edgeworth set forth the positive educational advantages of employing an intelligent woman and treating her as she deserved, Lady Blessington's tract is entirely pathetic in its appeal. Her picture of the abused governess resembles those posters of dogs begging not to be vivisected. This difference is fundamentally due, of course, to a difference of temperament, for Maria Edgeworth was eminently practical, while Lady Blessington was a romantic. Miss Edgeworth wrote about a governess because she really cared about education: Lady Blessington because it was her 'anxious wish to point attention and excite sympathy toward a class from which [more is] expected and to whom less is accorded than any other'. Her publisher, 'thinking only of the sale, bargained for its being interspersed with lively sketches';* and the theme certainly provides full scope for these. Clara Mordaunt was dismissed and engaged again so frequently, that *The Governess* might almost be described as a picaresque novel.

Clara Mordaunt was an orphan. Her father had run through a fortune and committed suicide, leaving her pennilessly dependent on an aunt who had been a mother to her since childhood. The story opens with this aunt, Mrs. Waller, showing Clara an advertisement: 'Wanted, in a highly distinguished family, a person as governess, to undertake the education of three young ladies of nine, seven and five. She must be of prepossessing appearance, of refined manners, and a perfect musician. She is required to instruct her pupils in French, Italian and English; geography and the use of the globes, with music, drawing and dancing; in all which branches of education she is expected to be proficient. Equanimity of temper and cheerfulness of disposition, joined to uninterrupted health, are indispensable requisites. She must understand cutting out and making the children's dresses. Salary 25 guineas a year.'

Leaving out the dressmaking requirements, we are reminded of Lord Melbourne who (asked by a Whig hostess to find her just such a paragon) replied that if he ever found one she would not become the enquirer's governess, but his

* Letter from Lady Blessington to her niece Mrs. Fairly, dated Nov. 5th, 1839, and quoted in Mr. Michael Sadleir's *Blessington-d'Orsay*.

own wife! Clara's Aunt Waller also thought the demands unreasonable: such 'a list of accomplishments, with moral and physical perfection', she declared, had never yet 'fallen to the lot of one human being. And yet for all these, the wages of a lady's maid are offered.' But Clara, who hated to encroach on her aunt's slender means, persuaded her that an interview could do no harm; so off went aunt and niece together to the house of Mrs. Williamson, a typically vulgar and inconsiderate employer.

'I have an objection', she said, 'to my governess receiving her relations or friends. I was bored to death by my last governess's family, who were continually coming to enquire for her; and though I did not permit them to see her, still it was very inconvenient to have those sort of people knocking at the door.' Which showed what sort of person Mrs. Williamson was herself, and appalled Mrs. Waller. However, Mrs. Williamson graciously conceded that Clara might be visited once a month, and Clara (alone with her aunt) insisted on accepting the situation. Mrs. Waller's parting words should have been borne in mind and acted on by many a governess: 'Exact proper conduct', she advised, 'from those around you, and do not submit to ill-treatment.'

The situation was not a happy one. The nursery-room looked out on roofs and was 'scantily and meanly furnished' with maps, an inky table-cloth, and coarse china which (said the maid) the governess was expected to replace if it got broken. Dinner was served anyhow on a tray, and fought over by the spoiled little girls; and Clara had some difficulty in getting fresh water to drink instead of beer. What with quelling the brats, reading aloud to Mrs. Williamson while her hair was brushed, and enduring insolence from the domestic staff, Clara's first day inspired '*ennui* and disgust'. Her 'gentle sway', however, soon produced 'a visible and salutary effect' on her pupils, and her struggle with the servants was brought to an end by the discovery of an old retainer in their midst. This man had worked for Clara's father in his prosperous days, and now told his fellow-servants how *grand* the new governess had once been, and how *good* she still was. Thanks to his good offices, the nursery-room no longer had its meals served hugger-mugger on a tray, but was sent 'a most comfortable dinner, with iced water, napkins and finger-glasses'. After dinner the housekeeper came herself with fruit, and the butler with two kinds of wine, which Clara prudently declined. Betsey, the nurse-maid, was also reconciled to Clara, who bid her 'always remember that a governess has need of all the civility of the domestics, as well as the kindness of her employers, to enable her to fulfil her arduous task'.

After Clara had put the children to bed in the room which she shared with them, she would read a volume of Shakespeare to the accompaniment of their snores—a grievance which the discovery of adenoids has perhaps alleviated for later governesses. She also had to read by a tallow-dip, for there were no wax candles in *this* nursery! Yet all might have gone smoothly, if not well, had not her 'arduous and painful duties' sometimes included taking Miss Williamson to the *salle à manger* for dessert. On these occasions the governess was given a chair at the bottom of the table. Mr. Williamson—the typical hen-pecked husband of a governess-bullying wife—offered her a glass of wine, but he was reproved by his spouse, who looked like a radish in her pink satin gown and *parure* of emeralds. The reproof on the first occasion was due simply to meanness, but later Mrs. Williamson grew jealous of the governess's attractions.

We shall scarcely be surprised at this, if we listen to the conversation of the ladies after dinner. 'What a pretty governess you have got', said Lady Thompson, 'just such a face as one sees a crowd round, at the Exhibition at Somerset House.' To which Lady Hancock added: 'Do you think it quite prudent to have so handsome a person under your roof?' But Lady Thompson knew that it was not so easy to find governesses whom even the husbands of radishes would not admire. 'It is now rather difficult', she complained, 'to find a plain woman, for since vaccination has become so general, one no longer sees a pockmarked woman, except of a certain age.' I had known that pockmarks had once been held desirable in servants as a guarantee that they could no longer catch smallpox and infect the household. But it had never occurred to me that they might also be a safeguard against moral infection!

Lady Thompson added: 'An acquaintance of mine was compelled to prohibit the governess from smiling, because she was always exhibiting her teeth.' After such warnings, it was no wonder if Mrs. Williamson regretted advertising for a person of prepossessing appearance and decided to keep an eye on Mr. Williamson.

Clara's second visit to the dining-room was even more embarrassing. Though she met her fate, in the person of Mr. Clarence Seymour, she was hardly aware of him as yet. On the other hand, she could not but notice the marked and coarse attentions of a young quadroon from the West Indies by the name of Hercules Marsden. Next day she received a note from him, beginning 'My angel', and offering her £500 if she would become his governess! Ostensibly, she was to be companion to his mother, who approached Mrs. Williamson on the matter, but poor Clara knew only too well what the situation would entail. Although a governess's position must have exposed her to such dishonourable proposals, this is the only example we shall meet of their actually being made. Mr. Rochester, it is true, proposed bigamous marriage to Jane Eyre, but Mr. Rochester was a law unto himself. Even Becky Sharp was offered marriage by Sir Pitt Crawley, and actually married his son.

Mrs. Williamson said she would not stand in Clara's way if she wished to go to Mrs. Marsden and, when Clara protested that she had no desire to leave, took the opportunity of delivering a little lecture. 'You are', she pointed out, 'well lodged, well fed, with nothing to think of except teaching the children, and making and mending their clothes; you have a good salary, and what I call an easy life, and yet you talk of arduous duties.'

A few days later the Williamsons moved to their country house, where the Marsdens and Mr. Seymour were to join them on the first day. Poor Clara was to start early by public coach, chaperoned only by Betsey; and no reader of romantic novels will be surprised to hear that Mr. Hercules Marsden forced his company upon her. Fortunately, however, Mr. Seymour, too, had heard the plans discussed at dinner, and insinuated himself quietly into the coach. 'Clara trembled, for she saw the blush of indignation crimson the lofty brow of Mr. Seymour, while the flush of fiery anger mounted the dark cheek of Mr. Marsden.' But an open quarrel was avoided, and the coach party arrived safely at the Williamsons' country seat. Here, where Clara longed to gaze out over the park, she and the children were assigned a bedroom overlooking the stable yard, with 'soiled paper' and 'scanty furniture'. But she was to sleep in it only for two nights. Next day she lost the children in the pleasure-grounds. And by the time Mr. Seymour had retrieved them for her, Mr. Marsden had waylaid her, and little Arabella had fallen on her face, Clara was in disgrace as a flirt and a frivol. Mr. Williamson, stricken with remorse at her forthcoming dismissal, made matters worse by sending her money, which she spurned. And in the morning the lady's maid brought her a letter of dismissal with a month's wages in lieu of notice. She left at once in the coach, and Mr. Marsden was only prevented by Mr. Seymour from pursuing her to London.

In the coach Clara made friends with an austere but kindly Quaker called Abraham Jacob and his daughter Rachel. She also dropped the purse which contained her little all. But even this mishap proved fortunate. For Mrs. Waller precipitately expired almost before Clara set foot in her Kensington villa, and Abraham Jacob arrived with the purse just in time to pick up Clara's fainting form and transport it to his home—Fair Lawn, at Clapham Common.

When Clara had sufficiently recovered from the shock of her aunt's death, her Quaker friend found her a situation as companion to an old lady with literary pretensions and governess to her adopted great-niece. Mrs. Vincent Robinson was an aged, raddled 'beauty' who wrote Della Cruscan verses, and had a *salon* of seedy spongers. She was a cross between Perdita Robinson in old age and Mrs. Leo Hunter. 'I wish', she said, 'to engage a person to instruct Ada Myrrha and to be my amanuensis also. Do you compose music? I want to have the songs I write set. I will give £100 a year.'

Poor Clara had to stick complimentary verses into albums, sing her own settings of Mrs. Robinson's songs at her parties (after having been starved to preserve her voice) and teach pathetic little Mary (*alias* Ada Myrrha) in the intervals. Once she had to accompany the old hag to the opera and as no one would face the ridicule of handing the old lady to her carriage, was sent to fetch her servants. In the crush-room she was, of course, accosted by Hercules Marsden and rescued by Clarence Seymour.

But her stay in this abode of artificiality and affectation was short and ended tragically. Little Ada Myrrha, ill from having been bitten by the lap-dog, was forced to take part with her great-aunt in a *tableau* of 'Poetry shielding Purity'. Sacrificed to the old lady's vanity and selfishness, the child died in spite of Clara's devoted nursing. Meanwhile, Mrs. Robinson herself had been bitten by her pet, and died soon afterwards of gangrene, aggravated by hydrophobia-phobia.

Clara was collected by Abraham Jacob and taken back to Fair Lawn, where she reflected on her 'knowledge of the vicissitudes and uncertainties of life, acquired since she had commenced the painful career of governess'. Her host, too, was giving the subject his serious thought, for he was making enquiries about another place for her and confessed: 'It moved me almost into wrath, to hear a meek and modest maiden like thee referred to, as though thou wert but meant to amuse, or teach another to amuse, the light hours of the man of pleasure. But such are the requisites too generally sought in a governess by unwise parents.'

Yet if Clara's career had been painful, she could not complain that it was dull. The two main bugbears of a governess's life—tedium and loneliness— were unknown to her. In all her situations she was seldom alone, and almost every day brought its own adventure. As for friend Abraham Jacob, he might have pursued his enquiries a little further instead of inveighing against frivolity. It is astonishing and a little discreditable, that so serious and sober a man should have landed his protégée in so many awkward situations.

Clara's next employer—the Marchioness of Axminster —was a great lady and an undoubted charmer. She and Clara took to each other at sight, and Clara was treated like a queen. Her rooms were comfortable and elegant; her pupil was docile and apt; the servants were attentive; and at two o'clock 'a light but excellent dinner, served with the utmost precision', was announced in a small *salle à manger*. 'A respectable footman waited on Clara and her pupil during the repast', which included dessert and two or three wines.

It would seem that Clara had everything a governess

could ask. But alas! there was a snake—a serpent of impropriety—lurking in this paradise. One afternoon Lady Axminster took Clara and little Lady Isabella in the carriage to Kensington Gardens, where they met a delightful gentleman called Lord Francis Carysfort. Lady Axminster introduced him to Clara 'with the same air of consideration with which she would have presented that gentleman to a lady of the highest rank, and he went through the ceremonial of taking off his hat, and bowing with as much politeness as if, instead of a humble governess, Clara was a person of the highest distinction'. All this was very gratifying; but it too soon became apparent, from Lady Axminster's manner and from little Isabella's artless remarks, that Clara's employer and new friend was involved (at the best) in a passionate flirtation with Lord Francis.

Soon afterwards Lady Axminster sat in the schoolroom while 'Lady Isabella went through her lessons. The patience and intelligence with which Clara assisted her pupil delighted the fond mother'—for Clara was not guilty of the incompetence usually ascribed to governesses of her type. When lessons were over, Lady Axminster confessed to Clara that she had arranged for Lord Francis to address his love letters under cover to the governess. Clara refused to be used in this way as a stooge in her Ladyship's *affaire*, but already the austere Lord Axminster had discovered the clandestine correspondence. As he had also been called upon to rescue Clara from Mr. Marsden in Hyde Park, he had naturally concluded that she was dissolute and corrupt. So back Clara went once again to Fair Lawn after persuading Lady Axminster to break with her lover.

Imagine Clara's surprise when Mr. Seymour came to stay with his old friend Abraham Jacob, and her chagrin when he was cold and distant to her! His coldness was due to his having seen at his club a letter addressed to her by the notorious rake, Lord Francis Carysfort. But out of loyalty to her late employer, Clara's lips were sealed. Life in the same house as the man she had learned to love became too painful for her, and she ran full-tilt into another situation.

Her interview with Mr. and Mrs. Manwarring took place in a hotel, while they were devouring a hearty breakfast. 'Can you', asked Mrs. Manwarring, 'instruct my children in every branch of education? I expect you to teach my daughters everything that young ladies ought or can be taught. What are your terms?'

Given this opening, Clara boldly demanded 50 guineas a year, and stuck to it in the face of the Manwarrings' outraged parsimony. 'Why', exclaimed the lady, 'there is a French governess at Lady Walker's who not only educates the children, but makes all her ladyship's dresses, and washes her lace, and she has only thirty pounds a year and finds her own tea.' Finally Mrs. Manwarring suggests a compromise: If Clara gets the salary she asks, will she make herself useful in assisting at plain work? To which Clara prudently replied: 'I should not like my doing so, madam, to be made a specific condition; but I should not be unwilling to occasionally assist.' After another haggle about laundry, she was engaged, and ordered to come to the hotel next morning *after* breakfast.

So, having been given breakfast next day by the more generous Quaker, she joined the Manwarrings at their hotel, ready to accompany them to their country house. Their manners were atrocious. 'Ring the bell, Miss Mordaunt', said Mr. Manwarring, giving this order with as much nonchalance as if she was a waiter or footman. 'Have sandwiches for *two* put up', said Mrs. Manwarring to the waiter. 'Mend my glove, Miss Mordaunt.'

Clara went to the chambermaid in search of needle and thread to mend the glove, and was asked to wait a minute in a bedroom. What was her horror to find that it was not only a man's room, but Mr. Hercules Marsden's—and that he was at that moment returning to it along the passage! With great presence of mind she locked herself in an inner closet, and remained there until he was called away. The Manwarrings were annoyed at being kept waiting, and thought her explanation fishy, but they were not interested in a governess's troubles except when these inconvenienced themselves. When, during the journey, it began to rain, Clara had to change places with Mr. Manwarring, and sit on the box. But, although she was shocked by his discourtesy, her physical discomfort was far outweighed by the relief of being virtually alone.

Her bed-chamber at Manwarring Park was 'destitute of all comfort'; and she learned—like many another governess—that 'there are few positions more calculated to produce depression of mind, than that of finding oneself, for the first time, in a house where one receives neither the politeness due to a guest, nor the friendly familiarity extended towards an inmate'. She compared her treatment here with that 'in the mansion of the Marchioness of Axminster', and also began to feel very hungry.

But her sojourn in this dreary room was shorter than in any other. She had not even seen her pupils before the Manwarrings entered with two Bow Street officers sent to arrest her on the charge of stealing £200 from Mr. Marsden's room in the hotel. At this dramatic climax to the story, I overreached myself, imagining that Hercules Marsden had 'framed' her in order to get her into his clutches. But the men were real Bow Street runners—the money had really been stolen—and things looked very black for Clara. Happily, however, the long arm of coincidence was stretched to save her, as it has saved so many heroines. First she discovered that one of the officers was a friend and admirer of Abraham Jacob, and then she was recognised by the Axminsters, who happened to be passing as she sat disconsolately in the chaise outside an inn.

By this time the Axminsters had become a reconciled and devoted couple, and the Marquis knew how much of this he owed to the wronged governess. Moreover--and this was even more to the point—he happened to be Lord Lieutenant of the County, and persuaded the officers to let him take their prisoner to his London mansion. Backed by such friends as the Marquis and the Quaker, Clara no longer had much to fear in court; but in the end she did not have to appear there, as a comic Irishman gave information about the real thief.

Though the Axminsters wished her to stay with them, first as their friend and then as their governess again, Clara insisted on going home with Abraham Jacob to Fair Lawn, where she soon found herself in Clarence Seymour's arms. Abraham Jacob said of Clarence: 'He is rich, yea, verily, the possessor of unbounded wealth.' This disparity of fortune did not distress Clara, but when Clarence added a title to his wealth and became Lord Seymourville, she was aghast. 'Known to many people as having the situation of governess in families whence she had been abruptly dismissed, and known to some twenty or thirty persons as having been made a prisoner on a charge of theft, how could she hope that so degrading a circumstance could long be concealed, or how bear, without dismay, the notion that it would be viewed as a stain on him whose rank she was to share?'

But the rewards of virtue, like the troubles of heroines, never come singly. Clara found herself heiress to an immense fortune on condition that she took the name of Bertie. She could now give herself to Clarence as a rich woman, and under a new, unsullied name. And he accepted the offering, saying playfully: 'I did not think, dearest Clara, that you were so proud. But remember, it was with the *Governess* I fell in love, and not the wealthy Miss Bertie.'

No victory, even of virtue, is complete in fiction unless it affords the heroine a public triumph over her enemies. This triumph came to Clara at the Ascot Races, where she sat with her betrothed in the Axminsters' box—the cynosure of all eyes, including those of the Marsdens, the Manwarrings and the Williamsons.

'Why', exclaimed Mrs. Manwarring, 'she's positively whispering and laughing with the Marchioness, as if they were equals; and see!—only look!—if there is not the Marquis, in all his pride and dignity, drawing her shawl over her shoulders.' Did Mr. Manwarring remember how he had turned her out of the carriage to sit on the box and face the rain in his stead? Whether he did or no, he let himself be bullied into 'exposing' her to the Marquis, and was snubbed for his pains. Hercules Marsden was involved in a brawl while trying to force his way into the Axminsters' box; and Mrs. Williamson contented herself with the admission that 'it can be no other than my *see-de-vong* governess whom I discharged'.

'Henceforth', says Lady Blessington, 'Mrs. Williamson and the Manwarrings ever treated the governesses who undertook the instruction of their children with more humanity; giving as a reason, that there was no knowing whether they might not, at some future period, become heiresses, or countesses, and so turn out useful acquaintances.'

I have spread myself over *The Governess* partly because the rarity of this forgotten book entailed my telling the story in some detail; but still more because it contains a wealth of sociological detail inextricably entangled with the plot. Lady Blessington, for all her airs and graces, is not above discussing schoolroom china or allowances for laundry. In her endeavour to emphasise the pathos of a governess's fate, she made a sincere effort to enter into Clara's feelings, and realised how large a part these squalid matters of beer and light and furniture played in the average governess's life.

Admittedly Clara was not a normal governess, even of fiction. Normal ones received no dishonourable proposals and were not arrested by Bow Street runners; nor did their employers so frequently die of dog-bites. Perhaps they wished they did! Compared with the dreary drudgery endured by Emily Morton, the next governess on our list, Clara's fate may seem to us to be almost enviable, even without the happy ending. Yet Lady Blessington, while she had to give her fashionable readers their ration of thrills, has supplied us with enough realistic detail to show how badly mere governesses (who were not romantic heroines) might be treated in her day. Although she exaggerated, Lady Blessington had perhaps heard employers talk almost as insufferably as the guests at the Williamsons' dinner party; and in her final 'moral' she gauged, more shrewdly than Maria Edgeworth, the loving kindness of fine ladies. Unlike Miss Edgeworth, she did not believe them to be perfectible: if ever they were to treat their governesses better, their motives would be snobbish and self-seeking. She knew, moreover, as well as you or I, that in real life governesses were neither rescued by Quakers nor pestered by quadroons; but that they *were* expected to mend the children's clothes, find their own tea, and accept the wages of a lady's maid.

CHAPTER II

EARLY VICTORIAN

Elizabeth Sewell, *Amy Herbert*; Charles Dickens, *Martin Chuzzlewit*; W. M. Thackeray, *The Book of Snobs, Vanity Fair*; The Brontës and Governesses: Anne Brontë, *Agnes Grey*; Charlotte Brontë, *Jane Eyre.*

THE transition from the early nineteenth century with its lingering eighteenth-century aroma, into the completely different early-Victorian atmosphere, is marked very strongly by our own transition from *The Governess* to the next book on our list. Elizabeth Sewell's *Amy Herbert* (1844), described in *The Dictionary of National Biography* as 'a well-written tale for girls, embodying Anglican views', is unlikely to be known by modern readers; nor need they be extravagantly ashamed of their ignorance. From our point of view, however, the very qualities which 'date' the book and narrow its outlook are valuable; for they centre the interest on Emily Morton, who is the very model of a martyred governess.

It should perhaps be explained at this point that I have made no systematic research into children's books; on the contrary, I have debarred 'juveniles'. But there are certain books such as Maria Edgeworth's *Moral Tales, The Daisy Chain* and Kenneth Grahame's *The Golden Age,* which must always have been enjoyed by many grown-ups. Among these, I think, we must count *Amy Herbert.* Although the characterisation is crude, it is bold and lively, and the manners and customs of a middle-class home are described in such detail as to provide plentiful material for our survey of the governess's social status.

Amy Herbert, from whom the story takes its title, and with whom young readers were no doubt expected to identify themselves, was a good little poor-relation who went to live with her odious cousins the Harringtons. Dora Harrington was proud, Margaret was vain; while little Rose was fortunate enough to die a violent death before Satan had left his stamp upon her. Their father was a nonentity, Mrs. Harrington was harsh and snoopy. This is neither our first nor our last instance of a nondescript husband married to a governess-baiting wife; we shall find that it is always mothers who are severe, while fathers (if important) are usually eccentric widowers, or crypto-widowers like Mr. Rochester.

Emily Morton looked after little Rose and helped the older girls with their music and drawing. When Amy asked to be introduced to the governess, they replied 'we never do it with her'. But Amy, carefully nurtured in a rustic cottage by a mother who was a real lady, was still not satisfied. She wished to know whether the governess was a lady, and received the answer 'certainly—she is the daughter of a clergyman', and Margaret added the comment (much in the manner of Emma Woodhouse): 'Of course she must be something like a lady, or Mama would not let her be with us.'

Yet having once got Emily Morton like a wage-slave into their power, the Harringtons were not concerned to treat her like a lady. It is true that two rooms were set aside for her use, but only because 'Rose always shared the same apartment'. They did not wonder how she spent her time or whether she was happy. 'Mr. Harrington scarcely thought of her at all; and Mrs. Harrington considered her as little above the level of an upper servant. Useful in a party to sing and play, and useful in teaching Dora and Margaret to do the same, but in other respects very slightly differing from the lady's maid.' She ate her meals in the schoolroom with the girls, who always addressed her by her Christian name while she in reply called them Miss

Harrington and Miss Margaret. 'Dora scorned her as an inferior', and Margaret 'envied her beauty and was angry with her straightforward simplicity'. All this was, of course, excessively painful to a girl as attractive and refined as Miss Morton; 'but there was a principle within, which soon brought her to a more patient spirit. She had no mother, no friends; her daily life was one of wearying mortification and self-denial; yet Emily Morton had never been heard to utter a single murmur.'

Lovers of fair play in fiction will be relieved to hear, however, that a happy ending was in store for her. When Colonel Herbert, Amy's long-lost father, ultimately arrived from India, Emily left the Harringtons and became Amy's governess in the rustic cottage. We must hope that in due course she found a man who appreciated meekness as well as beauty in his future wife. As for Dora and Margaret, they were left looking sadly through their music books and portfolios, and thinking 'that they should have no one for the future to take an interest in them as Emily had done'.

From this pious, simple tale we learn several things about the running of an early-Victorian home. The older girls, aged fourteen and twelve, ate with the governess, and the little one slept in her room. She also dressed little Rose and made herself generally useful to the others, besides giving them regular drawing and music lessons. In fact, she combined the duties of maid, nanny, nursery-governess and governess, and never went to the drawing-room unless summoned there to play or sing.

The governess of a neighbouring family is also mentioned, a tall, thin, inelegant Frenchwoman, dressed in Parisian fashion with a black wig and a cap covered with ribbons and artificial flowers, who sang and played the guitar. She and Madame de Rosier and Louise D'Argent are not the only French governesses whom we shall meet; this one, moreover, is in appearance a precursor of Madame de la Rougierre in *Uncle Silas.* But all our foreign governesses—at any rate in the nineteenth century—are French. The German governess, immortalised by Miss Ruth Draper, was an Edwardian innovation; nor had the Swiss—albeit the countrywomen of Froebel and Pestalozzi—yet shown a tendency to take the schoolrooms of Europe by storm.

Our next book describes a similar type of governess to Emily Morton, but describes her in a very different manner. Which is not surprising, since the book is *Martin Chuzzlewit*; and Charles Dickens had nothing in common with Elizabeth Sewell save his indignation at the abuse of governesses.

The scene opens outside a mansion in Camberwell where Tom Pinch's sister Ruth 'was governess in a family, a lofty family—perhaps the wealthiest brass and copper founder's family known to mankind'. When the Pecksniffs and Mrs. Todgers (of Todgers's boarding-house) went to visit her, they got 'at last into a small room with books in it, where Mr. Pinch's sister was at that moment instructing her eldest pupil—to wit, a premature little woman of thirteen years old. "Visitors for Miss Pinch!" said the footman, with a nice discrimination between the cold respect with which he would have announced visitors to the family, and the warm, personal interest with which he would have announced visitors to the cook.' Dickens knew how sensitively men-servants reflect the manners of their employers or, perhaps, how surely like tends to gravitate to like. Mr. Jarndyce's man would never have announced a visitor to Esther Summerson in this contemptuous tone, nor Sam Weller a visitor to the governess at Dingley Dell.

The children, too, were in this house taught to despise their governess and spy upon her; for the lady of the house 'was curious in the natural history and habits of the animal called Governess, and encouraged her daughters to report thereon '. On this occasion the child, whom Mrs. Todgers considered ' a young syrup ', was thinking to herself: ' Oh, very well, Miss Pinch, crying before strangers, as if you didn't like the situation '; and she was no doubt delighted when the contemptuous footman broke in with a message ' Missis's compliments to Miss Pinch, and begs to know wot my young lady is a-learning of just now '. For Miss Pinch herself, however, it was a disastrous visit, and she was ' so severely taken to task by the seraph's mother for having such vulgar acquaintances, that she was fain to retire to her own room in tears '. I suspect, though, that this proneness to tears should not be considered typical of ' the animal called Governess '—even when of the species Downtrodden—so much as of the whole genus ' womanly woman ' in Charles Dickens's works.

When Tom Pinch went himself to visit his sister, he was waylaid in the hall by a porter, probably the self-same footman, but now sitting in one of those bower-like wicker chairs which used to protect footmen from draughts when they sat in halls. ' Pray, does Miss Pinch live here? ' said Tom. ' Miss Pinch is Governess here ', replied the porter. ' Pray, is Miss Pinch at home? ' ' She's *in* ', replied the footman.

Finally, Tom is admitted into the presence of the brass and copper founder, his consort and seraph, who complains that ' Miss Pinch is always talking about her brother when she ought to be engaged upon my education '. Whereupon the *paterfamilias*, legs apart, no doubt, and coat-tails pushed up to warm his back against the fire, embarks upon a speech. This, I must admit, is an instance of a father taking an active part in the sport of governess-baiting. He had no doubt been put up to it by his wife, as it was only fit and proper that a man should scold a man. Not that the task was uncongenial! He launched his speech with fervour: ' Although I do not approve, as a principle, of any young person engaged in my family in the capacity of a governess, receiving visitors, it happens in this case to be well-timed. . . . Your sister has not the slightest innate power of commanding respect'. Imagine the feelings of this father when, desiring that his daughter 'should be choice in her expressions' and 'politely distant to her inferiors in society', he finds her 'addressing Miss Pinch herself as a beggar.'

'"A beggarly thing", observed the lady in correction.

'"Which is worse", said the gentleman triumphantly. "A beggarly thing. A low, coarse, despicable expression."

'"Most despicable", cried Tom.'

Then Tom let fly in one of those tirades of righteous indignation which Dickens so much enjoyed. 'Your governess cannot win the confidence and respect of your children, forsooth! Let her begin by winning yours, and see what happens. . . . She is as well bred, as well taught, as well qualified by nature to command respect, as any hirer of a governess you know. But when you place her at a disadvantage in reference to every servant in your house, how can you suppose that she is not in a tenfold worse position in reference to your daughters? Very partial they must grow to their studies when they see to what a pass proficiency in those same tasks has brought their governess!'

This last is an original argument, nowhere else (to my knowledge) adduced as a reason for respecting governesses. The whole scene is, of course, highly dramatised, almost caricatured. But though we have never met any of Dickens's characters in real life, we should recognise almost all of them if we met them in some fictional other-world. For they are not types but creations, living in their own right against their own background, and even this sketch of a self-made man's household in its suburban residence is drawn in the round. We believe in Miss Pinch's tears, though we deplore them. We even feel a pang of sympathy for her sobbed-at employers. Nor is the picture distorted out of all likeness to the real world. We have already seen just such a family in the Harringtons; and we shall find others in the works of Anne Brontë, Wilkie Collins, and even Anstey as late as 1893.

Thackeray's *The Book of Snobs,* published in 1847, is much more caricatured than *Martin Chuzzlewit,* and its characters do not in the same way exist in their own right. This is really neither surprising nor reprehensible, since the book was not a novel and therefore demanded no development of character. It was a collection of satirical sketches reprinted from *Punch,* in which sensitive readers might recognise portraits of themselves while the thick-skinned saw portraits of their neighbours.

The characters are frankly types, yet Miss Wirt the governess took to herself sufficient life to turn up again retrospectively as governess to the Osborne girls in *Vanity Fair.* As befits a governess in a Book of Snobs, Miss Wirt is our first example of a governess valued only as a Snob Exhibit. Her employers, Major and Mrs. Ponto, live parsimoniously in the country, striving to keep up appearances among their richer and more aristocratic neighbours—an endeavour in which Miss Wirt collaborates loyally. 'We only live', she says, 'with the country families. The Duke is abroad: we are at feud with the Carabases: the Ringwoods don't come down till Christmas: in fact nobody's here till the hunting season—positively nobody.' Such enthusiastic identification of her own interests with those of the family is repaid by the Pontos with fulsome flattery. When she plays the piano after dinner, her proud employer exclaims: 'What a finger! Glorious creature, isn't she? Squirtz's favourite pupil—inestimable to have such a creature. Lady Carabas would give her eyes for her! A prodigy of accomplishments.'

The accomplishments are, of course, just a part of the snob exhibition. As there is a visitor to be impressed Miss Wirt rounds off her performance with the oft-told tale of how, 'when I lived with the Dunsinanes, it was the dear Duchess's favourite [piece]. It was while hearing Jane play that, I remember, that dear Lord Castletoddy first fell in love with her! and though he is but an Irish peer, with not more than fifteen thousand a year, I persuaded Jane to have him.'

Boasting a governess who could bandy names from Burke so freely, it is no wonder that the Pontos—far from banishing her to the schoolroom—let her attend their dinner parties. She was the house's chief ornament; and the narrator, Mr. Snob, remarks that 'I who have been accustomed to see governesses bullied in the world, was delighted to find this one ruling the roost, and to think that even the majestic Mrs. Ponto bent before her.'

Tiring a little of the incessant routine of piano-strumming, the guest asked 'this great creature in what other branches of education she instructed her pupils'. Her reply comprised a curriculum far more ambitious than that of Miss Lee of Mansfield Park, with her Roman Emperors and precious metals. 'The modern languages', she began modestly, 'French, German, Spanish, Italian, Latin and the rudiments of Greek if desired. English, of course; the practice of Elocution, Geography and Astronomy, and the Use of the Globes, Algebra (but only as far as Quadratic Equations); for a poor, ignorant female, you know, Mr. Snob, cannot be expected to know everything. Ancient and Modern History no young woman can be without; and of these I make my beloved pupils *perfect mistresses*. Botany, Geology and Mineralogy I consider as amusements.' Yet when Mr. Snob looked into one of Miss Ponto's manuscript song-books, he found five faults of French in four words.

Squandering their meagre resources on such refinements,

the Pontos kept a poor table and were wretchedly served indoors and out. Indeed, so lacking were they in men-servants, that the Misses Ponto regularly rolled the lawn; and this unladylike occupation was passed off as being the latest fashion in physical training. For the Ponto family, in budgeting their income, had decided that they would 'live upon a fine governess and fine masters'.

A fine governess, in one sense, they certainly had. But with her all-inclusive curriculum one would have thought that they had no need for fine masters too. Masters and governesses were, of course, frequently combined, especially in grand houses and for older girls. The governess might be little more than a companion and chaperon, who sewed in the corner during the drawing-master's visit, presided over piano practice, and walked with her charges to the dancing-class. But it seems odd that the Pontos, living in the country, and possessed of a compendium of accomplishments in the person of Miss Wirt, should have considered masters necessary as well. If they had them, we may be sure that this was only to score off, or keep pace with, Lady Carabas, or because Miss Wirt herself demanded the social prestige of such auxiliaries.

Though Thackeray, as a satirist, necessarily exaggerated, there is no doubt a basis of truth in his exposure of Miss Wirt's pretensions: a satirist does not waste his shafts on empty air. Just as surely as Mr. Woodhouse required a governess who could be relied on to wrap up Emma's throat after she had the measles, so Mrs. Ponto wanted one who could fit her daughters for the marriage-market. Like a dog-handler who grooms, plucks and washes dogs for Cruft's, and teaches them how to show themselves to best advantage in the ring, Miss Wirt coached her pupils for their entry into Vanity Fair. She crammed them with aristocratic small-talk, taught them to play one piece of music with effect, and enabled them to recognise a smattering of words in various languages and sciences. For real education—*pace* Maria Edgeworth—there was no demand, since no one thought it necessary, or even becoming, for a lady. And as it was hoped that accomplishments would win girls wealthy husbands and lavish establishments, the old, homely education in kitchen and still-room was equally neglected.

Although *Vanity Fair* was not published as a whole until after *Agnes Grey* and *Jane Eyre,* it was appearing in monthly parts during 1847. It therefore seems chronologically legitimate as well as more sensible to consider it here before we pass from Thackeray to the Brontës. *The Newcomes,* it is true, also has a few small specimens of the genus Governess; so that we cannot round off Thackeray entirely. But we can at least pass to his immortal Becky while we are still in snobbish vein, and a smooth transition is afforded us in the person of Miss Wirt.

We have already referred to her appearance in this book as governess to the Osbornes, in which situation she was evidently more of a companion than an instructress, but we are told little about her except that she was paid quarterly, and that she introduced as drawing master a cousin of her own who had the audacity to make love to Miss Osborne. Her very presence, however, in a story placed in a period over thirty years before that of *The Book of Snobs,* brings us up against a problem affecting our whole treatment of *Vanity Fair.* Is it to be regarded as an historical novel, in the same sense as *John Halifax, Gentleman*? It is true that Thackeray was at pains to describe the setting and atmosphere of Brussels before and after Waterloo, and that Lord Steyne is a Regency rake as surely as Lord Kew in *The Newcomes* is a Victorian example of the breed. But even if Thackeray was sensitive to period atmosphere, and handled his manners and customs carefully, yet I think we have no reason to suppose that he investigated meticulously the status of governesses during the Napoleonic wars. He more likely took for granted that it was much the same then as when he wrote, and after our own investigation of Jane Austen's governesses it seems safe for us (in our turn) to assume that he was right.

Vanity Fair is the first great novel of which the heroine is a governess, and although Becky Sharp in this capacity is as unique as in the capacity of heroine, yet we must not forget her governess's career nor ignore the light it sheds upon the lives of her less spectacular colleagues. Although Becky, being unique, will fit into no tight category and conforms to no type, she is undoubtedly our first example of the sort of governess which I have called the Self-seeking Adventuress. Sir Pitt Crawley, too, is our first example of an eccentric employer. But Becky does not marry her boss. Despite her acuteness and lack of scruple, she misplays her cards, and when she leaves the schoolroom to become Mrs. Rawdon Crawley, her adventures have only just begun.

We must, however, begin at the beginning, when she left Miss Pinkerton's Academy and was taken home to Russell Square by her dear friend Amelia Sedley. There she met and captivated the nabob, Jos Sedley, and there, too, she first met George Osborne whose worthless heart she was later to seduce in Brussels. At first, however, he would have none of her. The Osborne home was a nest of snobs, in which Miss Wirt must have felt in her element, and George was as snobbish as his sisters. Watching her flirt with Jos, George described her to himself as 'a little nobody—a little upstart governess'; and reflected that 'a governess is all very well, but I'd rather have a lady for my sister-in-law'. In his mind, at all events, lady and governess were incompatible. He felt it to be a failing in his betrothed to introduce the girl into her home, and would have agreed with Mrs. Blenkinsop, the housekeeper, who confided to the maid: 'I don't trust them governesses. They give themselves the hairs and hupstarts of ladies, and their wages is no better than you nor me.'

Fortunately for all at Russell Square, Becky soon found a situation at Queen's Crawley, the seat of Sir Pitt Crawley, Bart. We are not told what testimonials she carried with her from Miss Pinkerton's Academy, but we can deduce their general trend towards perfection from the letter which Miss Pinkerton wrote to Mrs. Bute Crawley when that busy lady was in search of a governess for a friend. Two candidates were recommended, and 'either of these young ladies', wrote Miss Pinkerton, 'is *perfectly qualified* to instruct in Greek, Latin, and the rudiments of Hebrew; in mathematics and history; in Spanish, French, Italian, and geography; in music, vocal and instrumental; in dancing, without the aid of a master; and in the elements of natural sciences. In the use of the globes, both are proficient. In addition to these, Miss Tuffin, who is daughter of the late Reverend Thomas Tuffin (Fellow of Corpus College, Cambridge) can instruct in the Syriac language, and the elements of constitutional law. But as she is only eighteen years of age, and of exceedingly pleasing personal appearance, perhaps this young lady may be objectionable in Sir Huddleston Fuddleston's family.

'Miss Letitia Hawkey, on the other hand, is not personally well-favoured. She is twenty-nine; her face is much pitted with the smallpox. She has a halt in her gait, red hair, and a trifling obliquity of vision. Both ladies are endowed with *every moral and religious virtue*. Their terms, of course, are such as their accomplishments merit.' (It is worth noting before we leave this testimonial, that Miss Pinkerton clearly acted as a registry office for old girls, even when they must have left her school some ten years before.)

Much as Miss Pinkerton disliked and despised Becky as a penniless orphan and too clever by half, she must (for the honour of the establishment) have given her much such a testimonial as this. Becky was not as pretty as Miss Tuffin, nor as plain as Miss Hawkey; nor was she endowed with every moral and religious virtue. But she knew what she wanted, and had a pretty shrewd idea of how to get it; and she settled down complacently enough in her new home.

'I am to be treated as one of the family', she wrote to Amelia, 'except on company days, when the young ladies and I are to dine upstairs.' In lesson hours she took the wise course of saving herself trouble, and getting on easy terms with her charges. 'With the young people, whose applause she thoroughly gained, Becky's method was pretty simple. She did not pester their young brains with too much learning, but let them have their own way in regard to educating themselves; for what instruction is more effectual than self-instruction?' Madame de Rosier would have agreed with this theory, but not with Becky's application of it, for 'she and Miss Rose read together many delightful French and English works, among which may be mentioned those of the learned Dr. Smollett, of the ingenious Mr. Henry Fielding, of the graceful and fantastic Monsieur Crébillon the younger'. Of Miss Violet's peccadilloes she promised not to tell if Miss Violet would be a good girl and love her governess. In which respect Miss Sharp resembled Mrs. Grace, the lady's maid, rather than Madame de Rosier.

Lady Crawley, a sad invalid, kept her room. And when Mrs. Bute Crawley was not in the neighbourhood to interfere, Becky was 'almost mistress of the house'. It must have been a happy moment for her when she was able to repay George Osborne's snobbishness in kind: to his enquiries as to her welfare, she replied: 'We poor governesses are used to slights. At least in some families. You can't think what a difference there is, though. We are not so wealthy in Hampshire as you lucky folks of the city. But then I am in a gentleman's family—good old English stock. And you see how I am treated! I am pretty comfortable. Indeed, it is rather a good place. But how *very* good of you to enquire.' We must hope that George Osborne—spoiled darling of an opulent, vulgar city family—had not become too self-complacent to feel Becky's claws. She was expressing our familiar theory that a family's gentility may be gauged by its treatment of the governess, and she was expressing it, literally, with a vengeance.

When Miss Crawley, from whom all at Queen's Crawley had expectations, came to stay, Becky instinctively set herself to amuse and captivate the old tyrant. Up to a point she succeeded. When, for instance, the governess was as usual to be banished to the schoolroom during a 'county' dinner-party, Miss Crawley would not hear of such a thing. 'Not let Miss Sharp dine at table! I insist upon Miss Sharp appearing. Let Lady Crawley remain upstairs, if there is no room. But little Miss Sharp! Why, she's the only person fit to talk to in the county!'

Miss Crawley made a protégée of Becky, treating her with the easy familiarity of one whose wealth sets her beyond the reach of resentment or criticism. She encouraged Becky to use her sharp tongue in witticisms at the expense of the family, and in her own talk mingled flattery with arrogance. Secure in her rank and money, she fancied herself as a democrat: 'I consider you, my love, as my equal in every respect; and—will you put some coals on the fire, my dear; and will you pick this dress of mine, and alter it, you who can do it so well?'

But she was only a skin-deep democrat. When it was being broken to her that Becky had eloped with Rawdon, she did not speak of her as of an equal: 'I suppose', she said, 'this unfortunate Becky has been silly and sentimental—some apothecary or house-steward, or painter, or young curate, or something of that sort'—a list which throws a sudden gleam of light on the sort of people who might be carelessly assembled as the social equals of a governess. When she heard who was the actual object of Becky's 'sentimentality', equalitarianism was thrown to the wind. The old lady rallied to the family at which it had amused her to jeer with Becky, and cut poor Rawdon out of her will and out of her hard old heart.

It is a tribute to Becky's good sense that when she returned to Queen's Crawley as Mrs. Rawdon Crawley, 'with regard to her sisters-in-law Rebecca did not attempt to forget her former position of governess towards them, but recalled it frankly and kindly, and asked about their studies with great gravity. "At least she gives herself no airs, and remembers that she was our governess once", Miss Violet said, intimating that it befitted all governesses to keep their proper place.' While inwardly Becky was thinking: 'I have a gentleman for my husband, and an earl's daughter for my sister in the very house where I was little better than a servant a few years ago.'

She had indeed a gentleman for her husband, though a ruined one; and it is her unkindness to poor stupid, faithful Rawdon and to their little boy, which we find it hardest to forgive her. But we cannot any further pursue her remarkable career, except to notice that in due course Becky herself employed a governess. It is true that Miss Briggs was ostensibly her companion, chaperon or 'watch-dog'; but that she was also little Rawdon's governess is proved by Rebecca's claim that she was 'a capital mistress for him, and had brought him on famously in English, the Latin rudiments, and general learning'.

Miss Briggs is herself of interest in being the only instance which I have encountered of the superannuated governess. When the time came for her to retire, she was offered the position of housekeeper at Gauntley Hall. 'It was', we are told, 'a splendid position. The family did not go to Gauntley once in two years. At other times the housekeeper was the mistress of the magnificent mansion—had four covers daily for her table; was visited by the clergy and the most respectable people of the county—was the lady of Gauntley, in fact; and the two last housekeepers had married rectors of Gauntley. What words could paint the ecstatic gratitude of Briggs?'

All Thackeray's governesses were snobs: one of them was an adventuress. But at least they showed great spirit. We must leave them now, and turn to the Brontës, whose governesses were exploited rather than exploiting. Jane Eyre, it is true, showed quiet determination, but her cousins, the Rivers, were over-meek. As for Anne's Agnes Grey, she let herself be made into a doormat and a punch-ball.

Before studying her pathetic story, however, it would be wise for a moment to consider the attitude of this family to governesses and try to discover how far it is based on real life. Setting aside Charlotte's experiences in Brussels, since we are not here concerned with school teachers, we must remember that both she and Anne had been governesses in private houses. They might, therefore, be supposed to know what they were writing about. If Anne portrays a pitiably downtrodden governess, and Charlotte three potential ones, was not this because they had been humiliated themselves?

Charlotte wrote on this matter in a letter about a girl who was thinking of taking up a governess's career: 'No matter how brilliant and varied the accomplishments, if the governess has not the power to win her young charge, she will have a weary, wasting existence of it. . . . She will wish herself a housemaid or kitchen-girl, rather than a baited, trampled, desolate, distracted governess. . . . The demand on her knowledge will not often be larger than she can answer. But on her patience—on her self-control—the requirements will be enormous; on her animal spirits the pressure will be immense. . . . It is more physical and mental strength, denser moral impassibility that [governesses] require, rather than additional skill in arts and sciences. For twenty pounds per annum [the world] expects in one woman the attainments of several professors, but the demand is insensate.'*

In her last sentence, Miss Brontë was surely unfair: 'the world' (in the shape of many parents and most children) would probably greatly have preferred the animal spirits to the attainments, the 'denser moral impassibility' to the additional skill. But in her opening sentence she does, I think, put her finger on what was lacking in many unhappy governesses. They were without vocation. They disliked children and therefore could not teach them. At a time when few other means of livelihood were open to a gentlewoman, she could not choose but be a governess, however much she might dread the constant companionship of children. If she could not afford to live at home, nor make an equal match and have children of her own, then she must live in other people's homes and teach other people's children. And if these children felt her shrink from them, they tormented her, as a dog will bite a nervous postman's legs.

While stressing the hell that could be inflicted on a sensitive girl by thoughtless children—and most normal children, after all, are thoughtless—Charlotte Brontë implies that this hell may rather be a purgatory from which the governess may emerge strengthened as through fire. 'A governess's experience', she writes, 'is frequently indeed bitter, but its results are precious: the mind, feeling, temper are there subjected to a discipline equally painful and priceless.'† She does not, apparently, consider whether the children, too, are the better for growing up in a loveless,

* Quoted by Clement Shorter in *The Brontës and their Circle*.
† *Ibid*.

joyless schoolroom, and being allowed to torment or ignore a shrinking girl who cannot enter into their enthusiasms or open new worlds to them. Yet anyone who cared for children would consider them poorly served by such a governess.

The Brontës evidently disliked children, with the possible exception of Emily, whose little savages and spoiled darlings are always human beings with immense potentialities for good or evil. In this the Brontës were utterly unlike Maria Edgeworth, who won small children's hearts by lying on the floor and letting them crawl all over her! One can conceive of no family of girls less suited to be governesses than were the Brontës. In their own childhood they lived for the most part in worlds of their own imagining; though they had spirit enough, it was of the reserved, wild type which resents approach from strangers; they were pathologically sensitive; and they were conscious of powers which could only be wasted on children. They were, moreover, fanatically devoted to their home; and mutually self-sufficing to an extent which made it impossible for them to enter into the lives of other families.

It would be small wonder, then, if they were given a rough time in the homes where they found employment, and drew on their own harsh experience for their novels. Yet the only outside evidence which we have on Charlotte Brontë as a governess throws a very different light upon her treatment. It consists of a letter from A. C. Benson quoted in the late Miss E. M. Delafield's book, *The Brontës*. Charlotte had for some time acted as governess to some cousins of his, the Sidgwicks, and 'all that another cousin can recollect of her is that if she was invited to walk to church with them she thought she was being ordered about like a slave; if she was not invited, she imagined she was excluded from the family circle'.

It is true that this tiny sketch was made from memory

years afterwards by someone who knew Charlotte Brontë only slightly. Yet it rings true. It is an authentic picture of the psychological type who takes offence where none is meant. Most of us have met the type in real life, though not necessarily in a governess, and know how impossible it is to deal with, how subtly it can wreck a home. We shall find a fictional version of it later, when we come to *The Daisy Chain,* by Charlotte Mary Yonge. Psychologists encounter it only too often, and diagnose it as an inferiority complex or sexual repression according to their school of thought. But God forbid that I should psycho-analyse the Brontës! I quote the letter here only to show that if Charlotte so easily imagined injuries to her self-respect from real people, it was surely easier still to draw on her strong imagination when she was writing of her heroine's trials. And we may suppose that Anne, though a much less powerful creator, allowed her inferior fancy equal rein.

Agnes Grey was published in October 1847 under the pseudonym of 'Acton Bell', and formed the third of three volumes, the first two being *Wuthering Heights.* Agnes herself, like her creator and many other governesses of fact and fiction, was the daughter of a clergyman. When her parents' private income failed she was eager to help them by earning her own living; and the only way of doing so was to become a governess. Unlike Jane Fairfax she welcomed the idea, for she was bored by domestic duties and longed to explore the world outside the vicarage.

'How delightful it would be', she thought, 'to be a governess! To go out into the world; to enter upon a new life; to act for myself; to exercise my unused faculties; to earn my own maintenance.' Her idealism even embraced her potential charges, whom she no doubt imagined as milk-and-water Misses like Amy Herbert. 'I do not pretend', she told her parents, 'to be able to instruct great girls; but surely I could teach little ones; and I should like it *so* much: I am so fond of children. How charming to be entrusted with the care and education of children! To train the tender plants and watch their buds unfolding day by day.'

This outburst may appear to show that very sense of vocation whose absence we have deplored in governesses: but alas! her enthusiasm is dwelt on only to make the contrast with reality more striking. Her Papa's dry comment expresses much more nearly Anne Brontë's own feeling about a governess's career: 'Afflicted as we are', he said, 'surely we are not brought to that pass yet.'

The Greys' finances, however, got worse and worse, and Agnes became a perfect nuisance with her nagging. Eventually, Agnes continues, Mrs. Grey 'wrote to my father's relations, and consulted the newspaper advertisements'. Relations finally proved helpful, and 'at last it was decreed that I should take charge of the young family of a certain Mrs. Bloomfield; whom my kind, prim Aunt Grey had known in her youth, and asserted to be a very nice woman. Her husband was a retired tradesman, who had realised a very comfortable fortune; but could not be prevailed upon to give a greater salary than twenty-five pounds to the instructress of his children.' Even allowing for the value of money a century ago, this certainly seems little enough even in the abstract: for what poor Agnes had to put up with, it was a pittance indeed. For unfortunately Aunt Grey's assertions proved as misleading as Agnes's own dreams. The Bloomfield family was wholly odious. If we cannot perhaps sympathise with Agnes's sense of grievance on arrival, merely because she was sat down to a collation of beafsteaks and half-cold potatoes, we must agree with her that nice children do not tear fledgelings to pieces. Once again we can safely assert that the Brontës knew no nice children; and there is something even more unpleasant in this gratuitous cruelty of the little Bloomfields than in

Hareton Earnshaw of *Wuthering Heights* (who had been taught no better) hanging puppies from a chair as a wet afternoon's pastime.

The skeleton of Agnes's routine consisted of dressing the little girl and doing her hair; luncheon with the children, at which Mrs. Bloomfield joined them when her husband was away on business; and a supper of cold meat and bread, eaten by herself at half past nine. Little mention is made of lessons; most of the day was apparently spent in tagging after the children and trying to curb their sadistic orgies, in which their elders encouraged them. She was not allowed to punish them, and there were no regular hours. She became so exhausted, physically and emotionally, that after only fourteen weeks' employment she asked for a fortnight's holiday at Christmas, which was rather surprisingly granted.

From this holiday, owing to family troubles, she did not return. We soon find her in search of another situation, answering every 'Wanted a Governess' advertisement that appeared at all eligible. Her mother considered her thrown away on a family like the Bloomfields and at so low a salary. 'Your talents', she said, 'are not such as every poor clergyman's daughter possesses. Music, singing, drawing, French, Latin and German are no mean assemblage; many will be glad to have so much in one instructress.' (Yet as we have seen in the alleged accomplishments of Miss Wirt and Miss Rebecca Sharp, many a governess claimed to teach much more.) 'A family of some genuine, thorough-bred gentleman', continued Mrs. Grey, 'are far more likely to treat you with proper respect and consideration than those purse-proud tradespeople. I have known several among the higher ranks who treated their governess quite as one of the family.' Mrs. Grey was evidently familiar with the idea that a family's refinement may be gauged by its treatment of a governess, but she was unable to apply the theory in picking a suitable situation for her daughter. She *did* insist, however, that Agnes should ask £50 as salary, and Agnes herself stipulated in her advertisement for two months' holiday a year.

A new point arises in connection with these advertisements. Except in cases where a personal recommendation was available, such as Mrs. Elton's for Jane Fairfax or Aunt Grey's for Agnes, employers took their governesses as from a bran-tub and governesses went to their new homes with no idea of what they might expect there. Letters were formal and difficulties of travel no doubt made a personal interview impossible. By this hit-or-miss method it is no wonder if round pegs found themselves in square holes. Agnes may have thought that certain advertisements sounded eligible but, judging from results, she might just have well have dabbed at the paper with a pin. And when she received an answer to her advertisement, her only clues to the situation's eligibility were that washing was 'put out', and that 'next to unimpeachable morality, a mild and cheerful temper and obliging disposition were the most essential requisites'.

And so indeed they were in the self-assertive Murray family, for they were almost more disagreeable than the Bloomfields. Determined to start right this time, Agnes called her charges 'Miss' and 'Master', but they took this as only their due. These charges consisted of Rosalie, who was vain and thoughtless; Matilda, a horsey hoyden; and two boys. Incidentally, the hoyden is a constantly recurring type in Victorian novels, as it was in the eighteenth century. Horsiness in grown women like Surtees's Lucy Glitters denoted moral abandonment: in girls it involved bad manners, ignorance and coarse language. The little girl of to-day who looks after her own pony, lives for gymkhanas, and makes a religion of the Pony Club, would have been inconceivable in Victorian fiction.

With the Murrays, unlike the Bloomfields, Agnes had no lack of teaching. She had to teach the boys Latin grammar and *Valpy's Delectus* (whatever that might be) until they went to school; while with the girls, 'everything was neglected but French, German, music, singing, dancing, fancy-work and a little drawing'. Agnes might priggishly consider these to be frivolous subjects, but they made a lot of work for her. For during her solitary evenings she had to do all the dull parts of the fancy-work, copy the music, and finish the drawings that her pupils had begun.

She was, moreover, completely at the children's beck and call. 'I had all my meals in the schoolroom with my pupils, at such times as suited their fancy. Their hours of study were managed in much the same way. Sometimes Matilda and John would send the maid to call me up at half past five; sometimes I was told to be ready precisely at six, and discovered that they had changed their minds. While receiving my instructions they would lounge upon the sofa, lie on the rug, stretch, yawn, talk to each other, or look out of the window.' Ill-mannered cubs, certainly; yet even without sanctions a keen teacher should have made them enjoy their lessons more than this.

By Mrs. Murray Agnes was treated like a young servant-girl, and 'the servants regulated their behaviour by the same standards'. The family's friends and neighbours equally ignored her. After morning service 'Mr. Hartfield, the Rector, never spoke to me, neither did any other lady or gentleman who frequented that church; nor, in fact, anyone that visited Horton Lodge'. No wonder that she wrote: 'I sometimes felt myself degraded by the life I led.'

Nor did she give satisfaction for all her meekness. On one occasion she was obliged to hear a lecture from Mrs. Murray, in which the girls' offensive manners were attributed to her shortcomings, and she was contrasted with more efficient governesses. 'Who is to form a young lady's tastes, I wonder, if the governess doesn't do it? I *have* known governesses who have completely identified themselves with the reputation of their young ladies for elegance and propriety in mind and manners. The young lady's proficiency and elegance is of more consequence to the governess than her own, as well as to the world. When we wish to decide upon the merit of a governess, we naturally look at the young ladies she professes to have educated, and judge accordingly. The *judicious* governess knows this: she knows that, while she lives in obscurity herself, her pupil's virtues and defects will be open to every eye.'

During Agnes's stay at Horton Lodge she had mercifully made one friend, a curate as humble and neglected as herself. When she left her situation and retired with her mother to Scarborough she cherished both his memory and the flower which he had plucked her from a hedge. And when a hoped-for letter from him did not arrive she took herself to task in one of those downright, no-nonsense passages which might have been written by Charlotte rather than Anne. 'Was it come to this—that I should be *disappointed* to receive a letter from my only sister? "What a fool you must be", said my head to my heart, or my sterner to my softer self. "How could you ever dream that he would write to you? If you would but consider your own unattractive exterior, your unamiable reserve, your foolish diffidence! And now that you have been so foolish, pray repent and amend, and let us have no more of it."'

It is such rare, astringent self-criticisms which redeem a dull book from complete oblivion and prove its creator to be a Brontë. Before the end of the book Agnes Grey met her curate again, walking on the sands of Scarborough which Anne Brontë loved, and on which she looked out from her lodging windows when she lay dying there so soon afterwards.

We are apt to talk and think of the three Brontës as of a single constellation. It is true that their shared background and mutual devotion give them an intenser common radiance than is the case in other literary families. Yet when we scrutinise the galaxy more closely we are inevitably struck by the differing glory of its stars. Emily blazes in the white light of the spirit. Anne might be said to twinkle with homely realism—did not the word 'twinkle' carry an implication of humour that is unmerited. Charlotte, whose *Jane Eyre* we must now examine, smoulders with the hot light of romance, shot with cold flashes of intellectual power.

If we compare the childhoods of Jane Eyre and Agnes Grey, we find no suggestion that their creators drew their inspiration from a common source. Whereas Agnes was carefully reared by loving parents, Jane was up against the world from the very start. We cannot dwell here on her starved childhood, nor on Lowood as a school for governesses, save to compare it with what we know of Miss Pinkerton's Academy. For Lowood was wholly a 'charitable' institution; whereas Miss Pinkerton's was a school for young ladies, where future governesses—even articled pupils like Rebecca Sharp—mixed with the sisters and mothers of their future pupils. The curriculum of Lowood was also a great deal less pretentious. When Jane determined to seek a private situation, she described herself as 'a young lady accustomed to tuition', who is 'desirous of meeting with a situation in a private family where the children are under fourteen'. And she explained in parenthesis that as she was barely eighteen it would not do (even though she had been a teacher at Lowood) to undertake the guidance of pupils nearer her own age. 'She is qualified', continued the advertisement, 'to teach the usual branches of a good English education, together with French, Drawing and Music.' And she added the comment that 'in those days, reader, this now narrow catalogue of accomplishments would have been held tolerably comprehensive'.

This is a reminder that the action of *Jane Eyre* is supposed to antedate that of *Vanity Fair* by some years. In proof of this it may be noted that when St. John Rivers brought Jane 'a new publication' to read, it was not a volume of Tennyson, but Scott's *Marmion*, published in 1808. *Jane Eyre*, no less than *Vanity Fair*, is to some extent a period piece; and it is worth remembering before we criticise the violence and coarseness of manners in some of the Brontë novels, that *Jane Eyre* is set in the Regency period and *Wuthering Heights* in the reign of George III. If Charlotte Brontë was correct in her thesis that the demand for accomplishments had extravagantly increased with the years, then Thackeray must (as I suspected) have sketched his governesses' accomplishments from his own observation, rather than from researches into English society before Waterloo.

Anyway, Jane's advertisement was impressive enough to elicit a reply which baldly stated that 'if J. E. possesses the acquirements mentioned; and if she is in a position to give satisfactory references as to character and competency, a situation can be offered her where there is but one pupil, a little girl, under ten years of age; and where the salary is thirty pounds per annum'.

This is another and yet more flagrant example of an engagement entered into on the bare exchange of formal letters. It is true that references as to Jane's efficiency and character were sent to Mrs. Fairfax. But what guarantee had Jane, on her side, of Mrs. Fairfax's desirability as an employer? Permission for Jane to go into private service was certainly sought by Lowood from her aunt, who said she might do as she pleased; but having satisfied this convention the school authorities were quite prepared to send a young girl out into an unknown house without enquiry. Poor Jane herself was haunted by the fear of 'getting into some scrape', and wished the result of her endeavour to be 'respectable, proper, *en règle*'. She persuaded herself that Mrs. Fairfax's elderly handwriting was proof of this propriety and went into the unknown, 'a governess disconnected, poor and plain', little guessing into what sort of scrape she was really running her defenceless head.

Yet although she was courageous and idealistic, Jane did not suffer from the illusions to which childish Agnes Grey was prone. She was therefore agreeably surprised by her reception at Thornfield. 'She treats me like a visitor', Jane thought. 'I little expected such a reception; I anticipated only coldness and stiffness: this is not like what I have heard of the treatment of governesses.' Jane was installed that night in a bedroom which she was pleased to find 'of small dimensions, and furnished in ordinary modern style'. Next morning she was introduced to her pupil, and the existence of Mr. Rochester was explained to her. Then she and Adèle settled down to work in 'the library, which room, it appears, Mr. Rochester had directed should be used as the schoolroom. There was one bookcase left open containing everything that could be needed in the way of elementary works, and several volumes of light literature, poetry, biography, travels, a few romances, etc. I suppose he had considered that these were all the governess would require for her private perusal, and indeed they contented me amply for the present. In this room, too, there was a cabinet piano, quite new and of superior tone; also an easel for painting, and a pair of globes.' There is no doubt that the master of Thornfield liked to do things well!

In her pupil Jane Eyre was comparatively lucky. Adèle was not spoiled, as she had no one to indulge her; and far from ordering her governess about or tormenting her, she soon grew attached to her 'chère Mdlle. Jeannette'. But her inborn vanity and frivolity disappointed her governess, who would have preferred a studious and serious child.

On the arrival of Mr. Rochester, on Jane's friendship with him, the mystery, the declaration of love and the forbidden banns—on all this enthralling drama we cannot linger, since the story is peculiar to Jane Eyre among governesses. We must, however, consider Mr. Rochester himself, since he is the archetype of all eccentric employers. These, we shall find, are all men, and are either bachelors, widowers or mysteriously married. From the miserly Sir Pitt Crawley, through Mr. Rochester and Mr. Dorrit to the horrific Uncle Silas, they play a large part in the history of governesses. There was evidently nothing inherently improper in a governess caring for a widower's children. Becky Sharp, for instance, did not have to leave Queen's Crawley when Lady Crawley died although, had she not married Rawdon, she would no doubt have regularised her position by becoming Lady Crawley herself. Jane Eyre considered herself sufficiently chaperoned by the housekeeper; Mrs. Fairfax remained in the room during Jane's early talks with Mr. Rochester. And when he told her the risky story of his *liaison* with Adèle's mother they were safely out of doors, pacing up and down the long beech avenue. After the first conflagration he went away.

So Jane had evidently felt no embarrassment in her position by the time the house-party approached; when 'in the dining-room, the sideboard flashed resplendent with plate; in the drawing-room and boudoir, vases of exotics bloomed on all sides'. It was now, too, for the first time that she felt by contrast the loneliness and humiliation of a governess's life. Commanded to appear with her charge after dinner in the drawing-room, Jane withdrew to a window-seat from which she could observe the fine ladies and gentlemen and could overhear their conversation. Blanche Ingram, Jane's supposed rival, was setting her cap at Mr. Rochester, and with a proprietary air advised him on Adèle's upbringing. 'I suppose you have a governess for her', she says when he assures her that he cannot afford a school. 'I saw a person with her just now . . . there she is, behind the window curtain.' And although she must know that Jane may overhear, she arrogantly continues: 'You pay her, of course; I should think it is quite as expensive—more so; for you have them both to keep in addition. You should hear Mamma on the chapter of governesses. Mary and I have had, I should think, a dozen at least in our day; half of them detestable and the rest ridiculous, and all incubi—were they not, Mamma?'

'My dearest', responds the dowager, 'don't mention governesses; the word makes me nervous. I have suffered a martyrdom from their incompetency and caprice. I thank Heaven I have now done with them.'

When reminded that 'one of the anathematized race' was present, she coolly continues: '*Tant pis*! I hope it may do her good! I am a judge of physiognomy, and in hers I see all the faults of her class.'

Egged on by Mr. Rochester, who has his own reasons for exposing her as a heartless worldling, Blanche takes up the tale. 'I have just one word to say of the whole tribe; they are a nuisance. Not that I ever suffered much from them; I took care to turn the tables. What tricks Theodore and I used to play on our Miss Wilsons and Mrs. Greys, and Madame Jouberts! The best fun was with Madame Joubert: Miss Wilson was a poor, sickly thing, lachrymose and low-spirited, not worth the trouble of vanquishing, in short; and Mrs. Grey was coarse and insensible: no blow took effect on her.'

Mrs. Grey, in fact, was endowed with that 'denser moral impassibility' which Charlotte Brontë considered indispensable for a contented governess. Once again, employers are being judged (and condemned) by their treatment of their governesses. And once again I, for one, cannot help wondering whether the governesses were not a little to be judged by their pupils. No doubt Theodore, Blanche and Mary were horrid children, but could not a sensible girl have stuck it out and gradually made them fond of her? Could she not have diverted their high spirits into better channels? And if she had contrived to do so, might not Theodore and Blanche and Mary have grown up into wiser and happier human beings?

Another, and pleasanter, member of the party had evidently had a more sensible governess than the Ingrams, for Amy Eshton ('as fair as a lily') now puts in: 'Louisa and I used to quiz our governess, too; but she was such a good creature, she would bear anything: nothing put her out. She was never cross with us.' But that anyone else should take the floor is too much for Miss Ingram. 'I suppose now', she says, curling her lip sarcastically, 'we shall have an abstract of the memoirs of all the governesses extant. In order to avert such a visitation, I again move the introduction of a new topic.'

The humiliating house-party, with its charades and gipsies, came at last to an end, and Blanche Ingram left Thornfield for ever. Jane, too, left to attend the death-bed of her Aunt Reed. When she took her leave, Mr. Rochester said that she must have some money: '"I have given you no salary yet. Here", said he, offering me a note; it was fifty pounds, and he owed me but fifteen.' From which we may deduce that a governess's salary was (in some cases at least) paid twice yearly; an arrangement which must have made the giving of short notice quite impossible.

After Mr. Rochester's bigamous proposal of marriage, Jane ran away, and was taken in—half-dead from hunger and exposure—by St. John, Diana and Mary Rivers. Long before she discovered them to be her cousins, Jane had found that the girls were her fellow-sufferers by profession.

They were 'governesses in a large, fashionable South-of-England city, where each held a situation in families by whose wealthy and haughty members they were regarded only as humble dependants, and who neither knew nor sought out their innate excellencies, and appreciated only their acquired accomplishments as they appreciated the skill of their cook or the taste of their waiting woman'.

They were now studying German in order to obtain larger salaries, just as the Brontës did themselves. Jane pitied them from the bottom of her heart, and was thankful when St. John obtained for her the post of teacher in the village school. The work was 'plodding—but then, compared with that of a governess in a rich house it was independent, and the fear of servitude with strangers entered my soul like iron'. Considering how well she had been treated at Thornfield, this fear seems both unreasonable and ungrateful; for we must remember that Mr. Rochester had behaved to her with courtesy and consideration while he still thought of her as nothing but a governess. But she had heard from members of the house-party and from the Rivers what she might expect in other houses, and she was in love with Mr. Rochester. She therefore could not consider Thornfield typical; and she was eating her heart out to be back there with its owner. And back, in due course, she went, when he needed her; to become his wife and 'know what it is to live entirely for and with what I love best on earth'.

Here, surely, is the core of the problem of a governess's happiness or the reverse: that she was thwarted of her natural woman's life. The fonder a girl was of children, the more she must long for children of her own. The more she wished to be mistress of a house with her own things in it, the more she was oppressed by the splendour of other people's possessions. The more she loved society, the more lonely she felt. The fonder she let herself grow of her charges and their parents, the more she hated leaving them. The greater her love for books and music, the more her pupils' stupidity or coarseness galled her.

Her chances of marriage were much fewer than those of a cook or housemaid. For a governess was too much of a lady to marry a coachman or gardener, and her employers were constantly on guard against her possible designs on their sons and guests. Her field for courtship, as summarised by Miss Crawley in the case of Becky Sharp, was a narrow one: 'some apothecary, or house-steward, or painter, or young curate.' Occasionally, it is true, a governess would break through the guard and marry her employer or his son: Becky, for instance, and Jane Eyre herself. Others, again, made excellent matches outside the house where they worked. Poor Miss Taylor, for instance, after seeing her charges grow up, married Mr. Weston before it was too late for her to have a child of her own. Agnes Grey married a curate, within the bounds of Miss Crawley's list; and Hyacinth Clare, in *Wives and Daughters,* marries twice—the second time a most delightful widowed doctor. While Lady Blessington's Clara did best of all in marrying an earl.

But not all were as lucky as these. Many must have lost their hearts where there was no hope of honourable requital; and even those who found happiness in the end must have endured years of anxiety and heartbreak first. The unmatched, childless isolation of a woman constantly on the edge of a family circle, must surely have accounted for the unhappiness of more governesses than any other cause. It is strange, therefore, how few of our books so much as mention it. Vulgar employers, tormenting children, irregular hours, small salaries, pert footmen and even half-cold potatoes—all these are cited as evidence of the governess's unhappy lot; yet how lightly would even the worst of these have weighed on a normal girl had she felt certain of a husband, a home, and a child of her own awaiting her in the future.

Few of these hapless girls, moreover, seem to have found in their pupils an outlet for affection. Becky Sharp, perhaps, might have made something of the Crawley girls, had she had love and interest to spare for anyone except herself. But Miss Pinch's 'seraph', Agnes Grey's sadists, and Emily Morton's young Misses must have been hard to love. It is difficult to gauge how much is cause and how much effect: whether cruel children made sour governesses or self-centred governesses made heartless children. But it does seem a little odd that the governesses of all these disagreeable children were never hurt by their failure to win their love. They were susceptible to stabs at their pride rather than to blows struck at their hearts, and were pusillanimously reluctant to commit their affections. Had they met their charges more than half way and shown a little warmth even at the risk of getting burned, perhaps their generosity might have been rewarded. Jane Eyre was of the sort who would have done so, had she met with high-spirited, spoiled children—just as she did with a high-spirited, spoiled man. But Adèle, though affectionate and amenable, was neither a foe nor friend worthy of Jane's mettle. As for the rest of the afflicted tribe, they seem scarcely to have tried to win their children's hearts.

CHAPTER III

MID-VICTORIAN

W. M. Thackeray, *The Newcomes* ; Charles Dickens, *Little Dorrit* ; Charlotte M. Yonge, *The Daisy Chain*, *Womankind* ; Mrs. Henry Wood, *East Lynne* ; Wilkie Collins, *No Name* ; Sheridan le Fanu, *Uncle Silas* ; Mrs. Gaskell, *Wives and Daughters* ; Jean Ingelow, *Dr. Deane's Governess* ; George Eliot, *Scenes of Clerical Life*, *Middlemarch* ; Schools versus Governesses ; Anthony Trollope, *The Eustace Diamonds*, *Barchester Towers*.

It is almost with relief that we turn again to Thackeray, and to the governesses sketched with his inimitable bravura in *The Newcomes* (1855). These are included in the cast less for their own sakes than as foils to the leading actors; but their parts, though small, are character parts in a comedy of manners, and are therefore pertinent to our study.

The first of them was for a short time the pride of Mrs. Hobson Newcome of Bryanston Square. She had snob-value even in that fashionable neighbourhood, and was therefore raised far above Miss Wirt when she started her career in Bloomsbury. To the snob-exhibit she added a strong dash of the adventuress, and also a soupçon of the strict, governessy type which we have not hitherto encountered.

Clive Newcome as a schoolboy complained that, when he visited his aunt, he was made 'to dine with the children, and a great, cross, French governess, who is always crying and shrieking after them, and finding fault with them'. One day, when Clive and his father went to call, they saw the children in the Square gardens, and went to speak to them. 'That's the French governess', said Clive, 'the one with the mustachios and the yellow parasol'; and her strictness and snobbishness were both displayed to the Colonel, as she explained: 'One cannot too early inculcate *retenue* and decorum to young ladies in a country where demoiselles seem forever to forget that they are young ladies of condition.' Her snob-value to her employers was emphasised when Mrs. Hobson Newcome herself joined the party and introduced her: 'Madamaselle Lebrun, le Collonel Newcome, mong frère.' And she added in a whisper to the Colonel (who had already, from innate good manners, treated the lady like a queen): 'My children's governess and my friend, a most superior woman.' Turning again to the governess, she interpreted untruthfully: 'Nous parlong de Napolleong, Mademoiselle, dong voter père a été le Général favorry.'

This claim of Mademoiselle's was, of course, more than enough to make Mrs. Newcome parade the governess as her friend. But it proved to be unfounded. For Mademoiselle, as I have said, had a dash of the adventuress (or rather the impostor) in her Gallic composition. Poor, deceived Mrs. Newcome complained afterwards how 'that wretched Frenchwoman, Mademoiselle Lebrun, turned out, oh frightfully! She taught the girls the *worst* accent, it appears. Her father was not a Colonel; he was—oh! never mind! It's a mercy I got rid of that *fiendish woman* and before my precious ones knew *what* she was.'

Lady Ann Newcome seemed to share Mrs. Hobson's failing for alternating between enthusiasm and disgust. 'Her daughter [Ethel] had had so many governesses—all darlings during the first week, and monsters afterwards—that the poor child possessed none of the accomplishments of her age. She could not play on the piano; she could not speak French well; she could not tell you when gunpowder was invented; she had not the faintest idea of the date of the Norman Conquest, or whether the earth went round the sun or *vice versa*. She did not know the number of counties in England, Scotland and Wales, let alone Ireland; she did not know the difference between latitude and longitude.' Which shows not only the useless nature of much of the information imparted to young ladies, but also how easily a governess's security might be wrecked by the mere caprice of her employer.

The governess in possession at the moment is a Miss Quigley, to whom the Colonel 'behaves with splendid courtesy' and 'makes a point of taking wine with her. If Ethel makes her uncle purses, guard-chains, antimacassars, and the like beautiful and useful articles, I believe it is in reality Miss Quigley who does four-fifths of the work as she sits alone in the schoolroom, high, high up in that lone house, when the little ones are long since asleep, before her dismal little tea-tray and her little desk, containing her mother's letters and her mementoes of home.'

For Thackeray can, when he pleases, pile on the pathos as thick as any of them: and, indeed, it is a genuinely pathetic picture rendered all the more so by contrast with his cynical portraits of more cynical governesses. But it is pleasant to hear that Miss Quigley's sojourn with the Newcomes lasted long enough to include a journey abroad to fashionable Baden. There she met the Irish governess of La Duchesse d'Ivry's little girl, 'Miss O'Grady, with the richest Milesian brogue, who had been engaged to give Antoinette the pure English accent'. (Between her and Mademoiselle Lebrun, England and France were quits in the traffic in vulgar accents.) When Miss Quigley and Miss O'Grady were introduced, 'the Irish Protestant governess scowled at the Irish Catholic—there was a Boyne Water between them'.

Their mutual distrust raises a point which we have not yet considered, but which must have provided a minor grievance for many governesses. Just as their charges were expected to play happily together for no better reason than that they were all children, so governesses were expected to get on like wild-fire merely because they followed the same calling. Often, no doubt, they had much to talk of—if only the shortcomings of their employers—and enjoyed each other's company. But it must have been galling to have their instant friendship taken for granted; and often they had to walk warily at first. A strange governess might prove to be a spy, an informer—even a stool-pigeon—who would curry favour by slandering a colleague or would try to replace her.

Miss O'Grady proved, in fact, to be our first example of the Governess Villain unless, of course, Becky Sharp really meant to murder Jos Sedley in the end. But she was a villain on a mean and petty scale. For she not only wrote poison-pen letters for her employer, telling Ethel Newcome about Lord Kew, but she afterwards blackmailed his lordship on her own account while he was on his honeymoon. A governess, who (as we saw in *Jane Eyre*) was assumed to be deaf in company, and who inevitably knew much of what was going on in the family, must have had many opportunities of blackmail. Perhaps this source provided—for a few of them—their superannuation pension and the additional luxury of a delayed revenge.

One more candle-gleam of light is shed by the observant Thackeray on the position of the governess in a big house. This, as we have seen, was something between drawing-room and servants' hall, between mistress and maid, and tended towards her being very much alone. But in the assumed presence of the Almighty, where for once all might be considered equal—here, surely, she might be at one with the whole household? But no! Even at family prayers, when the master takes his place before the Bible, and the domestic staff ranges itself against a row of dining-room chairs—even here, Thackeray assures us, the isolation is maintained, and 'the governess worships a little apart'.

Before we leave the great novelists of the 'forties and 'fifties and break entirely new ground, we must return for a moment to Dickens, whose *Little Dorrit* was published serially from 1856 to 1857. Those who can ignore or forgive the complexities of its plot and love its main characters as dearly as they deserve, will remember that Mr. Dorrit—after emerging from a lifetime in the Marshalsea—sought a woman to rub from his daughters the roughness of a prison upbringing.

He was recommended to a Mrs. General, 'a lady in the varnishing trade', who handled the interview with a masterly hand. She was particularly delicate on the subject of her salary. 'I am not a governess', she assured him. 'I cannot, therefore, put a price upon services which it is a pleasure for me to render, if I can render them spontaneously.' As there were two daughters to be 'finished', it would in this case 'be necessary to add a third more to the payment (whatever its amount may prove to be) which my friends have been accustomed to make to my bankers'. From this roundabout approach the fact somehow emerged that her friends had been accustomed to pay her £300 per annum. For accompanying the two Dorrit girls on a grand tour, Mrs. General was accordingly paid £400 per annum, which seems a very handsome reward indeed for the pleasure of rendering spontaneous services.

Mrs. General's 'way of forming a mind was to prevent it from forming opinions', and her ultimate goal was 'the formation of a surface'. She was addicted to Podsnappery; but her version of Mr. Podsnap's dictum—'I don't want to know about it, I don't choose to discuss it: I don't admit it.'—was adorned with the addition of alliteration. 'Nothing disagreeable', she considered, 'should ever be looked at. A truly refined mind will seem to be ignorant of the existence of anything which is not perfectly proper, placid and pleasant.' Her criticisms were wholly negative and destructive: 'Fanny', she complained 'at present forms too many opinions. Perfect breeding forms none, and is never demonstrative.' Even on a grand tour, she considered, 'it is better not to wonder'—in which she proved herself a disciple of Mr. Gradgrind no less than of Mr. Podsnap.

Her positive teaching related entirely to deportment; and even then, to the management of the face rather than the feet or figure, whose existence it was surely much better to ignore. It is above all her advice on lip-control which has won her immortality and an inalienable place in cross-word puzzles: 'Father is rather vulgar, my dear. The word Papa, besides, gives a pretty form to the lips. Papa, potatoes, poultry, prunes, and prism. . . . You will find it serviceable, in the formation of a demeanour, if you sometimes say to yourself in company—on entering a room, for instance—Papa, potatoes, poultry, prunes and prism, prunes and prism.'

We may, perhaps, agree with Mrs. General that she was not a governess. Like so many Dickens characters she was neither a type nor a real person, but a portent—a symbol, if you will, of all that was most soul-destroying and inhuman in female education. The snob governess at least strove to impart a veneer of accomplishment to her charges: Mrs. General merely applied a polish. Under the smooth surface there might or might not be a veneer, but there would certainly be no sound foundation. If Mrs. General succeeded in her aim, the supposedly solid core of character would have been eaten away by ignorance, pretence and selfishness.

The Daisy Chain, by Charlotte Mary Yonge (1856), is a very different proposition from *Little Dorrit* and *The Newcomes.* For Charlotte Yonge was no genius; and her gifts, though considerable, were rather for domestic scenes and historic reconstruction than for satire or strong emotion.

But we must not jump to the other extreme and assume that, because it was written for young people and under the influence of John Keble, *The Daisy Chain* necessarily resembles *Amy Herbert.* It is true that both authors hoped to instil High Church principles into their young readers; but their gifts for telling a story and teaching a lesson differ widely. Miss Yonge's imaginative power soars as much above Miss Sewell's as it falls short of Thackeray and Dickens.

Although *The Daisy Chain* was written for young readers, it was not written down to them. Idealistic in aim, it is realistic in treatment. Although the May family are given to good works and good words, they are none the less a real family with real governesses. Dr. May is an intelligent and conscientious doctor in a country town. Early in the story his carriage is overturned and his wife killed; while Margaret, the eldest girl, is crippled and lingers on a sofa until she dies at the end of the book. Her *fiancé* is drowned at sea after a wreck from which Harry May, the jolly midshipman brother, returns unharmed. The eldest brother becomes a curate. The second girl makes a worldly and unhappy marriage, while Norman, the clever one of the family, nearly loses his faith at Oxford but recovers it in time to become a missionary. The real heroine is Ethel May, Norman's friend and the doctor's intellectual companion. She is clever, good, enthusiastic, plain, impetuous and unladylike. The five younger children cannot be described in detail: readers must take my word for it that they provide a nursery-full of personalities.

At the outset the small children are cared for by a nurse. Norman, Harry and another brother attend the Grammar School; while a daily governess, Miss Winter, teaches Flora, Ethel and the younger girls. Miss Winter is an excellent example of the governessy governess. Strict, repressive, and holding narrow ideas on education, she is not a suitable teacher for Ethel. Margaret, from her sofa, explains this to her younger sister: 'Dear Mama thought Miss Winter an excellent governess for the little ones, but hardly up to you', she says. And this is perhaps not surprising, since Ethel's ambition was to keep pace with her beloved brother Norman in construing Sophocles and writing Greek and Latin verses; while for Miss Winter the conceptions of bluestocking and gentlewoman were simply incompatible. She would tear poor Ethel away from her enthralling struggle with cube-roots to make her answer Mrs. Mangnall's Questions, and when Ethel spouted Shakespeare, complained: 'That is declaiming. It is not what one wishes for in a lady.' She was 'formal' and 'precise'; and 'Ethel's eagerness was checked by Miss Winter's dry manner, producing pettishness.' Yet Ethel was sensible enough to appreciate her good intentions and to cherish respect and affection for her. She realised, moreover, that her own clumsiness and absent-mindedness were unbecoming in a lady. Not that Miss Winter was a Mrs. General. She did not wish to produce a polish so much as self-control and good sense. 'Though it may not be the fashion to say so', she once confessed, 'I consider good needlework far more important than accomplishments.'

Above all, there should be no enthusiasm. Ethel was a good girl, as well as a clever one, and she had conceived the idea of building a mission church in a neighbouring colony of poor and barbarous miners. Not only did she work for years to raise money to build the actual church, but she visited the parish herself and taught the children in her own Sunday School. This was too much for Miss Winter, who considered it 'beyond what befits a young lady of her age'; and she strove to endow Ethel with her own 'dry experience and prejudiced preciseness'.

The Mays are the first family since the Harcourts in *The Good French Governess* to take the education of women seriously: to consider the general needs of growing girls, and the special needs of individuals. Miss Winter herself, as we have seen, despised those accomplishments which were the stock-in-trade of Jane Fairfax, Miss Wirt and Emily Morton. She wished to form old-fashioned wives and mothers rather than society ladies. But though the Mays were at one with her in the belief that accomplishments are not enough, they aspired to fill the gap with something more than needlework—at any rate for Ethel. Ethel had an active, understanding mind which needed to be fed and stimulated with Sophocles, cube-roots and missionary projects; and it was to the credit of her parents, sister and brothers that they did not want to see her powers curbed by Mrs. Mangnall's Questions.

One day the Doctor took Ethel with him to visit a patient, Mr. Rivers, who lived in a big house outside the town. Here she found conservatories full of exotics, spacious rooms, quiet servants, all the amenities and luxuries unknown in her own crowded home. And here, too, as sweet and beautiful as a flower from one of her father's own greenhouses, was Meta Rivers. Longing for girls of her own age, Meta welcomed Ethel as a friend; and the whole May family was soon made to feel at home with her. Having lived a very sheltered life, the noisy inrush was a revelation to her. But her loneliness up till then had been consoled by a governess.

Mrs. Larpent was really more of a companion than a governess. She provides an admirable specimen of the loved and trusted *confidante,* that species of governess of which Emma's Miss Taylor was our first example. When Norman first saw them together they were 'on such sister-like terms' that he 'could hardly believe her to be the governess, when he thought of Miss Winter'. Yet she would not have satisfied Dr. May's desire to fit his children for life, nor have provided intellectual companionship for

Ethel. It was not Sophocles or cube-roots that filled her long, leisured hours with Meta. It was not towards a tough Sunday School that they took their walks. Far from it. When they were first discovered together, Meta and her governess were cutting leaves out of leather: 'Our holiday work', said Mrs. Larpent. 'Meta has been making a drawing for her Papa, and is framing it in leather-work.' This occupation would surely have been condemned by Ethel as trivial, and by Miss Winter as an accomplishment. Yet it did not prevent Norman from falling in love with Meta in due course, nor Meta herself from facing the hardships of a missionary's wife.

When Miss Winter left the Mays, the Doctor replaced her with an orphan 'who had been qualifying herself for a governess, and needed nothing but age and finish'. Ethel, by now, had left the schoolroom and had undertaken the running of the house. To her, therefore, fell the task of coping with the sensitive spirit of Miss Bracey, the new governess. And it was no easy task, for Miss Bracey must certainly have read *Agnes Grey* and *Amy Herbert,* and have made up her mind to be a downtrodden, humiliated member of the depressed class of governesses.

'She was obliging and intelligent', and Ethel would have been glad of the equal companionship of a girl so near herself in age. She therefore did her utmost 'to make Miss Bracey feel at home—and like a friend—in her new surroundings'. But Miss Bracey preferred her grievance; she would not be deprived of martyrdom. Nor did she suffer in silence. 'The governess was one of those morbidly sensitive people who cannot be stopped when once they have begun arguing that they are injured.' Worse than this, she developed an unbalanced love for her new home and its inmates. She did not, indeed, fall in love with Dr. May: there is no evidence that *Jane Eyre* had been included in her preparatory course of reading. But she had a 'crush' on Ethel and 'demanded a manifestation of sympathy and return to her passionate attachment that perplexed Ethel's undemonstrative nature'. Even kindnesses were resented. 'It was one of Miss Bracey's idiosyncrasies to be hurt whenever Mary was taken out of her hands.' She was jealous of the little girls' love, and suspected that her methods with them were thought unwise. She accordingly took offence when, at a bazaar, the Doctor considerately took them off her hands for a while. 'Her feelings', Ethel protested to her father in despair, 'are always being hurt. If any one of us criticises anything the girls have done, if there is a change in any arrangement, if she thinks herself neglected, she will argue with me until we are both half dead.'

Wise Dr. May urged Ethel to go on being kind in her own way, and also to try to put herself in the governess's shoes. 'Remember', he said, 'that dependence is prone to morbid sensitiveness. We do not know what it is to be among strangers, uncertain of any claim to their esteem or kindness. Each trifle seems a token one way or the other.'

As an experienced physician Dr. May had often taken off the lid and looked into his patients' minds. He knew just what made a governess so vulnerable that pin-pricks became stabs, and kindness reeked of patronage. If he had heard the story of Charlotte Brontë and the Sidgwicks, he would have recognised that she and poor Miss Bracey were sisters under their skins. Charlotte Brontë, as a novelist, shared his insight to some extent, but as a woman (and a governess) she could not use it on herself. Indeed, her very power of imagination only served to magnify and distort the 'tokens' of kindness and unkindness in the Sidgwick family; and the supposed slights rankled, until she was able to sublimate them in her novels. She suffered, too, the added bitterness of knowing herself wasted on her work, though this superior knowledge was possibly a secret solace, too.

There is no doubt that Miss Bracey, at any rate, derived comfort from being (as she fancied) misunderstood. 'My feelings have always been over-sensitive', she said, with a sort of complacency when next she cornered poor Ethel in the schoolroom for a heart-to-heart talk. But in the end Ethel's patience and good sense were rewarded by Miss Bracey's reform, which was helped by the fact that the governess had a friend in a similar position, but 'in a family less considerate than the Mays'. Towards her, at least, Miss Bracey could assume an attitude of unquestioned superiority; and she helped to cure herself through her attempts to cure her friend. She took to writing to this friend, urging her to be more enduring and 'repeating all Ethel's pieces of advice'. In the process of passing on, they assumed for herself a new validity; for, as every good governess knows, we never learn anything so well as when we teach it to another.

Like Maria Edgeworth, Charlotte Mary Yonge wrote about governesses in the abstract, as well as in her novels. In 1876, twenty years after *The Daisy Chain,* she published a collection of studies called *Womankind,* in which she devoted some thought to the matter. She introduces a new element to our researches by insisting that no girl under twenty-five should henceforth be employed to teach children over fourteen unless she had got a diploma. Such diplomas had been obtainable since 1848 at Queen's College, Harley Street, which was founded primarily for the purpose of training governesses; while the Oxford and Cambridge local examinations established in 1858 had later on been opened to women. If a girl could not attain to this standard, said Miss Yonge, she should either teach small children only, or adopt some other profession such as nursing.

In spite of *Punch,* which for many years maintained that workhouses, the streets and lunatic asylums were replenished from the ranks of sweated governesses, Miss Yonge was as optimistic about governesses as Miss Edgeworth had been eighty years before. I think the two good ladies can have numbered only gentlefolk among their friends. Miss Yonge pooh-poohed the 'old, stock complaint' of 'insolence to governesses'. In real life she had heard only of two instances: one of 'a thoroughly vulgar employer', the other of 'a servant who was sharply rebuked, and, I think, dismissed'. In fact she considered that governesses were seldom exploited except by the kind of employers who would be equally offensive to their families and friends; and it is of especial interest to us that she held the 'pathetic governess' type of book to be largely responsible for the myth. Not that she shut her eyes to the difficulties of daily life. The governess, she urged, must share her pupils' hours and not be hurt when inevitably excluded from the grown-ups' gaieties. The mother, although 'afraid of boring her husband with a stranger', could yet contrive to make a companion of the governess, and to share and supervise the teaching. Elder daughters could often find a delightful friend in their little sisters' governess; or, failing that, could make her happier by taking her books, flowers and 'bits of news'.

To employers in general, Miss Yonge said that 'there is no need to be sentimental' about the governess. 'Treat her as a lady with a vocation, your equal in breeding, and your superior in certain acquirements.' To governesses she said astringently that 'whether the condition of governesses ever receives the change that is talked of, depends not on their employers, but on themselves'. Finally, governesses should remember always that their calling is not only a profession, but a vocation. 'The governess who teaches history and geography, and hears scales practised, with the conscientious care of one who has the fear of God before her eyes, is just as much a handmaid of the Church, as if she were a nursing or teaching sister in a community.' A high ideal, certainly, if a little bleak. Whereas Miss Edgeworth dangled before her rationalist governess the female equivalent of some snug Deanery, Miss Yonge seems to offer her High Church novice only the prospect of retirement to a spiritual convent cell.

It is certain that neither Ethel nor Meta from *The Daisy Chain,* would have allowed their growing girls to read *East Lynne* by Mrs. Henry Wood. But perhaps their governesses hid a copy under their gloves and handkerchiefs, and devoured this improper story of another governess after their innocent charges were asleep. Few educated people read it to-day, though they may have seen it acted by a touring company and have quoted the pathetic phrase 'he never called me mother'. For *East Lynne* survives as a period piece and a legendary best-seller.

The style is so bad as to repel at first; yet if one perseveres, it exercises a morbid fascination—a contagious influence. Sir Ernest Gowers, when he was compiling his delightful *Plain Words,* would have found it a mine of officialese, wherein every horrific circumlocution is included. Mrs. Henry Wood never used a short word where a long one would do as well. It is as if she had looked up every word in Roget's *Thesaurus,* and always chosen the most unlikely alternative from his fantastic array of synonyms. She uses 'transpire' instead of 'happen', 'be cognisant of' for 'know', 'premise' for 'foresee', 'deem' for 'think', and 'style' in the sense of 'call'. In the pages of *East Lynne,* as in a policeman's notebook, people do not go to bed, but 'retire to rest'. They do not tell the news but 'communicate the tidings'. Mrs. Wood is not above such vulgarisms as 'so thoroughly the gentlewoman', 'of a morning', and 'all of a twitter', the last being said by a man in the very midst of a dramatic crisis. Her characters are forever changing colour like so many chameleons. Faces are livid or suffused with crimson; hearts have to be held down by clasped hands; nerves vibrate; and pulses thrill or quicken. And when Mrs. Wood relaxes from dramatic tension and plumps for some colloquial relief, she does it thoroughly. 'Talk of her having looked ill!' she observes to the reader, 'you should have seen her now.'

Setting aside the intricate sub-plot about a murder, *East Lynne* is the story of Lady Isabel Vane as maiden, wife, mother, outcast and governess. She was beautiful and highly born—everything, in fact, that a heroine with such a name should be; and when she married Mr. Archibald Carlyle, wealthy and virtuous owner of East Lynne, the match was no more brilliant than she deserved. It is perhaps a little strange that East Lynne itself, which gives its name to the book and is the scene of so much drama, should not have been remarkable. It was not a stately home, and hid no mystery, but was merely a commodious Victorian residence. Lady Isabel became the mother of a beautiful girl and boy, and would seem to have had all she could desire. But during a solitary holiday at Ostend she was thrown into the company of Sir Francis Levison, and as he was a wicked baronet, she was naturally undone. She eloped with him, only to discover (too late) his worthlessness, and Mr. Carlyle's excellence. In one way it was all to the good that Sir Francis was soon thrown from a dog-cart to his death. But in the same accident she herself was shattered and horribly disfigured. In a remote cottage somewhere in France, she recovered from her injuries—save only a scarred face and broken heart. From the papers she learned that her very compromising death had been assumed, and (in due course) that Mr. Carlyle had remarried. Too proud and too ashamed to make known her survival, she found herself thrown upon the world without a penny and without a name.

What, then, could be more natural than that she should decide to become a governess—and a French governess at that? Under the name of Madame Vine, and with her face permanently hidden by layers of veils, she took service with an English family at some German spa. We are told nothing of her position here, except that she could learn nothing about her family because the English newspapers were not sent up to the governess. It is not made clear whether this omission was due to inconsiderateness or because the French governess was not expected to read English papers.

After a time she heard through other English residents that the new Mrs. Archibald Carlyle of East Lynne was requiring a governess for her step-children and, as might be expected, she jumped at the opportunity of seeing her little ones again. Difficulties which to us might seem insuperable were nothing to her. She was convinced (and rightly) that no one would recognise her: the veils and the foreign accent would successfully baffle even her husband. Nor was she afraid of the effect of these appurtenances upon the children. We have noted before how irresponsibly parents engaged governesses whom they had never seen regardless of their influence on their charges. The Carlyles reduced this irresponsibility to the absurd. Even when they saw her, it apparently never occurred to them that small children might be puzzled—even frightened—by the companionship of a woman who was permanently draped in an unusual grey costume, and whose face was hidden (indoors as well as out) by an impenetrable veil. And to do them justice, the little Carlyles accepted the mystery with true English phlegm and grew very fond of Madame Vine.

When she first had the situation described to her Lady Isabel was told: 'You will be treated as a lady, and have all things comfortable. The salary is seventy guineas.' On arriving at East Lynne, she found everything arranged for her in a manner fitting so handsome a salary. A fire was burning in her private sitting-room, and she was offered another in her 'commodious and well-furnished bedroom'. She was expected to share neither bedroom nor schoolroom with her charges. In the sitting-room, on her first night, supper was set out, with a copper tea-urn probably 'bought for the use of the governess. She might have known, by the signs observable, that the governesses at East Lynne were regarded as gentlewomen; treated well and liberally. Yes: for East Lynne owned Mr. Carlyle for its master.'

Many as were her trials, Lady Isabel was spared the horror of seeing her children maltreated by their step-mother. Barbara Carlyle was kind and sensible. She held the theory that a mother should not concern herself with the trivial daily doings of her children, but should remain for them someone special and apart to whom they looked for guidance in such serious matters as religion. She therefore gave the new governess a free hand, and was kind enough to her by any normal standards.

Before we condemn her for occasionally inflicting pain, we must remember that (thanks to the veils and the accent) she did not know that Madame Vine was the children's mother and that she herself was therefore bigamously married! She meant no offence, for instance, when she said: 'You will come into the drawing-room by and by with Miss Lucy, Madame Vine. We wish to hear you play.' Yet the governess pondered bitterly: 'Miss Lucy! and it was spoken in the light of a command.' Barbara's mother, too, was kind and considerate. When she came to visit the Carlyles she would go and sit for a few minutes with Madame Vine, for 'she feared that governesses must be very lonely'. In time, moreover, Barbara made a friend of the governess. One day she told her about the murder mystery in which her brother had been implicated: 'You will understand, Madame Vine', she ended, 'that this history has been given you in confidence. I look upon you as one of ourselves.'

The strain of controlling her emotions before her loved ones became almost unendurable for Lady Isabel when she nursed little William through his long and fatal illness. Even then, though he never called her 'mother', she retained the material and spiritual veils until the end. But the strain told upon her, and after the child's affecting death she became ill herself. Grateful for her devotion, Mrs. Carlyle was most thoughtful and generous. She would not hear of Madame Vine leaving East Lynne: 'You have made yourself ill, waiting upon poor William, and you must remain here and take holiday until you are cured. You will soon get well, if you will only suffer yourself to be properly waited on and taken care of.' For 'Barbara could not fail to perceive that she was a thoroughly refined gentlewoman, far superior to the generality of governesses. She would raise her salary to anything in reason if she would stay.'

The engagement was ultimately terminated by the governess's death. She left her situation through no fault of her own, and the character she took with her—as Madame Vine, if not as Lady Isabel Vane—was highly satisfactory. Perhaps little William welcomed her in her new place, and learned to call her 'mother'.

The case of Lady Isabel Vane, *alias* Madame Vine, is *sui generis,* and we can consign her to no category of governess. She is certainly not, as Mr. G. M. Young asserted, the apotheosis of the governess who was 'snubbed, bullied, loving and usually quite incompetent'. She was loving enough, it is true, but she was not incompetent, and any snubs she received were due entirely to her false position. The inconsiderateness (to put it mildly) was all on the side of the governess. For it is unfair to employers to risk their married happiness—their very married *state,* indeed—and unkind to pupils to suck their emotional blood in secret like a vampire.

But *East Lynne* cannot be considered a serious contribution to either the psychology or the sociology of governesses. Even the few concrete details as to salary and rooms are suspect as elements in Mrs. Henry Wood's nightmare vision of life in high society. I said that *The Daisy Chain* was written for young people, but not written down to them: in the same way *East Lynne* may be said to have been written for housemaids and not written down to them. Had it really been written by a housemaid, her impression of a governess's life might have been extremely valuable, but as it was written by a lady novelist *East Lynne* contributes no more to the social history of the nineteenth century than does *Forever Amber* to that of the seventeenth.

Wilkie Collins's *No Name,* published in 1862, is as dramatic as Mrs. Henry Wood's farrago of nonsense, and far more genuinely exciting. But at the same time it is much more convincing on details of everyday life. The story opens in the middle-class home of the Vanstones, and we are almost immediately introduced to the governess, Miss Garth. 'Her hard-featured face; her masculine readiness and decision of movement; her obstinate honesty of look and manner, all proclaimed her Border birth and Border training. The self-possession of her progress down the stairs and the air of habitual authority with which she looked about her, spoke well for her position in Mr. Vanstone's family.'

The family consisted of Mr. and Mrs. Vanstone and two daughters, now grown up. Since Norah and Magdalen left the schoolroom, 'the entire arrangement of the household' had been left in Miss Garth's capable hands. Wilkie Collins had evidently studied the theory of the downtrodden governess, but did not think it had universal application. For he says of Miss Garth: 'This was evidently not one of the forlorn, persecuted, pitiably dependent order of governesses. Here was a woman who lived on ascertained and honourable terms with her employers—a woman who looked capable of sending any parents in England to the right-about, if they failed to rate her at her proper value.'

She was undoubtedly accepted by the Vanstones at her own valuation, which she had made good through years of honest devotion. She held 'the position of a high authority on all domestic questions'; and Mrs. Vanstone wrote to her of their 'long and intimate friendship'. Even when the strange and shocking truth was revealed, that the seemingly respectable Vanstones had never been man and wife—even when the girls were left penniless orphans (and illegitimate penniless orphans at that)—even then Miss Garth did not lose command of the situation. Indeed, her true worth was made known in this crisis. She told the girls that they must go and live with her in her sister's boarding school until they found work, and altogether behaved like a sensible and loving mother. Norah, at least, appreciated this, and wrote of her as 'our dearest friend, our second mother'.

Unfortunately Magdalen had a gift for mimicry, together with too strong a dose of the dramatic temperament. Stage-struck, she ran away and actually earned a living by her impersonations. But her adventures, and her relations with Captain and Mrs. Wragge, though they make up the bulk of the book, must not detain us here. It is enough to say that Miss Garth, who was no straitlaced prude, never despaired of her pupil's outcast state.

Norah, on the other hand, was afflicted with no such striking talents as her sister. Brought up for marriage, yet without a dowry, she could of course do nothing but become a governess. Her first experience of the business showed that Wilkie Collins did not reject the oppressed governess theory in its entirety; for poor Norah became 'the hired victim of an old woman's insolence, and a child's ill-temper'. Norah, in one of her many letters, wrote that the children's grandmother 'made my life very hard to me. My inexperience in teaching was a constant subject of remark to her.' Luckily, however, Norah was not entirely defenceless. Although she was, like so many governesses, an orphan, she had Miss Garth in the background to encourage and support her; and Miss Garth knew from experience how governesses should be treated by gentlefolk. So when Norah's first job became intolerable, she was able to leave it and find another. The second situation was with unusually charming and tolerant employers. They did not object to 'followers', but allowed their governess's young man to visit and court her in their house. Nor did they draw the line at Magdalen, by now a vagrant *artiste* of dubious reputation; but sent a maid with Norah when she went to look for her erring sister.

All Wilkie Collins's material on governesses rings true. He could, when he wished, create fantastic characters in the *genre* of his master, Dickens: for instance, Captain Wragge in this book, and Count Fosco in *The Woman in White*. He could strain probability—even possibility—when the needs of a complicated plot required it. But his ordinary characters are plain and foursquare enough, sometimes so ordinary that they scarcely come to life at all. For whereas Dickens paints a scowl, grimace or expression of rapture on every face in his crowded canvasses, Collins distorts only the central group. We can therefore accept as true to life his three examples of a governess's position, as we can never accept those of Ruth Pinch or Mrs. General. And when he shows us one case of a bullied governess, against two treated with friendship and respect, we may tentatively rest assured that this was a reasonable and usual proportion.

Once again we find that the main factor in the situation

is the human relationship. A governess's happiness depended not on copper tea-urns or modes of address, but on her own integrity and her employers' human understanding. Miss Garth was respected because she respected herself, and even the insolent grandmother would not have dared to bully her. As for Norah, she was scarcely more used to teaching in her second place than in her first, but because her inexperience was not flung in her teeth she no doubt taught much better. I suspect that every employer eventually got the governess whom she deserved. While a governess with character would, in the end, find or mould a family to her liking, even though she might get some hard knocks in the process.

Sheridan le Fanu, like Wilkie Collins, was a mystery-monger and creator of 'characters'. He was perhaps an even greater conjurer of atmosphere. In his short stories he often explored the supernatural, but the horrors of *Uncle Silas,* the novel which concerns us here, are caused entirely by human avarice and cruelty. This first-rate thriller, published in 1864, is not forgotten yet. Not only has it been recently republished, but it has also reached a different public through the medium of film. And in many ways it is an admirable story for filming, for the strong types, often violent action, and natural dialogue, give it dramatic intensity. Yet no film can recapture the slow serenity of ordinary days; and it is the contrast of this mid-Victorian routine with growing mystery and culminating crime, which constitutes the magic of *Uncle Silas*.

The heroine and narrator, Maud Ruthyn, is a young girl brought up in seclusion by her widowed father, a recluse and a Swedenborgian. When Austin Ruthyn learns that he may die at any moment, he is concerned to find his daughter a companion. 'This won't do', he says, 'you must have a governess. Your French is pretty well, and your Italian; but you have no German. Your music may be pretty good—I'm no judge—but your drawing might be better. I believe there are accomplished ladies—finishing governesses, they call them—who undertake more than any one teacher would have professed in my time, and do very well. It is nearly six months since Miss Ellerton left you—too long without a teacher.'

Had Austin Ruthyn's sole anxiety been not to neglect his daughter's accomplishments, all would have been well. Unfortunately, he wanted a governess for her partly because he felt he was neglecting her himself. And this neglect was due to his preoccupations. Death hovered over him; and before he could make his peace with Swedenborg's over-populated Heaven, there was a wrong on earth that he felt called upon to right. He had a younger brother, Silas, who had been a rake, run through a fortune, married a barmaid, and finally been suspected of an unsavoury and brutal murder. Though Silas had never been charged with this crime, through lack of evidence, the mud had stuck. He had been cut by the county and dropped by his friends, and now lived in complete retirement with his son and daughter on an estate in Derbyshire belonging to his brother Austin. In recent years he had ostensibly reformed; and in letters to his brother had convinced him of a leaning towards Swedenborgianism.

Austin Ruthyn was a proud man, and the slur on his brother's reputation was also a blot on the family escutcheon. He had never believed Silas to be a murderer, and his dissipations had long been a thing of the past. How better could he put Silas right with the world than by bequeathing Maud—a great heiress—to her uncle's sole guardianship until she came of age? As Silas would automatically inherit Maud's fortune should she die before her twenty-first birthday, Austin's confidence in Silas must be patent to all the world. It was an ingenious plan, which

Austin kept locked in a secret cupboard until the time came for reading his will. Maud, of course, knew nothing of all this. But a portrait of Uncle Silas as a young man had already won her romantic allegiance, and she had solemnly promised her father to do all in her power to clear her uncle's name.

Maud was sitting in the drawing-room one day when she saw an apparition on the terrace—a gaunt, grimacing woman for whom she conceived an immediate terror. Imagine her consternation when the apparition proved to be Madame de la Rougierre, her new French governess! 'Every girl of my age', she observed, 'knows how much is involved in such an advent. Was it really the arrival of a governess? Was that apparition which had impressed me so unpleasantly to take the command of me—to sit alone with me, and haunt me perpetually with her sinister looks and shrill gabble?'

In the course of our survey we have seen many governesses from their own point of view. We have heard them criticised by parents, laughed at by visitors, derided by pupils, and admired by fathers and elder brothers. But never before have we seen a new governess through the eyes of a highly strung, intelligent girl who has got to live with her. At last we are presented with the pupil's side of the medal, and find (as I have already hinted) that it has its own discomforts, anxieties and fears.

Consider how different the life of Meta in *The Daisy Chain* would have been, had Mrs. Larpent been sullen and tyrannical: imagine the fate of Emma Woodhouse had Miss Taylor been vain and vulgar. An only girl, living with a widowed father in the country, was pathetically dependent on her governess both for intellectual stimulus and human comfort. The governess was her only female adviser in physical ailments, niceties of etiquette, matters of clothes and taste, and even in affairs of the heart. She had to read with her, sit with her, walk with her, eat with her, and sometimes even sleep in the same room. If her father was a hypochondriac like Mr. Woodhouse or an eccentric like Mr. Ruthyn, a sensitive girl would shrink from troubling him with complaints about the governess. If he was a tyrant, she would be afraid to set up her own opinion. In her ignorance, too, she might believe that all governesses were the same, or fear that a change would be for the worse. So even if Madame de la Rougierre had been merely an uncouth and disagreeable woman, Maud would have had plenty of cause for apprehension. But she was far worse than this. She was a spy for Uncle Silas, planted by him in the house to find out how the land lay, steal the will, and even trap poor Maud into a forced marriage with Dudley Ruthyn, Silas's son. We are not told how she was insinuated into the household: possibly Silas had seen an advertisement inserted in the paper by his brother. At all events, she was 'highly recommended and perfectly qualified'; for Madame de la Rougierre is our first example of a really wicked governess, and your true villainess is never at a loss for unimpeachable credentials.

Not only did Maud herself feel 'more than an apprehension of her temper and fear possibly abused authority'; the servants, too, detested her at sight. 'I wonder', asked Mrs. Rusk, the housekeeper, 'why honest English girls won't answer the gentry for governesses, instead of them gaping, scheming, wicked furreigners? And who did she live with? Where was her last family? Madame de la Rougepot, *I* call her.'

Unfortunately for Maud, Madame contrived to worm her reptilian way into the confidence of her employer. Though she bullied Maud in secret, she was always solicitous for her charge's comfort when they walked together on the terrace outside Austin's study. She would complain to him of Maud's 'contumacy and temper'; and it was always her word, not Maud's, that he accepted. She deceived Maud, too, about her real nature. Even her thwarted attempt to have her abducted in a coach by the coarse-grained Dudley, was passed off as a drunken assault; and Madame's share as a decoy was not suspected. But Maud, though she told herself not to be hysterical, continued to fear and detest her governess, as well she might. For Madame, though she was (in a sense) a figure of fun—with her wig, her scrawny figure, her cheap finery and atrocious accent—was at the same time wholly horrible. From her first grimacing appearance outside the window, until the coal-hammer shattered her skull, she was the embodiment of evil—'a great, gaping reptile'.

Nevertheless, governess and pupil settled down into a tolerable routine, until Lady Knollys came to stay. Lady Knollys (Maud's Cousin Monica) was a sensible, middle-aged woman, worldly but kind. She took Maud under her wing, and immediately told her that she looked a fright in her old-fashioned dress. '"And why", she asked, "does not Madame make your dresses? I wager a guinea the woman's a milliner. Did she not engage to make you dresses?" "I—I really don't know. I rather think not. She is my governess—a finishing governess, Mrs. Rusk says." "Finishing fiddle! Hoity-toity! And my lady's too grand to cut out your dresses and help to sew them! And what *does* she do? I venture to say she's fit to teach nothing but devilment."'

Evidently French governesses were expected to employ their national gift for dress on the adornment of their pupils (though all the French governesses we have met were conspicuously unattractive)—and even to help with the actual sewing. It would seem, moreover, that Lady Knollys had as law an opinion of 'the anathematized race' as Lady Ingram in *Jane Eyre*. But no! she saves herself from the charge of injustice by making a clear distinction between good, bad and indifferent governesses. 'A governess', she says, 'may be a very useful or a very useless person; but she may also be about the most pernicious inmate imaginable. She may teach you a bad accent and worse manners, and heaven knows what beside.'

So far Lady Knollys did not know just how pernicious an inmate lurked in her cousin's house, for on her arrival, Madame had taken to her bed with a bottle of brandy and an unspecified complaint. 'I am, of course', she whined to Maud, 'only a poor governess, and such people perhaps ought not to have pain—at least to show what they suffer. It is permitted to die, but not to be sick.' In spite of her protests, however, Lady Knollys forced her way, with remedies, into the governess's room, drew back the coverlet, and was shocked by what she saw. For she had known Madame before under another name, and had known no good of her. Madame, on her side, braved out the discovery as best she could, and hastened to tell her side of the story to Austin Ruthyn.

Outside the bedroom, Cousin Monica questioned Maud: 'Who sent her?' 'I really don't know; Papa tells me so little—he arranged it all himself, I think.' On which Lady Knollys commented bitterly: 'It is very odd, how people *can* be such fools'—an observation which we ourselves have made from time to time on the irresponsibility of parents.

In spite of her knowledge of Madame's past (which the reader is never allowed to share) Lady Knollys completely failed to shake Austin Ruthyn's confidence in the woman. She quarrelled with him on the question and left in a hurry —not before warning poor Maud against Madame, whom she considered 'very deep, daring and unscrupulous', and even capable of poisoning Maud's food! Mercifully Austin Ruthyn's eyes were opened when Maud saw Madame de la Rougierre tampering with his desk. The false key was extracted from her and she was sent packing, without a character and vowing vengeance on her pupil. The reign of terror was at an end, but only for a while.

Shortly afterwards Austin Ruthyn died, the will was read, and Maud went to live with her Uncle Silas. What Austin called 'the ordeal of purification' was to be accomplished. Just as Madame was a grotesque, hideous, coarse-grained villain, so Silas Ruthyn was by contrast silky, elegant and sinister. He was a gourmet, a hypocrite and a hypochondriac. He had a soft voice, ingratiating manners, white hair, and strange, hypnotic eyes; and he was subject to attacks of suspended animation induced by opium.

He was careful not to frighten Maud at first. He was kind and gracious, and let her spend her time at liberty with her cousin Milly. Milly was a hoyden, who had been brought up innocent of governesses, running wild with gamekeepers and stable-boys. She wore navvy-boots, and her talk was a mixture of dialect and schoolboy slang. Yet as she was affectionate and clever, Maud delighted in imparting to her all that past governesses had taught herself. But the idyll came to an end with the reappearance of Dudley Ruthyn. Silas Ruthyn cherished the humane intention of trying to marry Maud to his son, before he was reduced to the sad necessity of murdering her. Maud was repelled by Dudley's race-gang courtship, and therefore the second plan had gradually to be put into operation. Maud began to feel herself a prisoner, and frightening things occurred with unpleasant frequency.

Above all, Madame de la Rougierre turned up again—first as a face at the window of Uncle Silas's sickroom, where Maud was keeping watch; and then in a secluded bed-room, whither Maud had wandered—Madame de la Rougierre herself, with her wig pushed back off her bald head, her skirts above her knees, and her legs plunged into a footbath.

The baffling, truly terrifying climax cannot be described here; it must be read—and that not too soon before bedtime. For the rest of the story Madame was in no sense a governess. She was a gaoler, a keeper, a ghoul. And it was not through self-sacrifice, but through her old habit of drinking, that she finally died in her pupil's place. Even though she did not know that actual murder was intended, one can hear her dying screams unmoved by pity.

The importance of Madame de la Rougierre in our catalogue of governesses lies in her being our only real criminal. Becky Sharp was an adventuress; Miss O'Grady dabbled in blackmail; and we shall in due course have to face a ghostly governess who burned with the sluggish flame of evil. Only Madame de la Rougierre was a spy, a thief, a murderer's tool, and (it is hinted) a white-slave trafficker.

Yet how admirably was a governess placed to be what burglars call an 'inside stand'! She could hear more secrets, worm out more information, than any servant; and she was often left in charge of the house when the owners were away. Madame de la Rougierre's story makes one wonder more and more how people could employ governesses on such slender knowledge; they seem to have valued their property as little as they valued their children's welfare. And that—for most fictional employers of governesses—was very little. It was luckier for them than they deserved, that fictional governesses were almost invariably honest.

As we close *Uncle Silas* and pick up *Wives and Daughters,* we pass from a world of lonely houses and neglected estates into the busy, tidy atmosphere of a country town. Mrs. Gaskell was still at work on this delightful book when she died in 1865, and it is mellow with a life's experience of middle-class people.

It is true that Hollingford had its big house, the country seat of Lord and Lady Cumnor and their family.

But it also had its tea-drinking ladies who would have felt equally at home in Cranford. And among its worthiest citizens ranked Mr. Gibson, the surgeon. Mr. Gibson's first wife had died young, leaving him with an only daughter, Molly; and though he had strong ideas about education, and often took his little girl with him in the dog-cart when he went his rounds, he had no time to spare for regular teaching. He wished Molly to grow up a good, simple, sensible girl (as indeed she did) and would therefore have no truck with 'finishing governesses' and their accomplishments. Instead, he engaged a Miss Eyre, who lived near by with her widowed mother and orphaned nephews and nieces. Miss Eyre bore no resemblance to Jane of the same name. She was 'a respectable woman, the daughter of a shopkeeper in the town'; and was 'a "lady" in the best sense of the word, though in Hollingford she only took rank as a shopkeeper's daughter. She was sensitive and conscientious, and knew the evils of an ungovernable temper.' This last qualification, however, was hardly needed with so sweet-tempered a child as Molly, who grew devoted to Miss Eyre, and upheld her loyally against the jealous grumblings of her old nurse. She was an eager pupil, too, whose only complaint was that Miss Eyre could not (or would not) teach her all she wished to learn. For Miss Eyre's teaching methods were somewhat circumscribed by Mr. Gibson's theories, which he had expounded to her at the outset.

Among her duties, he had told her, was included the exertion of a civilising influence on his assistants—medical students who lived in the house and helped in the surgery and dispensary in return for all that he could teach them. 'Now, Miss Eyre', he began, 'you are to remember this: you are to make good tea for the young men, and make them talk without stammering and giggling.' More important, however, were the precepts—mostly negative—laid down for her guidance in Molly's education. 'Don't teach

Molly too much: she must sew, and read, and write, and do her sums; but I want to keep her a child, and if I find more learning desirable for her, I'll see about giving it to her myself. After all, I'm not sure that reading or writing is necessary. Many a good woman gets married with only a cross instead of her name; it's rather a diluting of mother-wit, to my fancy; but, however, we must yield to the prejudices of society, Miss Eyre, and so you may teach the child to read.'

Mr. Gibson, of course, genuinely admired the 'mother-wit' of his cottager and farmer patients, and wished Molly to grow up with their sterling qualities rather than the affectations of fine ladies. But at the same time he was something of a tease. It seems probable that his real idea of female education was not quite so old-fashioned and limited as this little lecture would suggest. No doubt he knew that his Molly was an intelligent child, endowed with normal curiosity and intellectual energy, which would be stimulated rather than deadened by a little judicious thwarting. If this were so, and he was really playing a subtle game of bluff, he certainly won it. For though Miss Eyre, while teaching Molly to read and write, 'tried honestly to keep her back in every other branch of education', Molly was not to be robbed of her birthright. 'It was only by fighting and struggling hard that bit by bit Molly persuaded her father to let her have French and drawing lessons.' But she fought triumphantly, and 'being daunted by her father in every intellectual attempt, she read every book that came her way'.

When Molly was twelve years old, she went to a fête at the Tower, Lord Cumnor's house, and made the acquaintance of another governess strongly contrasted with honest, home-spun Miss Eyre. Hyacinth Kirkpatrick (*née* Clare) was at this time only visiting her former employers at the Tower; but she had previously taught French to Lady

Cuxhaven, the Cumnors' married eldest daughter, and been governess to the younger girls. She had then married a Mr. Kirkpatrick, a clergyman, since whose death she had kept a small private school. She had a daughter, Cynthia, of about Molly's age; and was now on the look-out for another husband who would save her from a school-marm's drudgery.

Hyacinth Kirkpatrick (of whom her former pupils always spoke, rather disrespectfully, as 'Clare', *tout simple*) was silky, soft and graceful as a Persian cat. Little Molly fell in love with her at once; and so, some time later, did Molly's father. It was natural, perhaps, that he should fall an easy prey to the very type which he so much disliked, and which was so incapable of valuing him or making him happy; and he did Molly an unkindness, too, when he made Hyacinth her stepmother. Not that Hyacinth was cruel or wicked. She was just a howling snob and fathomlessly selfish, but she was not very clever nor 'always quick at resources, though tolerably unscrupulous in the use of them'. In fact, she was a more attractive, less intelligent and less hard-boiled Becky Sharp, with about one eighth of Becky's redeeming vitality.

Mr. Gibson, then, was not marrying a downright adventuress, but it would have been as well for his peace of mind could he have overheard a conversation at the Tower one day between Lady Cumnor and her daughters on the subject of their former governess. 'She is not very wise, certainly', began Lady Harriet, the second daughter, 'but she is so useful and agreeable, and has such pleasant manners.' For Clare had been clever enough to know that her best line lay in being obliging and not standing on her dignity, and her reward had been to be treated as one of the family—albeit on the family's own, rather haughty, terms.

'I should have thought', went on Lady Harriet, 'that anyone who wasn't particular about education would have been charmed to keep her as a governess.' This last remark was aimed at her mother's educational indifference, but it was also—as we know by now—a shrewd hit at many another mother and many another governess. 'You gave us the best of masters', she added, to make amends, 'and Clare to dragonise and keep us up to our preparation; but then you know, or rather you didn't know, some of the masters admired our very pretty governess; and there was a kind of respectable, veiled flirtation going on, which never came to anything.'

Clare was indeed a flirt—a quality which she passed on to her adorable daughter Cynthia. But perhaps this was, on the whole, an advantage in a chaperon. She at least deflected possible attentions from her charges—unlike Miss Wirt who (it may be remembered) introduced as drawing-master a cousin who dared to make advances to Miss Osborne.

It is evident that Lady Cumnor must be ranked among the irresponsible parents; for not only was she ignorant of what went on in the schoolroom—she also frittered away the governess's time by using her as a secretary. 'You used', continued Lady Harriet, 'to call Clare away from us at the most critical times of the lessons, to write your notes and add up your accounts, and the consequence is, that I'm about the most ill-informed girl in London. Only Mary was so capitally trained by the good, awkward Miss Benson.'

Here Mary herself—the eldest daughter, and now Lady Cuxhaven—put in a word. 'I was so little with Clare in the schoolroom. I used to read French with her; she had a beautiful accent. Both Agnes and Harriet were very fond of her. I used to be jealous for Miss Benson's sake, and perhaps that made me fancy that she had a way of flattering and indulging them—not quite conscientious, I used to think.'

But Mary had not been far wrong. Clare certainly had a way with her, and had flattered herself into her younger pupils' favour. She had known that to discuss with them matters beyond their years is (with growing girls) the subtlest and most potent form of flattery. And in indulging their curiosity she had also indulged her own egoism; for she had affected to confide in them as equals and women of the world. 'I was her confidant', said Harriet, 'in her loves with poor Mr. Kirkpatrick. I know of three offers she had besides. Clare and I are always great friends.'

It was certainly a tribute to Clare that Lady Harriet, an intelligent and sensitive young woman, remained her friend and visited her after she had become Mrs. Gibson. On these occasions all the snobbish self-consciousness was on Hyacinth Gibson's side. When the hostess found it necessary to apologise for her small drawing-room, Lady Harriet merely laughed at her grand ideas: 'Well', she said, 'perhaps your schoolroom was larger, but remember how bare it was of anything but deal tables, and forms, and mats.'

Although Hyacinth Clare ceased to be a governess when she became a wife, she still trailed clouds of pretentiousness from her old life. Perhaps she was not the first governess to be spoiled for a middle-class home by her sojourn in great houses. The downtrodden governess, it is true, was usually overawed and downcast by the luxury in which she took no real part: to her, 'be it never so humble, there's no place like home.' Agnes Grey, Emily Morton and Jane Fairfax all suffered from this nostalgia for humble roofs. But there were certainly others, such as Becky Sharp and Hyacinth herself, who were dazzled by the 'pleasures and palaces' through which they had roamed. Even though the schoolroom might be bare, yet the salon in which they sometimes played the piano was crammed full of red plush, glittering lustres and hothouse plants; and though they did not really belong to these surroundings, they built their castles-in-the air on the same model. In fact, they got ideas above their station.

It would not have mattered so much if Hyacinth had merely compared Mr. Gibson's modest parlour with the marble halls at the Tower; unfortunately, she was critical of the human furnishings as well. Though quite incapable of appreciating her husband's intellectual gifts and moral qualities, she disliked his bourgeois habits. It was ungenteel to smell of cheese, and therefore he must forgo his favourite supper: a gentleman did not eat in the surgery with his students, and therefore he must waste his time over kick-shaws in the dining-room.

Yet although she was selfish, lazy and highfalutin, the second Mrs. Gibson had no real vice in her, so that they all got on together tolerably well. And when her daughter Cynthia came home from school, she captivated Mr. Gibson and his daughter as surely as she captivates readers to this day. We cannot follow her tangled love-affairs, which caused poor Molly so many heart-burnings, nor the scrapes from which Molly devotedly saved her. But it is interesting to note that Cynthia—when her affairs were more than usually involved—once threatened to become a governess in Russia. 'I've heard', she said, 'of a situation as English governess in Moscow, in a family owning whole provinces of land, and serfs by the hundred.' The threat was never carried out, but I cannot help wondering whether, had she gone, she might not have ended up as governess to Dasha Pavlovna in *The Possessed* by Dostoievsky. Dasha's patroness, the redoubtable Varvara Petrovna, had made up her mind to educate her protégée as if she were her own daughter, and 'at once set aside a sum of money for her, and sent for a governess, Miss Griggs, who lived with them till the girl was sixteen, but she was for some reason suddenly dismissed'. Perhaps Cynthia might have stayed longer, and it is fascinating (though idle) to speculate on her possible relations with the inmates of that house and town.

Mrs. Gaskell's world and Dostoievsky's existed side by side in time, but their creators were worlds apart. Not only were they different in sex, race and language; not only had they different traditions, backgrounds and conceptions of the universe; but they were as spiritually contrasted as two contemporary individual souls could be. And yet, despite all this, it remains possible to imagine Cynthia straying from the one world into the other. This bare possibility, to my mind, constitutes proof of the excellence of both these books. I had nearly written 'greatness' instead of 'excellence'; but *Wives and Daughters* is not a great book, only excellent of its sort. Both Mrs. Gaskell and Dostoievsky had integrity in their very different spheres; they wrote of life as they saw it, and were true to their own vision. Because of this integrity their characters live and their worlds exist. Therefore Cynthia, a living being, could have moved from one real world into another, and taken her humble place as English governess among the incomparably greater characters of *The Possessed.*

Studies for Stories, by the poetess Jean Ingelow, appeared first in 1864; but as they were republished several times before 1888, they were among the books which Molly Gibson in *Wives and Daughters* might have read aloud to her own children. Among them was one called *Dr. Deane's Governess* which would have appealed especially to Molly, because Dr. Deane was just such a sensible, kindly man as Molly's own father, Dr. Gibson. Doctors, indeed, emerge with flying colours as employers of governesses; Dr. May, Dr. Gibson and Dr. Deane, though all widowers, were none of them eccentric, and all three of them demanded an unusually high standard of educational intelligence.

When Dr. Deane's wife died he was left with four children—a boy of six, and three older girls—for whom he must engage a governess. Feeling that even the highest testimonials would not enable him to trust a stranger, he looked round among his patients' daughters, and soon decided that Ann Salter would be just the girl. Ann was the only daughter of a small farmer, who had grown up something of a tomboy among her ten brothers, until her grandmother sent her to a neighbouring school. Even then, while she fitted herself to earn her own living, she spent her holidays on the farm, and her 'excellent spirits and love of outdoor life' had been among her chief recommendations to the doctor. She was a healthy, intelligent girl; and when she first went to the Deanes was 'as ready for any sort of expedition or amusement as the children themselves—such a hand at nutting!—in such spirits at hop-picking time!' She dined with the family and came down to the drawing-room at eight-thirty, after the last child was in bed. She loved the friendly, easy life after the pinching and coarseness of the farm; and in the conversation of the doctor and his friends she found the intellectual stimulus and good taste needed to complete the work of her school. But though she enjoyed it all hugely, she never learned to think herself too good for her own family.

One day Dr. Deane's orphaned niece Fanny came home from school to live with them; and thenceforward Ann Salter's whole demeanour changed. The doctor bluntly complained to her that she now walked about with her head hanging down, and had 'the air of appearing to think that it is quite derogatory to smile'. She had no illness or worries, but admitted to depression; and the doctor—who held that genuine 'depression of spirits comes from dyspepsia, or from a disordered liver'—could not account for the mysterious change. He could not guess that Miss Salter's new pose of pensive languor was copied from a popular print called *The Governess*; nor that she thought it humiliating to be paid her salary when the servants received their wages; nor that she confided to a journal the imagined slights inflicted on her.

The source of the trouble, of course, was Fanny, who had devoured too many books about pathetic governesses. Fanny was affectionate and compassionate. She made a dear friend of Ann Salter and lent her some of the romances; then she discussed them with her, and encouraged her to keep a journal like those penned by governess-heroines. Worse still, Fanny was imaginative, and had lived more in books than in real life. And all her reading led her to assume that Ann must be a highborn lady who had come down in the world, and whose delicate refinement was vulnerable to every slight. Although Ann herself knew very well that by becoming a governess she had gone up in the world rather than down, she did not disillusion Fanny about her origin; and after reading some of the books, and crying over them with her dear friend, she came to believe wholeheartedly in the humiliation of her position.

When Dr. Deane at last found a clue to what was going on, he dragged out of Fanny the plot of one of those 'many interesting stories that had a governess for their heroine'. In this book, said Fanny, 'the heroine is a tall, dark-eyed lovely creature' (Ann's hair was inclined to sandy) 'brought up in the greatest luxury, and accustomed to associate with refined people. And the story goes on to say that the people at her first place are very vulgar, and treat her with the greatest insolence and harshness. She is very unhappy, but bears it all with the sweetest meekness.' Fanny had to confess that the story 'ends not quite so naturally as it begins', for the governess 'marries a young baronet, who is struck with the pensive sweetness of her face, as she takes the children out for a walk. But the most interesting part of her story is her journal, with the description of all her lonely feelings; really, it is quite harrowing to read it—such beautiful resignation, and, at the same time, such melancholy.'

This journal had had so moving an effect on Ann, that it had driven her out of bed early every morning to emulate its pathos. She had been rather hard put to it to scrape up grievances; but had found a few which seemed to call for pity. '*Wednesday the 2d.* No room for me at the table—had to dine with the children. Fanny was distressed, and said, "I daresay, dear, that being accustomed to good society, you feel keenly the dullness of your present life"; and she was so sympathising that I could not help shedding a few tears. . . . *August 3d.* I do not like the new housemaid's manner; it is too familiar, and adds to the discomfort of my position. I do sometimes feel a wish that some other than the peculiar trial of dependence, and the slights and annoyances it gives rise to, had been appointed for me.'

Knowing that he could only help the governess through Fanny, Dr. Deane decided to shake some sense into that young lady; and being a man of action, he thought it wiser to disillusion her by confronting her with facts. He therefore took her on his rounds to visit Ann's home, an ugly, red farmhouse which lacked (in Fanny's eyes) even the redeeming features of thatch or gables; and there she met Ann's cheerful, hardworked mother, who was eloquent about Ann's good fortune in earning her own living as a governess.

On the way home, Fanny admitted to her uncle that she had been mistaken about Ann's birth; but she maintained that Mrs. Salter had been wrong 'in saying that Annie is independent, because she earns her own living'. Surely, urged Fanny, 'that is the very thing that prevents her from being independent. You know, uncle, that servants and governesses and people who live in gentlemen's houses, are always called their dependants.' The doctor explained to her that this confusion was caused by an ambiguous use of the word 'dependent'. He himself was dependent for a living on his own efforts to please his patients. 'Miss Salter and I', he argued, 'are both dependent and independent; independent of other people's exertions, and dependent on our own.' And he very gently pointed out that the real dependant in his house was Fanny herself, since like 'all young ladies living at home and doing nothing', she depended on him for her allowance.

Fanny promised the doctor that she would behave to Ann with just the same warm friendship as before. But both girls felt some constraint now that the truth about Ann's home was known; and it was perhaps fortunate that Ann was called home to nurse her father, who had had an accident. Back on the farm—scalding milk-pans, plucking fowls, churning butter, stirring puddings, and generally sharing the endless labour of a farmer's wife—she realised that there are harder fates than to be a governess. She missed the fun and companionship of the doctor's house, and often wished herself back in the schoolroom. She told Fanny of this, and of her hope that she might one day return; and Fanny arranged to keep her place warm for her by herself undertaking the education of her little cousins. At the end of the agreed six months, however, Ann Salter had become engaged to an intelligent miller, whom Fanny had once encouraged her to despise. Fanny had now learned better, and rejoiced with her on this prospect of great happiness. Nor was Fanny sorry on her own account; for by this time she had proved her ability as a teacher, and had become dependent for her happiness on her work as Dr. Deane's governess.

Miss Ingelow's story amusingly exposes the harm done to governesses by reading books about their supposedly cruel fate. 'The books, you know', said Fanny, 'almost always represent a governess as lovely and ill-used.' It is fascinating to wonder what these misleading books may have been. Fanny and Ann had almost certainly read *Amy Herbert,* and possibly *Agnes Grey.* They may have been familiar with the works of Jane Austen. I doubt if the doctor would have approved of *Jane Eyre*; and I should have thought that *The Governess,* by Lady Blessington, would have smacked too much of Regency manners to find its way into a mid-Victorian schoolroom. Yet the journal and the young baronet in Fanny's novel certainly suggest a romantic atmosphere, to which *The Governess* has so far been our nearest approximation. And as Dr. Deane was no doubt too busy to censor Mudie parcels, the girls may have got hold of many books which he would have thought unsuitable.

Fanny, talking vaguely of 'the books', had the honesty to modify her 'always' into 'almost always'; and it is possible that she may have read *Vanity Fair* and *Little Dorrit,* in which the governesses were neither lovely nor ill-used. Of all our books, I should have thought the likeliest for her to have read would be *The Daisy Chain*; and she could so easily have identified herself with Ethel May, the daughter of a widowed doctor. If so, she would scarcely have idealised Ann Salter, any more than Ethel idealised Miss Bracey. Perhaps she had read it at school and put it away with other childish things; since when, her lending library must have provided her with many novels of the 'pathetic governess' type. With some of these we are familiar; but there were no doubt others too silly and too ephemeral to leave any trace behind them.

George Eliot might be expected to include many governesses within her wide sweep and keen analysis. Yet there is slight mention of them in her books. The omission is perhaps due to her habit of antedating her stories. As a social historian, she gained detachment and proportion by writing of the past: as a novelist, she supplied everyday detail from memories of childhood and created characters from those human emotions which do not change from reign to reign. It followed, therefore, that if she had had no governess as a child nor known one well in after years, she would be unlikely to make any of her heroines a governess. For she could not document a governess's amorphous duties, as she documented Lydgate's work in Middlemarch by studying reports on sanitation; nor was her imagination here stimulated by experience.

The allusions to governesses in *Scenes of Clerical Life* are few, meagre and negative. One of them is in *Janet's Repentance,* when a gossip accounts for Janet's marriage by saying that she 'had nothing to look for but being a governess'; and there is another in *The Sad Fortunes of the Reverend Amos Barton.* It may be remembered that the sadness of these fortunes was due in part to the Bartons' innocent friendship with an adventuress called the Countess Czerlaski. Now the villagers and local gentry assumed that her title was entirely bogus and that the Bartons were deceived about her in this as in all else. But in point of fact 'her husband had been the veritable Count Czerlaski, . . . whose fine whiskers, fine air and fine romantic fortunes had won her heart ten years ago, when, as pretty Caroline Bridmain, she was governess to Lady Porter's daughters, whom he initiated into the mysteries of the *pas de basque* and the lancers quadrilles'.

As for *Middlemarch,* although I knew that it held no important governesses, I snatched at the chance of reading my favourite book again. I sometimes think that I would sacrifice all Victorian fiction except *Wuthering Heights* and half-a-dozen Dickens, if I might keep this conspectus of provincial life, with its humour, its irony and its tragic stride. Published in 1871, it deals with the late twenties and early thirties of the nineteenth century; and I ought perhaps on that account to have considered it in my early nineteenth century section. But there is so little detail in it about governesses that there seems no need to be portentously accurate about chronology.

All but one of the inhabitants of Middlemarch and the surrounding villages took a poor view of a governess's career. The Vincys employed one to teach their younger children. At an evening party where Mayor and Mrs. Vincy were surrounded by their handsome family and genial friends, 'everything looked blooming and joyous except Miss Morgan, who was brown, dull and resigned, and altogether, as Mrs. Vincy often said, just the sort of person for a governess'. Rosamond, the eldest girl, dismissed her as 'uninteresting and not young. One wonders what such people do, without any prospect. To be sure, there is religion as a support.' This was an easy assumption for Rosamond, who felt sure of never needing any support for herself beyond that of her own self-will. But Rosamond was at that time absorbed in her trousseau, and interested in Miss Morgan only as a seamstress—for 'she does the open hemming very well'.

The Vincys had governesses forced on their attention from another angle, and a more acute one. Fred Vincy was in love with Mary Garth, who was looking after their common connection, old Peter Featherstone. And though she got more kicks than ha'pence from the old curmudgeon, Mary nursed him because she liked that 'better than being a governess'. But Mrs. Vincy thought that she was after the old man's money, and described her as 'a dreadful, plain girl—more fit for a governess'.

In George Eliot's mind, as in those of her characters, there is some confusion between a governess in a private family and a school teacher: the word 'governess' is used indiscriminately of either calling. Mary had evidently tried both and found them wanting, though she liked teaching classes better than single children. She shared George Eliot's sense of duty and gave conscientious scruples as her main reason for hating to be a governess. 'I have tried being a teacher, and I am not fit for that: my mind is too fond of wandering on its own way. I think any hardship is better than pretending to do what one is paid for, and never really doing it.' Mary is surely unique in seeing the matter from the employer's viewpoint rather than her own: where other governesses pitied themselves as sweated labourers, she doubted her own capacity to give employers their due money's worth.

Mrs. Garth had little sympathy with Mary's objections, for she herself had been a teacher and enjoyed it: 'Teaching seems to me to be the most delightful work in the world.' Whether she had, before marriage, 'taught school' or been a governess proper, she had by so doing earned the contempt of the Middlemarch middle-class snobs, who thought that 'an intimacy with Lindley Murray and Mangnall's Questions was something like a draper's discrimination of calico trade marks'. Because she loved teaching and wanted money to pay her boy's apprenticeship premium, Mrs. Garth took up teaching again after her marriage, and though her unconventional dame-school cannot honestly be forced into my study of governesses, it is irresistible. 'She had sometimes taken pupils in a peripatetic fashion, making them follow her about in the kitchen with their book or slate. She thought it good for them to see that she could make an excellent lather while she corrected their blunders "without looking"—that a woman with her sleeves tucked up above her elbows might know all about the Subjunctive Mood or the Torrid Zone.'

I have said that the word 'governess' was often used indiscriminately of teachers in private families and mistresses in schools; and at this period it was evidently not uncommon for girls to try their hand at both sorts of teaching. Mary Garth, for instance, had done so, and her choice reminds us that, parallel with the literary history of governesses, there runs the literary history of girls' schools. Let us pause here a moment to trace their journey side by side. How have schools and governesses compared so far—economically, educationally and socially? And what has each of them offered to parents, to pupils and to the teachers themselves?

There were, I think, three main types of girls' schools during the first three-quarters of the nineteenth century, at different social levels and offering very different educational wares. First there was the finishing school for young ladies, of the sort which turned out Miss Fanshaw in Maria Edgeworth's story of *The Good French Governess.* In such a school emphasis was laid on deportment, fashionable accomplishments and a smattering of the arts and sciences. It was no doubt expensive. Nabobs and mill-owners sent their girls to these academies, hoping that they might be asked to stay with titled school friends in the holidays and eventually marry scions of the aristocracy. In this category was Miss Pinkerton's Academy in *Vanity Fair.* It is true that Miss Pinkerton manufactured governesses as well as *débutantes*; but the parents of Miss Tuffin and Miss Hawkey no doubt made great sacrifices to send their daughters there. It was, indeed, an investment; for a governess's snob-value would thereby be considerably enhanced. Some of the future governesses, moreover, paid a part of their fees by their work as pupil-teachers. To these schools were also sent, I think, girls whose parents could not be bothered with them at home, and wished to get them married as soon as possible. But although a few of the aristocracy and landed gentry may have been included, it was evidently a sign of social superiority to be educated at home. Although Amelia Sedley went to Miss Pinkerton's, her patronising friends the Osbornes were educated at home by masters under the supervision of Miss Wirt.

The second type of school was humbler. It was usually situated in a small country town, and attended by the daughters of local tradesmen and farmers. Such was Miss Goddart's school in *Emma,* which was 'not a seminary, or an establishment, or anything which professed, in long sentences of refined nonsense, to combine liberal acquirements with elegant morality upon new principles and new systems—and where young ladies for enormous pay might be screwed out of health and into vanity—but a real, honest, old-fashioned boarding-school, where a reasonable quantity of accomplishments were sold at a reasonable price, and where girls might be sent to be out of the way and scramble themselves into a little education, without danger of coming back prodigies'. Here, again, girls were sent to be out of the way. Most of them were members of large families, whose mothers could not teach them while minding the shop or running the farm. But among these might occasionally be placed a love-child, until a husband or a situation could be found for her. Emma's protégée, Harriet Smith, was such a one—although her father was a tradesman, and not the nobleman whom Emma's imagination had conjured up.

It may be remembered that in *Jane Eyre* Mr. Rochester was advised by Blanche Ingram to send Adèle to school; and when he said that he could not afford to do so, she assured him that a school would be cheaper than a governess. Here, I suspect, Mr. Rochester and Miss Ingram were at cross-purposes; *he* was thinking of a pretentious academy like Miss Pinkerton's, while *she* had in mind an old-fashioned school like Miss Goddart's. Possibly she suspected that Adèle was Mr. Rochester's daughter rather than his ward, and thought that a cheap school would be a convenient *oubliette* for her. Had Blanche married him, she might even have insisted that Adèle be disposed of in this way. But although these country schools must have been used to some extent as depositories for unwanted children, the bulk of their pupils were born in wedlock to the middle classes. To such a school, in later years, went Ann Salter who became *Dr. Deane's Governess* in Miss Ingelow's tale; and they must have turned out many admirable governesses for families which did not want a snobbish façade or fancy accomplishments.

The third type of school was the charitable institution, of which Lowood in *Jane Eyre* was the most perfect and horrible example. The pupils in these schools were either orphans, semi-orphans or the daughters of professional-class parents who had come down in the world. Admittance was presumably gained through influence; and freedom was won by settlement in a situation. For they were factories which turned out from their assembly-lines a succession of governesses—well-taught (indeed the teaching at Lowood was sound, if limited), but friendless, penniless and destined to be downtrodden.

Let us now consider these three types of school from the worldly parent's standpoint. Selfish, indifferent or embarrassed parents might pack their girls off to any of the three; and so might such ruthless guardians as Jane Eyre's Aunt Reed. The *nouveaux riches* who wished to educate their daughters a cut above themselves might choose a finishing school where the girls would make valuable friendships and be fattened for the marriage-market. But the most socially secure would, I think, prefer to keep their girls at home, with all the advantages of the best masters. The mixing of all classes in a school could, after all, be only to the disadvantage of the highest class; while poise and *aplomb* could be learned better at home than from a socially isolated schoolmarm.

Even parents who were not snobbish—who accounted health, character and education more valuable than worldly wisdom—had to weigh the advantages of school against those of a governess. Their problems were discussed by Charlotte Mary Yonge in *Womankind* (1876). The best education for girls, she thought, was by parents with the help of teachers; failing that, 'a good governess or elder sister superintended by the parent'. Third and last came 'a really good school', which was at least better than 'an inferior governess left to herself'. It is, however, said Miss Yonge, very hard to find 'a good school that is not so expensive as to be out of the reach of large families'. (Large families, of course, usually included sons who were the first charge on family budgets.) If adequate teaching is provided, a school will be either very expensive or very large; and in a large boarding-school there lacks both privacy and 'confidence between the head and the members'. She therefore thought it better for large families to employ a qualified governess; and suggested that smaller families should arrange to share one. If such home education was found inadequate for older girls, it would be safe to entrust them for the last two years to the rough-and-tumble of school after their characters were formed.

In discussing the merits and demerits which commended a school or a governess to parents, we have also been implicitly considering the pupil's standpoint. But we have still to wonder what might be the relative advantages of school teaching or a private situation from the point of view of a governess. Mary Garth is the only governess of fiction who has articulately weighed the pros and cons; and if the others made a conscious choice, they came down on the side of private work. I suspect that in this choice they were often influenced by parents, who thought the position of a governess more sheltered and refined. Jane Eyre, of course, chose to be a governess of her own free will, because she wanted to see the world—which, for her, was anywhere but Lowood. But when, later on, she became the mistress of a village school, she felt herself free by comparison with Diana and Mary Rivers who were still compelled to 'earn the dependant's crust among strangers'. Many governesses must, like the Brontës themselves, have dreamed of starting their own schools; failing that, the choice was between two servitudes. Between the tyranny of mothers and the tyranny of headmistresses there was little to choose. Even a headmistress—like Miss Temple at Lowood, before it was reformed—might be the thwarted agent of a governing body.

With so little evidence, we can only fall back on the obvious conclusion that a good place as a governess was better than a bad school, and *vice versa*. But we should remember that most girls' schools (before Queen's College started its pioneer work in 1848) were very bad indeed. And that as they were few in number compared with homes, the chance of drawing a horse in the Schools Sweepstake was very much less than that of a lucky number in the Governess Lottery.

'Poor little Lucy Morris' is not really the heroine of Anthony Trollope's novel *The Eustace Diamonds* (1873). The leading lady is undoubtedly Lizzie Eustace, *née* Greystock, whose dealings with her late husband's diamonds give the book its name. But Lucy is the most attractive character in the book; and although she 'had quietly submitted herself to the position of a governess', she was (as her lover, Frank Greystock felt) 'better than all the rest'.

Lucy was an orphan. Her parents had been friends of the Greystocks of Bobsborough, where Lucy as a child often stayed with Admiral Greystock and his brother, the Dean. She had therefore grown up in intimate friendship with the Admiral's daughter Lizzie and the Dean's son Frank, who were both to play such large parts in her life. Left penniless, she had at the age of eighteen 'gone out to be a child's governess', and it was 'thought a great thing' for her that she should at the outset be 'hired to teach English, French, German and something of music' to the two youngest daughters of old Lady Fawn, at Fawn Court, Richmond.

'Lady Fawn and her daughters lived very much out of the world . . . and did not go much into society.' But they were well contented, being a respectable, kindly, evangelical family of stay-at-homes who found sufficient stimulus and human intercourse within the family circle. Just because they possessed all the domestic virtues, their home was an ideal one for a governess. She did not have to be banished to the schoolroom during parties, nor left behind when the girls went into society. On the other hand, it was precisely Lady Fawn's domestic virtues which made her somewhat strict about a governess's conduct. It was not from snobbishness that she forbade 'followers'; but because she felt a maternal responsibility for any girl under her care. She also suspected that 'a governess, if she were given to falling in love, could hardly perform her duties in life'.

When Lucy went to Fawn Court she already felt something far deeper than her childhood's affection for Frank Greystock, and had noticed a corresponding warmth in him. Frank's mother, too (had Lucy known it), had observed a change in Frank's attitude to Lucy; and although she had no inkling that he might be serious, had warned him against going too far. 'She is', said Mrs. Greystock, 'as sweet a girl as ever lived, and a perfect lady. But with a governess, unless you mean to marry her, you should be more careful than with another girl, because you may do her such a world of mischief. If Lady Fawn knew that she had an admirer, Lady Fawn would not let her come into her house.'

In this, of course, the Dean's wife was correct. Lady

Fawn did not turn Lucy out because of Frank; but she soon put an end to his visits. She 'fully appreciated her treasure and was conscientiously anxious to make Lucy's life happy. But she thought a governess should not be desirous of marrying, at any rate till a somewhat advanced period of life.' So although Lizzie Greystock, now the widowed Lady Eustace, was allowed to drive to Richmond to visit her old friend Lucy, Frank Greystock was (after a few visits) very gently forbidden the house. Lady Fawn explained all this to Lucy while she 'kissed her, and purred over her, and praised her'; and though Lucy had by now irrevocably given her heart to Frank, she agreed that 'a governess should make up her mind to do without a lover'. So she determined to identify her interests with those of the Fawns, and was so successful that 'her presence in the house was ever felt to be like sunshine'. Before long she 'had catalogued the library, she had planned the new flower-garden—though Lady Fawn thought she had done that herself. She had been invaluable during Clara's long illness. She knew every rule at croquet and could play piquet.' Even Lord Fawn, the only son, who was 'a Peer of Parliament and an Under-Secretary of State, consulted her frequently, and made no secret of his friendship'. Yet although 'there was no fear that his feelings towards the governess would become too warm', Lord Fawn proved eventually to be the fly in Lucy's ointment.

For Lord Fawn and Frank Greystock were at loggerheads. Frank, who was Member of Parliament for Bobsborough, was put up to oppose a measure sponsored by his lordship; and when Lord Fawn came to Richmond for a week-end and complained to his female relations of Frank's speech, Lucy was rude to him in Frank's defence. When Lady Fawn reasoned with her afterwards, Lucy apologised. 'I know', she said, 'how good you are to me. I know you let me do things which other governesses mayn't do—

and say things; but still I am a governess, and I know I misbehaved to you.' To which the kind old lady answered: 'My dear, you are more like another daughter to me than anything else. To me and my girls, who know you as a lady, you are as dear a friend as though you were—were anything you may choose to think. Lucy Morris is to us our own dear, dear little friend Lucy.'

And so indeed she was. We have seen many cases of arrogant employers and have censured them for not treating their governesses as equals. The case of Lucy Morris is the first in which the governess was not only treated as a social equal, but really *was* one. For she came not only from the same social class as her employers, but the same social world. Many a governess from a country vicarage (Agnes Grey, for instance) was by birth her employer's equal or even superior; but if she had lived in poverty and obscurity, her birth would pass unnoticed in the rich family for which she worked. Her pride might even cut her off from them more sharply. Lucy's position among the Fawns was completely different. The Deanery, in which she had been almost an adopted daughter, was no more retired than Fawn Court —probably less so. Lucy's old companion Lizzie Greystock had done well for herself. She had married a baronet and been left a rich widow, and was soon to become intimately involved with the Fawns; while Lucy's friend Frank Greystock was a rising barrister and a Member of Parliament, who met Lord Fawn on his own ground. There was therefore no condescension about Lucy's reception as one of the family, for she was entitled by birth and upbringing to equal treatment. Not that all employers would have recognised the fact; Lucy was certainly lucky to work for anyone as sympathetic as Lady Fawn. But we shall see that in spite of all the kindness she met with, Lucy's life at Fawn Court did not always run smoothly; and that her position as an extra daughter bred complications of its own.

The next complication was Lord Fawn's impetuous engagement to Lizzie Eustace. Lucy was told of it at once because, as Lady Fawn said, ' there can be no reason why Lucy should not know all that concerns our family '. Knowing Lizzie of old, Lucy was not enthusiastic about the news; and events proved her to be right. For Lizzie refused to surrender the famous Eustace diamonds to her late husband's executors; and Lord Fawn refused to abide by the engagement unless she gave them up. Relations between the betrothed were already strained when Lizzie came to Richmond to stay with her future mother-in-law, and they boiled up to bursting point before the fortnight's visit had run its course. Lucy, of course, was claimed as an old ally by Lizzie, who even tried to bribe her to act as a spy. But worse was still to come. Although Frank Greystock might be exiled from Fawn Court as an admirer of the governess, he had every right to go there as the cousin and legal adviser of Lady Eustace. He arrived one day when Lady Fawn was out, and took the opportunity of walking with Lucy in the shrubbery and telling her that he loved her.

On hearing this, Lady Fawn was distressed rather than angry. She assured Lucy that she was ' revelling in hopes which would make her miserable ', since ' Mr. Greystock, a Member of Parliament, could not marry a governess '. Lucy had to admit that Frank had not actually proposed; and Lady Fawn was horrified when ' the girl persisted in declaring her love for the man, and yet did not even pretend that the man meant to marry her! And this, too, was Lucy Morris, of whom Lady Fawn was accustomed to say to her intimate friends that she had altogether ceased to look upon her as a governess. "Just one of ourselves, and almost as dear as one of my own girls." ' Here was another disadvantage in being treated as a daughter. The same standards were applied to Lucy as to Augusta or Lydia;

and parents notoriously expect and exact more from their own children than from others. Poor Lucy felt that she was in sad disgrace.

Frank, meanwhile, was making up his mind in the Inner Temple. His cousin Lizzie's fortune, if he married her, would forward his career; and he believed that he might marry her in spite of her engagement to Lord Fawn. Lucy, in comparison, had little to recommend her from a worldly standpoint. 'She was not beautiful—hardly even pretty—small, in appearance almost insignificant, quite penniless, a governess.' If he married her he would not only have to cut down expenses and change his way of life; he would also have to face such contemptuous comments as: 'Oh, Heaven! —there has Frank Greystock gone and married a little governess out of old Lady Fawn's nursery!' Yet because he loved her and could be happy with no one else, he sat down and wrote a letter asking her to be his wife.

When Lucy had read the letter, she flung herself into the arms of Lady Fawn, who exclaimed: 'I think our little wise one has lost her wits.' When she heard of the proposal, Lady Fawn gave permission for Frank to visit Lucy at Fawn Court. 'But I shall be glad', she added, 'just to say a word to him. Of course, you are in my hands, and I do love you so dearly, Lucy! I could not bear that anything but good should happen to you.' There were no more lessons that day. The schoolroom hummed with girlish confidences; and Lady Fawn 'purred, and congratulated, and gave good advice'.

It seemed as if all Lucy's dreams had suddenly come true; but alas! she still had some formidable nightmares to encounter. Not only did Frank neglect her, so that the Fawn girls secretly 'thought that as a lover he was very slack'. He also made himself unpopular at Fawn Court by espousing his cousin Lizzie's cause in her quarrel with Lord Fawn about the diamonds. He and Lizzie were closeted together more than seemed necessary or proper for a man and woman engaged to other people, even though they were cousins. And when he went up to Scotland to shoot grouse on Lizzie's moors, things looked very black for everyone at Fawn Court.

Lord Fawn came to Richmond one week-end and complained that Frank had been 'most insolent' in pressing Lizzie's claims on him and insisting that he should behave as her future husband. Lucy let fly in defence of her lover, and his lordship 'condescended to be full of wrath against his mother's governess'. In an interview with Lady Fawn after this scene, Lucy said that she had better go away, whereat Lady Fawn protested: 'You know that I don't wish you to go away. But if you behave badly, of course I must tell you of it.' She kissed Lucy and left her; and that night Lydia Fawn went to Lucy's room and 'the two girls talked the matter over for hours'. Lucy rose early next morning and waylaid Lord Fawn in the garden. But instead of apologising, she only made things worse; and Lord Fawn 'like a great child' (as Lucy thought) at once went to 'tell his mother what that wicked governess had said to him'.

Poor Lady Fawn 'was divided in her judgment and feelings between the privileges due to Lucy as a girl possessed of an authorised lover, and the very much greater privileges which attached to Lord Fawn as a man, as a peer, as an Under-Secretary of State. . . . Lucy no doubt had a lover; but perhaps that fact could not be taken as more than a balancing weight against the inferiority of her position as a governess.' Perhaps after all it would be more comfortable for everyone, including Lucy herself, if she were to leave Fawn Court. But where then could she go? 'She had no home but such a home as she could earn for herself by her services as a governess, and in her present position it was almost out of the question that she should seek another place.' If, on the other hand, she stayed, what line was to be taken with her? 'She might be scolded and scowled at, and put into a kind of drawing-room Coventry for a time—so that all kindly intercourse should be confined to schoolroom work and bedroom conferences. She could be generally " sat upon ", as Nina would call it. But as for quarrelling with her—making a real enemy of one whom they all loved—that was simply impossible.'

Such were the problems which resulted from making a friend of one's governess. Perhaps Clara Hittaway, the married daughter, was right when she said that they had all been 'soft about that girl', and that 'a governess with a lover never does suit'. But the real crux, as Lady Fawn knew, lay in the governess's relations with the men of the family. She tried, rather clumsily, to explain this to Lucy: 'Though to me and the girls you are as dear as any friend can be, and can say just what you please—. Indeed, we all live here in such a way that we all do say just what we please —young and old together. But you ought to know that Lord Fawn is different.' Lucy understood her employer's feelings and respected them. Yet she could not answer for herself should his lordship next week-end again insult her lover. So she insisted on leaving, and wrote to tell Frank of her decision.

Now 'Frank knew as well as Lady Fawn that she could not go into another family as governess', and that her rightful home as his betrothed was with his mother at Bobsborough Deanery. But Mrs. Greystock, when she was told of Lucy's predicament, was reluctant to harbour her. Since she knew of Frank's engagement, indeed, her attitude to Lucy had hardened. 'Poor dear little Lucy Morris was as good as gold. Mrs. Greystock was quite willing to admit that.' But she was 'a little chit of a thing. Her position was simply that of a governess. Mrs. Greystock declared to her daughter that no one in the whole world had a higher respect for governesses than she had. But a governess is a governess—and for a man in Frank's position such a marriage would be simply suicide.' It was therefore arranged that Lucy should go for six months as companion to Lady Linlithgow, a dowager connected by marriage both with Frank and Lizzie.

Frank, meanwhile, had been dallying with Lizzie in Scotland. They had been seen embracing in a cave; and Mrs. Hittaway (determined to break her brother's invidious engagement) had heard the unsavoury gossip, and passed it on to Richmond. Fawn Court was more upset by the news on Lucy's behalf than on Lord Fawn's. He, after all, would be well rid of Lizzie; whereas they feared that Lucy might die if Frank abandoned her. Lady Fawn told Lucy a little about the rumours, and begged her to stay among friends who loved her: 'If anything went wrong with you here, you could come to me as if I were your mother.' And as she talked 'she held Lucy by the hand, and no one looking at them would have thought that Lucy was a governess and that Lady Fawn was her employer'.

But Lucy persisted in going to Lady Linlithgow, who was told the fact of her engagement, though not the name of her *fiancé*. Her new employer, in spite of gout and grumpiness, was not unkind, but she asked a lot of questions. She asked, for instance, if Lucy had had a salary of fifty pounds a year with the Fawns. Lucy was glad, for her old friends' sake, that she could claim to have had a salary of eighty pounds a year, adding that she had also had a great deal more. 'I had', she said, 'downright love and affection. . . . I don't suppose any governess was ever so treated before.' Nor was it long before Lady Linlithgow wormed the identity of Lucy's lover out of her. 'So that's it, is it', commented the dowager drily. 'You've done me the honour of making my house your home till my own sister's nephew shall be ready to marry you.'

But it was her own thoughts, not her employer's crotchets, that made Lucy wretched at this time. She read in the papers about the various adventures of the Eustace diamonds; and then Lady Fawn wrote to tell her there was no doubt that Frank was making love to Lizzie. Lucy did not know, of course, that Mrs. Hittaway had written to her mother: 'It was not to be expected that such a man as Frank Greystock should marry your governess. I think Miss Morris would make a very nice wife for a country clergyman. . . . But she has no style.' But she was so heartbroken by Frank's neglect that she 'doubted even whether ever again she could become serviceable as a governess, and whether the energy would be left to her of earning her bread by teaching adequately the few things that she knew'. In spite of good advice, however, she hung on to a forlorn hope; and she would not write to Frank to release him even when that cat Lizzie sent for her and told her that it was her duty to do so.

Although Lady Linlithgow asked her to remain after her six months, Lucy went back to Fawn Court to stay until a place could be found which should be 'in every sense unexceptionable'. On the morning of her first day there, Lady Fawn and her elder daughters went out driving. 'Lucy was busy among the others with books and maps and sheets of music', when an agitated maid announced a gentleman in the drawing room to see Miss Morris. She was agitated, because she remembered trouble about a 'follower' when Miss Morris had been there before; and 'now, on the very first day, just when my lady's back was turned, here was the follower again'.

Knowing who it must be, Lucy went to him just as she was in her old 'pale grey, well-worn frock' which she had put on that morning 'as a testimony that she had abandoned the idea of being anything except a governess'. Opening the drawing-room door, she found herself in

Frank's arms, and immediately forgave him everything. Lady Fawn, on her return, welcomed him as a prodigal, and so did the girls. 'The lover was not the lover of one of themselves, but of their governess. And yet all his sins were forgiven him. The fatted calf was killed.' And when, fifteen months later, her hand was joined to Frank's by the Dean of Bobsborough, Lucy was surrounded by 'a bevy of Fawn bridesmaids'.

The story of Lucy Morris is the story of a governess who was loved and made much of. It proves that even when a girl was treated as one of the family, her position might become intolerable. Lucy is among our most attractive governesses, and she certainly found in Lady Fawn the employer she deserved. A word of praise should also be given to her pupils and their elder sisters. Seven rather plain young women 'running down from seven-and-twenty to thirteen' might have resented the intrusion of an attractive girl into their narrow circle. It is true that Lucy's attachment to Frank put her out of the running with other men; but still Augusta, Amelia and the rest might have hated her as the Ugly Sisters hated Cinderella. Instead, they rejoiced or agonised with her throughout the ups and downs of her romance, and attended her at her wedding. Their sympathy and generosity warm the cockles of our hearts, and throw a cheerful glow over the whole employer-governess relationship.

As we have seen, the Dean's wife at Bobsborough held that 'a governess is a governess', meaning by that that she was 'a little chit of a thing'. She must have spoken from experience, though not from Christian charity; for a cathedral town is surely a hotbed of potential governesses. One would have expected Barchester, for instance, to abound in them. Yet no governess appears in *Barchester Towers,* even in a walking-on part. The book contains, however, two significant references to the governess's calling, both proving it to have been held in as low esteem in Barchester as it was in Bobsborough.

One instance occurs during a tense scene between Mr. and Mrs. Quiverful. Mr. Quiverful has just been tricked by Mr. Slope, the Bishop's odious chaplain, into surrendering all claim to the wardenship of Hiram's Hospital. When he tells his wife, protesting lamely that they must wait for some other preferment to fall vacant, the mother of his fourteen children breaks out passionately, 'Wait! Shall we feed the children by waiting? Will waiting make Bessie and Jane fit even to be governesses?'

The second reference forms part of an estimate of Mrs. Grantley, the Archdeacon's wife. It is said of her that 'though much the wealthiest of the ecclesiastical matrons of the county, she had so managed her affairs that her carriage and horses had given umbrage to none. She had never talked too loudly of earls and countesses, or boasted that she gave her governess sixty pounds a year, or her cook seventy.'

The Eustace Diamonds was written sixteen years later than *Barchester Towers,* and in those years the sum mentioned for a governess's salary had risen by twenty pounds. This advance may have been due to economic factors; but I doubt if it was really an advance resulting from the passage of years. It is likelier that Mrs. Grantley would have paid sixty pounds in 1873, and Lady Fawn (an exceptionally good employer) eighty pounds in 1857. Though Mrs. Grantley had more money to spend than the other Barchester ladies, she still needed to apportion her outlay among various commodities. She valued her husband's stomach at ten pounds a year more than her daughters' education, and knew that indifferent governesses were easier to come by than good cooks. Even after this economy had been effected, her governess was still a more expensive example of her kind than adorned the other schoolrooms of Barchester. It probably never occurred to her that a governess had had to spend on her own education those years in which the cook had been earning wages as a kitchen-maid; nor that the governess had no clothes provided for her. Lady Fawn, on the other hand, considered all these things. She could never have been happy in Lucy Morris's company knowing that her salary was less than the cook's, and less than the Fawn girls' dress allowances.

CHAPTER IV

LATE VICTORIAN

Samuel Butler, *The Way of All Flesh*; Mrs. Alfred Hunt and Violet Hunt, *The Governess*; Sir Arthur Conan Doyle, *The Sign of Four, The Copper Beeches*; Joseph Conrad, *Chance*; Kenneth Grahame, *The Golden Age*; Hugh Walpole, *Jeremy*; Harold Nicolson, *Some People*; Henry James, *The Turn of the Screw, What Maisie Knew*; F. Anstey, *The Man from Blankley's*.

ALTHOUGH *The Way of All Flesh* by Samuel Butler is strictly a period piece, it is so much a satire of the whole Victorian Age that it can as well be placed at the end of the century, when it was written, as in its exact setting. Butler used satire in self-defence, to clear away the stuffy atmosphere which hampered the exercise of his faculties. He had suffered personally from Victorian hypocrisy, and all he asked of society was that it should let him be. If his attacks also served to right the wrongs of other people, too, it was only incidentally, and the wrongs righted were only those of people who wanted to be left alone as passionately as he did himself. Among these, of course, are many children. It is therefore natural that Butler should have attacked hidebound and torturing education both in schools and at home, that pharisaical parents and hectoring schoolmasters should be ruthlessly deflated.

It does not necessarily follow that he should mention governesses. Yet there are two in *The Way of All Flesh*, although so slightly sketched as to have no names. The first was governess to the Allaby girls when young Theobald Pontifex went to stay with them; and she had made of their drawing-room a veritable Siren Island for the undoing of susceptible young men. Christina Allaby, when singing, 'at every pause added an embellishment of arpeggios from one end to the other of the keyboard, on a principle which her governess had taught her'. As for the governess, 'she, indeed, had been a rarely accomplished musician; she was a pupil of the famous Dr. Clarke of Cambridge, and used to play the overture to *Atalanta,* arranged by Mazzinghi'. The resemblance to Thackeray's Miss Wirt, that 'glorious creature, Squirtz's favourite pupil—a prodigy of accomplishments'—is striking; and her musical method of getting her pupils married was equally successful, even though 'it was some time before Theobald could bring his courage to the sticking point of actually proposing'.

Theobald himself, when he became a father, was so heavy a one that one can imagine little scope for a governess within his educational system. Yet little Ernest, the potential rebel, was attended by one. As he was at that time about seven, and already did some of his lessons with his father, she must have been what we should now call a nursery governess—as, of course, were Emily Morton, Agnes Grey and others. Only one instance of her relations with little Ernest is recorded. In the course of a history lesson he asked her 'what a natural child was—were not all children natural?' "Oh, my dear", said she, "a natural child is a child a person has before he is married."' Although a constant inmate of nurseries, she had evidently remained quite ignorant of the workings of a child's mind. The prospect of immediate fatherhood so alarmed poor Ernest, that he consulted his godfather on the matter. 'And you have told your governess about this?' he asked. 'Yes, but she puts me off and does not help me: she says it will not come for many years, and she hopes not then.'

This is a truly Freudian example of prudish evasion producing confusion and consequent fear; and we must hope that not many governesses were as blind as Ernest's. Perhaps it is only another case of an employer getting the governess he deserved. Theobald was so blind and overbearing himself that he frightened his governess into frightening his child. It is certainly another example, and a pathetic one, of a pupil's helplessness. The governess was set over Ernest as one among his innumerable elders and betters, whose word—however silly—was law. What she said, went; and though she said it at random, it went straight home to his innocent psyche and festered there.

The late Mr. Ford Madox Ford explained in his introduction to *The Governess,* by Mrs. Alfred Hunt and Violet Hunt, that Mrs. Hunt began this book in the 'eighties or early 'nineties, when she was trying to adapt her style to the new fashion of short novels. She had, he said, excelled in the leisured, detailed manner of the old three-decker; and it was in this manner that she embarked on her study of a sensitive young governess in a vulgar north-country family. Then, feeling that she could not successfully infuse into it the 'shortness, vim and snap' demanded by her publishers, she put the book aside; and it was afterwards finished by her daughter, Violet Hunt, and published in 1912 under their joint names.

The result of this double authorship is not entirely happy. *The Governess* starts as a quiet, old fashioned study of a downtrodden governess which reminds us of *Agnes Grey*; and ends as a melodramatic murder story. It succeeds in neither of these *genres*; but it has a few realistic details and touches which are worth noticing, even though it is impossible to give even an outline of the complicated plot.

The opening is conventional. Barbara Wynne was delicately nurtured, and accustomed to abundant pin-money and servants to wait on her. When her father was ruined, she found a situation as governess in the north of England with a rich family called Dulverton. The children regarded all governesses as their natural enemies, and were encouraged to spy and tell tales by their mother, who is by far the best drawn character in the book. During lesson hours the schoolroom door was left open so that Mrs. Dulverton could hear if the children cried; and in the evening she would walk down the corridor towards the schoolroom quarter, jangling her bugled dress against the walls. She resented any reminder of the fact that Barbara had once been richer and more socially distinguished than herself; and when Barbara lent Bertie (Mr. Dulverton's son by his first wife) some ultramarine with which to finish a water-colour, she let it be known that no governess should possess a colour costing a guinea a cake. There was also a continual battle about clothes. Barbara was not allowed to wear her white cambric dresses in hot weather, because of the expense of washing them; and although the olive-green silk which she usually wore in the drawing-room passed muster, she once ventured to wear a *feuille d'octobre* gown which Mrs. Dulverton knew must have cost thirty pounds, and which she assumed Barbara had put on to captivate the son from Oxford.

Barbara did indeed captivate him, so that his attentions became 'oppressively demonstrative' and caused bitter jealousy in the heart of Bertie, the stepson, with whom Barbara was in love. We may perhaps spare some sympathy for Mrs. Dulverton when she complained: 'It seems to me that both my sons are fascinated by this governess! Two in one family is too many.' But she had no pity for Bertie and still less for Barbara, caring only for her beloved younger son: 'I don't care a pin how much she falls in love with him, so long as it does not prevent her doing her work.'

Barbara had a salary of sixty pounds a year, paid quarterly, and had to be given a quarter's notice. But as the former governess had received only forty pounds a year, Mrs. Dulverton recouped herself for this extravagance by getting rid of an old nurse who had formerly supervised the children's playtime. Barbara was therefore never free from these ' bangaboutsome ' children until after they had gone to bed. Even then she was often expected to sing or do her needlework in the drawing-room while her employers slept. And as Bertie said to her, ' better an oil-clothed schoolroom floor with an occasional rug on it, and peace and quietness, than a drawing-room downstairs with no alternative but to go to sleep '.

Bullied by the mother, blackmailed by the children, pursued by the undergraduate son and misunderstood by the stepson whom she loved, it is small wonder if Barbara's nerve began to break. As Bertie later explained to her mother: 'The situation was one which must work upon the nerves of any delicate girl. . . . The hours which she worked were very long. . . . My young sisters and brothers . . . are exceedingly bright, clever and malicious children; they know how to say wounding things and they are, I am sorry to say, adepts at malicious tale-bearing. . . . My step-mother exceedingly disliked Miss Wynne and took no steps to make her life agreeable.' Barbara certainly had plenty to make her anxious and bitter as she sat in the evening ' by a small bad fire, and the light of one doubtfully smelling lamp '. And even when she was asleep she was tormented by a recurring dream in which—driven beyound endurance—she struck one of the children and trembled in fear of the retribution which her impatience would bring upon her head. This dream is, I think, the most original and telling point in an otherwise undistinguished book.

In spite of Mrs. Dulverton's determination to get her hanged for murder, Barbara in due course found the happy ending which awaits most governesses in fiction. The children rallied to her defence; her father restored his fallen fortunes; and Bertie—learning at last that she had loved him all the time—presumably married her. And as (in the words of Jack, whom she had coached so efficiently in Latin) she was ' a dear good girl and a right good plucked one ', we may be sure that she was kind and contented as a wife and mother.

Among the territories which I originally fenced off when demarcating a manageable field for my researches was the densely-wooded hillside of detective stories. Although many a governess, I am sure, lies hidden among the scrubby undergrowth of crime, I have no intention of tracking them to their hide-outs. But a few giant trees—the classics of detection—tower old and vigorous above the thickets; and the noblest of them all is Conan Doyle's creation, Sherlock Holmes. Therefore I must remind any readers who have followed me so far, that the first Mrs. Watson was by origin 'a needy governess'.

Miss Morstan appeared as a client in *The Sign of Four,* on an afternoon when Dr. Watson was at his most obtuse, and Holmes at his most lethargic. 'She was a blonde young lady, small, dainty, well-gloved, and dressed in the most perfect taste. The dress was a sombre, greyish beige, untrimmed and unbraided, and she wore a small turban of the same dull hue, relieved only by a suspicion of white feather in the side. I have never looked upon a face which gave a clearer promise of a refined and sensitive nature.' Given such a quakerish costume, which 'bore with it a suggestion of limited means', we should not be surprised to hear either that Miss Morstan was a governess, or that she was involved in a dark and Oriental mystery. I cannot describe—much less unravel—the mystery; but keeping within my terms of reference will only recount what we know about Miss Morstan as a governess. This, alas, is very little: for instance, no child is ever mentioned in connection with her work. But she bore some of the distinguishing marks of her kind.

'My father', she told them, 'was an officer in an Indian regiment, who sent me home when I was quite a child. My mother was dead, and I had no relative in England.' So that when her father disappeared for good and all, the day after his arrival in England, she was left as poor and dependent as one could wish. Some time later she 'entered the family of Mrs. Cecil Forrester in the capacity of governess', and there she had remained for over six years. She was now seven-and-twenty, 'a sweet age, when youth has lost its self-consciousness and become a little sobered by experience'.

Not all employers would have fancied a governess who received anonymous letters, and an annual gift of a 'very large and lustrous pearl'. But to her other merits as an employer Mrs. Cecil Forrester added a supreme one when dealing with such a case. She herself had once thrown herself on the mercy of Sherlock Holmes, and conceived an admiration for his powers, so that when Miss Morstan was bidden to a mysterious assignation, her employer directed her without hesitation to 221A Baker Street for escort and advice.

That evening, Miss Morstan ('muffled in a dark cloak') set off with her two squires on a series of drives through the murky, lamp-lit streets of London, which led finally to a corpse at Pondicherry Lodge, Upper Norwood. Though her 'demeanour was as resolute and collected as ever', Dr. Watson (already over head and ears in love) 'endeavoured to cheer and amuse her by reminiscences' of his adventures in Afghanistan. In the garden of Pondicherry Lodge he found himself holding her hand, and was not repulsed. But as he drove her in yet another four-wheeler to Mrs. Forrester's house in Upper Camberwell, he did not exploit his advantage. Evidently she was disappointed: 'She has told me since', he writes, 'that she thought me cold and distant upon that journey.' But he remembered that 'she was weak and helpless, shaken in mind and nerve'; while the promise of a fortune which that night's work had held out to her, further restrained the half-pay army surgeon from a declaration. When they reached Camberwell 'it was nearly two o'clock. The servants had retired long ago, but Mrs. Forrester had sat up. She opened the door herself, a middle-aged, graceful woman, and it gave me joy to see how tenderly her arm stole round the other's waist, and how motherly was the voice in which she greeted her.'

There is no need for me to consign Miss Morstan to any category of governesses: Dr. Watson himself has done it for me. 'She was', he wrote, 'clearly no mere paid dependant, but an honoured friend. As we drove away I stole a glance back, and I still seem to see that little group on the step—the two graceful, clinging figures, the half-opened door, the hall-light shining through stained glass, the barometer and the bright stair-rods. It was soothing to catch even that passing glimpse of a tranquil English home in the midst of the wild, dark business which had absorbed us.'

Next day Dr. Watson went again to Camberwell to report progress to both ladies. '"It is a romance", cried Mrs. Forrester. "An injured lady, half a million in treasure, a black cannibal, and a wooden-legged ruffian". "And two knight-errants to the rescue", added Miss Morstan, with a bright glance at me.' It is to be feared that she was a little forward; and purists might (on the strength of those 'knight-errants') consider her unfit to teach English grammar to her charges.

Miss Morstan was evidently something like a daughter to her employer, who called her Mary. Nor was she relegated to the schoolroom—if schoolroom there was in this house where barometers and stair-rods, rather than children, constituted a 'tranquil English home'. When, later on, Dr. Watson called with the treasure-chest, Mrs. Forrester was out, and Miss Morstan was sitting in the drawing-room 'dressed in some sort of white diaphanous material'. When the box was opened and found empty, the Doctor was emboldened to propose; and 'whoever had lost a treasure, I knew that night that I had gained one'.

There we must leave Miss Morstan, who as Mrs. Watson was to fight a losing battle against the ascendancy of Sherlock Holmes over her husband. Perhaps she gave way the more willingly to his truancies because she was herself a potential detective. Or so, at any rate, Holmes thought. When she first outlined her case—eschewing all tangents, and marshalling the relevant documents—he said to her: 'You are certainly a model client. You have the correct intuition.' And at the end, when Watson broke the news of his engagement, Holmes said: 'I think she is one of the most charming young ladies I ever met, and might have been most useful in such work as we have been doing. She had a decided genius that way.' This was high tribute from Sherlock Holmes, himself the master-genius. And though he said of himself that he could never marry, lest he bias his judgment, it seems a pity that he could not take Mrs. Watson into a business partnership. At first, perhaps, the bridegroom would have objected to her running risks; but later, when he reverted to his bachelor habits and left her so much alone, the arrangement might have been of advantage to them all.

We have already seen, in connection with Madame de la Rougierre, how strong a position a criminal governess held in a house. And surely the converse is equally true? If a female detective could be planted in a house of mystery as governess, few of her employers' secrets could escape her vigilant eye, her sharp ears, and her deductive powers. I am afraid Miss Morstan, with her 'sweet, brave nature' and her 'decided genius' for detection, was thrown away as the neglected wife of a G.P. whose heart was seldom with *her*, and never in his practice.

Mrs. Watson was not the only governess who found her way to Baker Street. Violet Hunter, the heroine of *The Copper Beeches* (from *The Adventures of Sherlock Holmes,* 1891) was another, and she found herself in two minds about accepting a situation at the princely salary of a hundred and twenty pounds a year. She had gone one day to 'a well-known agency for governesses in the West End called Westaways', managed by a Miss Stoper; and when she had been ushered from the ante-room into the inner office, had found sitting by Miss Stoper a fat man who (on barely seeing her) exclaimed: 'That will do. . . . I could not ask for anything better. Capital! Capital!' After this abrupt opening, suggesting the slave-market rather than the employment-agency, he asked her about salary; and when she said she had received four pounds a month in her last place, denounced this as 'rank sweating' and offered her a hundred pounds a year. Her charge, he explained perfunctorily, was 'one dear little romper just six years old. Oh, if you could see him killing cockroaches with a slipper. Smack! Smack! Smack!' Her teaching duties, however, would not be heavy, the first essential for the post being 'the deportment of a lady'. But his wife would be much obliged if she would sometimes wear a special dress which they would give her; and he must insist that she should cut off her hair before she came.

This was the stumbling-block. Although the child sounded unalluring and the wife eccentric, if not mad, yet 'very few governesses in England are getting £100 a year'; therefore Miss Hunter would not have hesitated but for the final clause. 'As you may observe, Mr. Holmes', she said, 'my hair is somewhat luxuriant, and of a rather peculiar tint of chestnut. It has been considered artistic. I could not dream of sacrificing it in this off-hand fashion.'

But Miss Stoper, who had no doubt been offered a handsome rake-off, had threatened to cross Violet Hunter's name off her books; and when the girl got home to her lodgings (she was, oddly enough, an orphan!) and found her tradesmen's bills unpaid, she began to think better of turning down so lucrative a post. (How many governesses, obliged to support themselves between engagements, must have been driven by dwindling resources into accepting the first thing that offered!) So that when she got a letter from the strange Mr. Rucastle, raising his offer to a hundred and twenty pounds, she succumbed. But she thought it wiser, before cutting off her hair and taking the train to Winchester, to put her problem to the famous Sherlock Holmes.

And Sherlock Holmes let her go, though he thought it fishy that employers should give £120 a year 'when they could have their pick for £40' and muttered afterwards to Watson that he would not like his own sister to go to such a place. He told Miss Hunter that she could wire for him to come if she found herself in any scrape; and she did so when she became too puzzled by sitting in the window in an electric blue dress while Mr. Rucastle told her funny stories. But we cannot here discuss what was hidden in the disused wing of the Copper Beeches, or why Miss Hunter found in her room a coil of chestnut hair exactly like her own. When he had heard her story, Holmes said: 'You seem to have acted through all this matter like a very brave and sensible girl, Miss Hunter'; but the most sensible thing she did was to send for him. Soon after his arrival the mystery was solved, the prisoner rescued, and Mr. Rucastle savaged almost to death by his own mastiff. 'As to Miss Violet Hunter', Watson concludes, 'my friend Holmes, *rather to my disappointment,* manifested no further interest in her when once she had ceased to be the centre of one of his problems, and she is now the head of a private school at Walsall, where I believe that she has met with a considerable success.' The italics are mine; and I put them in because those four words suggest so subtly a hypersensitiveness in Dr. Watson to those of his friend's clients who chanced to be attractive governesses.

Although the book was published in 1914, the action of Joseph Conrad's *Chance* dates back to the late nineteenth century. Scenes laid in the neighbourhood of the Docks suggest a London of four-wheelers and trams which is much the same as Sherlock Holmes's London, so that chronologically it may well follow the wooing of Mrs. Watson and the mystery of the Copper Beeches. Otherwise, of course, there is nothing in common between Sherlock Holmes and *Chance*, which is a psychologically serious book full of wisdom and beauty, pity and terror. The story, told by Conrad's inimitable method of indirect approach, is pieced together from confidences, observation and conjecture by the narrator, Marlow; and it is the story of a girl called Flora de Barral whose early life was wrecked by a series of unlucky human chances.

Her father was a loathsome fraudulent financier; her mother, a crushed nonentity; Mrs. Fyne, her only friend, was a conscientious, arid feminist. Even her devoted husband, Captain Anthony, came near to ruining their marriage by his mistaken generosity. But the character who gave the *coup de grace* to Flora's innocent childhood, and permanently undermined her confidence, was an evil governess whose surname Marlow never learned. This anonymity, this impersonal existence as 'Mrs.— or Mrs. What's-her-name', tends only to intensify the woman's sinister significance; for it suggests that she was less a cruel human being than the agent of those malevolent powers which tortured Flora's girlhood.

Mrs. Fyne, the feminist, first got to know Flora when she was a little girl. Flora's father had bought a country house and banished to it his wife and child, together with a large staff and a governess who claimed to have had a situation with a duke. The powers of evil, like supernatural card-sharpers, had already won a trick by forcing this card upon de Barral. There was no shortage of governesses at that time and many would have been glad to teach the daughter of a millionaire. From among these he might easily have chosen 'a perfectly harmless, naïve, usual, inefficient specimen of a respectable governess'. (Marlow evidently had no high opinion of the tribe!) Or again he might have found 'a commonplace, silly adventuress', or even 'have chanced on a model of all the virtues or a repository of all knowledge'. But the powers had planned otherwise for Flora and decreed that he should hit upon 'a plotting governess with the trick of a "perfect lady" manner (severely conventional) and the soul of a remorseless brigand'.

Even so evil a chance might not have mattered had the governess's employers been more normal. Flora's tragedy lay in the circumstance that all the human factors in her early life were complementary, and nicely adjusted for her overthrow. From the first, the governess despised Mrs. de Barral; and when that lady died from neglect, de Barral—despite a fine show of possessive sentiment—cared so little for his child that he might have left her to languish indefinitely in that gloomy country mansion, had not the governess put her foot down. After dealing with a duke, she was not going to stand any nonsense from an upstart financier; so she 'bullied de Barral in a very lofty manner' until he installed her with her charge in an expensive establishment at Brighton. Here she reigned supreme, and spent his money 'in extra-ducal style'. He would visit them sometimes at week-ends and walk silently on the beach with Flora. But as he had risen to opulence from humble origins and still lived outside society, and as he did not at all want a nearly marriageable daughter on his hands, he more and more deferred to the governess's wishes and did not see that she was 'an intriguing person hatching a most sinister plot'.

This plot was to marry Flora to a young cad whom the governess called her nephew, but for whom she cherished an infatuation. So reckless, so blind was this passion that she hoped to retain her hold on him by buying him with Flora's money. She did not even take much trouble to disguise her plans; for she was arrogantly assured of her domination over de Barral. Mrs. Fyne, who chanced at this time to be staying in a hotel next door, at once suspected what was up when she saw the 'nephew' coming for week-ends and being sent out riding alone with Flora. But other neighbours who did not know the governess so well, saw nothing untoward in these visits. For the governess had built up an imposing façade of respectability. Brighton and Hove had become accustomed to the 'extraordinary, stiff-backed thin figure all in black'. And although Flora 'was stared at in public places as if she had been a sort of princess', her governess ('playing with cold, distinguished exclusiveness the part of a mother to the fabulously wealthy Miss de Barral') saw to it that her charge should make no friends who might feel themselves in duty bound to interfere.

Although she was 'severely practical—terribly practical', Miss de Barral's governess had overestimated her own mastery of the situation; for she had assumed her employer to be as practical as she was herself. She never guessed that he squandered on South Sea Bubbles the money which, by clever advertising, he had extracted from the public. So she had no inkling of the impending crash until her 'nephew' Charley told her of the rumours, only a day before the story broke. Had she been merely practical and cared only for money, she would now have cut her losses and sought a new situation, getting a good reference from de Barral before the prosecution started. But she had more to lose in the de Barral crash than her present command of cash or even her future security. She was a 'woman of forty, an age in itself terrible', and she had pinned her last passionate hopes on the marriage of Charley to an heiress. Now that her bait had lost its sordid charm, she knew that she had lost him too; and all the pent-up envy and bitterness of a thwarted life was to be vented on the nearest, tenderest victim.

In this unnamed woman we encounter for the first time a psychopathic governess. Though we have met many who felt acutely the contrast of their lives with those of their employers, and a few (like Becky Sharp) who hastened to obliterate that contrast, Flora de Barral's governess is the first victim of what should surely be the occupational mental disease of governesses. If the psycho-analysts are right, then the conditions under which governesses spend their lives are calculated to produce in them sexual starvation and repressions of all sorts, liable at any moment to break out in vile abuse and cruelty. Yet for some reason—perhaps Victorian prudery—none of our governesses so far has shown any symptoms of this very natural strain. Becky was coldly calculating, untroubled by strength of feeling for anyone except herself. Jane Eyre, it is true, had very powerful emotions; but she had even stronger principles with which to master them. The rest of our governesses, apparently, had no ungovernable emotions to contend with.

And yet, as Marlow asked: 'Why shouldn't a governess have passions, all the passions, even that of libertinage, and even ungovernable passions?' This governess had certainly banked up such passions for many years and fanned them with contempt for her employers. Marlow suspected that 'she had always disliked intensely all her charges including the two ducal (if they were ducal) little girls'. And for her charges' parents she felt not only dislike, but venomous envy and contempt. Unlike Becky Sharp, she would never have tried to ' better ' herself by marriage with a man whom she did not feel to be her better in some way other than financially. Even if de Barral ' had made advances, this governess would have repulsed him with scorn '. Not only was she arrogant, but she was, furthermore, too much the creature of her passions to give or sell herself to a man who could not satisfy her cravings. All her life she had watched others enjoying sensations and emotions which, she felt, she could have enjoyed more thoroughly herself. She had been denied indulgences which should have been hers by right, as an intelligent, handsome woman. So it was ' no wonder that . . . she clung desperately to her last infatuation '.

When Charley had given her the tip about de Barral's failure, she packed up everything of value that she could cram into her trunks, drew from the bank all the money that de Barral had placed at her disposal, and prepared herself for a last word with Flora. When Charley appealed to her, saying ' you might behave decently at the last, Eliza ' (for the poor, lost creature had at least a *Christian* name) ' she set her lips in cruel obstinacy '. For she had improvised a drama of revenge, and was determined that no decent feelings should rob her of this last emotional orgy. Her plan was to shatter, in one brutal scene, her innocent charge's faith in her father, in human nature, and (above all) in herself. A plan in which, as we shall see, the monster succeeded to terrible perfection.

The scene took place in the drawing-room, where Flora had been having a delightful water-colour lesson with a visiting master. The governess swept in, dragging the reluctant Charley in her wake; and to imagine Flora's feelings we must remember that ' there had been between them an intimacy of relation as great as it can possibly be without the final closeness of affection '. Flora did not love her governess; but the woman had been for years an integral part of her everyday existence. Even while Mrs. de Barral was still alive, the governess had been the moving spirit in the household; and since then she had stood as the unquestioned representative of order and security. For Flora, she was the only criterion of values, the sole interpreter of life. Small wonder, then, that the girl froze in horror when, instead of a cold, protective goddess, there bore down on her a fury of unreasoning, unmerited revenge. As she told Mrs. Fyne afterwards, Flora 'received suddenly the feeling of being personally attacked'.

She cried out once; then stiffened into a silent terror which merely titillated the governess's lust to hurt. When the woman asked her violently 'whether she imagined that there was anything in her, apart from her money, to induce any intelligent person to take any sort of interest in her existence', Flora could not answer. 'When she was viciously assured that she was in heart, mind, manner and appearance an utterly common and insipid creature', she was too appalled to feel conscious anger. But the words pierced all the deeper into her subconscious as 'she stood, a frail and passive vessel into which the other went on pouring all the accumulated dislike for all her pupils, her scorn of all her employers (the ducal one included), the accumulated resentment, the infinite hatred of all those unrelieved years'.

One can imagine how, through all those years, a sense of wasted powers had smouldered under her professional poise, her formal kindness. All the time, she had cherished her hatred and nourished it. And because this hatred was so strong, the hurt which it inflicted on the girl's soul was crippling. Yet still Flora did not protest until the fiendish woman called her 'the child of a cheat and a swindler', at which she cried out in anguish: 'You mustn't speak like this of Papa.'

After her tormentor had left the house Flora sought refuge in the hotel next door with Mrs. Fyne, who put her to bed and tried to comfort her. But alas! this theoretician, this scrupulous stickler for truth, felt it to be against her principles to give the child the only assurance which might have healed her. When Flora begged: 'Oh! Mrs. Fyne, don't tell me that she wasn't mad', her well-meaning friend, sitting 'by the bedside of that brutally murdered childhood', withheld from her the harmless, but so necessary lie. 'She is a vile woman', Mrs. Fyne assured her; but she refused to admit the saving possibility of madness.

And so, through the years of girlhood spent with her father's common relations, and even after her marriage to Mrs. Fyne's sailor brother Captain Anthony, Flora had to carry the burden laid on her once for all by her wicked governess. One result was to make her whitewash and idealise her vampire of a father. While he was in prison she read the story of his trial and persuaded herself that he was the innocent victim of a conspiracy. More harmful by far was the appalling doubt sown by the governess, her 'ineradicable suspicion of herself and others'. After all, as Marlow said: 'How could one have expected her to throw off the unholy prestige of that long domination? She could not help believing what she had been told; that she was in some mysterious way odious and unlovable. It was cruelly true—*to her*. The oracle of so many years had spoken finally.'

Very horribly, she even became to some extent that which she had been told she was. She was so withdrawn, unfriendly and *farouche* that it was difficult indeed for anyone to love, or even like, her. And Mrs. Fyne, with her feminine grudge against a world of men, was not the friend to humanise her and draw her out. Only Captain Anthony, who loved her, was able to reach the core of her which the governess had left unharmed; and even he could not give her back her power to love and to be loved until the two of them had been through many and great tribulations.

The Golden Age, by Kenneth Grahame (1895) is a very different story—dreamy and whimsical, and redolent of the 'nineties and the *Yellow Book.* Though written in a sense for children, and still read by them with enjoyment, it is self-consciously written from the child's-eye view by a nostalgic grown-up. One feels that Kenneth Grahame went down on hands and knees to recapture the spirit in which his children looked up to the dim height of the adult 'Olympians'.

If it seems strange to couple the Golden Age of childhood with the Yellow Book of sophistication, let us remember that Sir Max Beerbohm (ever sensitive to social atmosphere) recognised in the 'nineties a decadence of the nursery no less than of the drawing-room and studio. 'The 'nineties', he wrote in his delicious essay called *A Cloud of Pinafores,* 'wish children to be children, and nothing more'; and he contrasted this wish with the old-fashioned endeavour to make children behave (and even look) like miniature men and women. This new craze, he diagnosed, was due to a craving for simplicity. 'It is probable', he went on, 'that the efforts to keep children simple by leaving them free, will but exterminate simplicity at last. It is only oppression that can keep human beings as they are. . . . Miss Caroline and Master Richard, driven to bay by their elders, set their back against the nursery wall and were simple to the last. But Jock and Millicent, encouraged in all their childishness . . . will very soon become self-conscious. . . . Introspection has set in already, and soon every high chair will hold its lisping Rousseau or Marie Bashkirtseff.'

Kenneth Grahame wrote amid this cloud of pinafores in the spirit of this craving for simplicity. But he wrote of children who were still oppressed by unappreciative grown-ups. Selina, Edward and the rest were still snubbed, chivvied and misunderstood, and still regarded their elders as unpredictable bores and tyrants. It is small wonder, therefore, that their governess was of the 'governessy' type —the dictator of the schoolroom ever ready with dates and tables, with decrees and punishments. Even the time-honoured status of orphanhood was transferred from her to her defenceless and downtrodden charges. Yet from the little we are told about Miss Smedley she would seem to have been a kind enough young woman, albeit a little priggish.

That she was young and not unattractive is established negatively by her effect on Uncle George, who was promising well from the children's point of view until she appeared on the scene, when his 'manner at once underwent a complete and contemptible change. His interest in rational topics seemed . . . to flag and ebb away; and though Miss Smedley's ostensible purpose was to take Selina for her usual walk, I can vouch for it that Selina spent the morning ratting . . . ; while if Miss Smedley walked with anyone, it would appear to have been with Uncle George.'

The children naturally could not understand their uncle's dereliction: 'We who from daily experience knew Miss Smedley like a book—were we not only too well aware that she had neither accomplishments nor charms—no characteristic, in fact, but an inbred viciousness of temper and disposition? True, she knew the dates of the English kings by heart; but how could that profit Uncle George, who, having passed into the Army, had ascended beyond the need of useful information?'

Evidently Miss Smedley was old-fashioned enough to ignore the theory that children should be left to their sweet simplicity, untroubled by discipline or facts. Even if she had secretly adhered to it, she could scarcely have upheld it openly; for if children are to run wild, and to learn only from the books of Life and Nature, then a governess's occupation is gone. There must be grammars and primers on the ink-stained schoolroom table, and children must be forcibly fed with their unpalatable contents. But not all books, according to Miss Smedley, are wholesome for children if taken in large doses. On the subject of fairy stories she would have found a stalwart supporter in the Good French Governess; and it is on her explanation of them that I base my certainty that she was priggish. This is what happened: 'Charlotte was sadly out of spirits. Having "countered" Miss Smedley at breakfast by an apt quotation from her favourite classic'—a book of fairy stories—'she had been gently but firmly informed that no such things as fairies ever existed. "Do you mean to say it's all lies?" asked Charlotte bluntly. Miss Smedley deprecated the use of any such unladylike words in any connexion at all. "These stories had their origin, my dear", she explained, "in a mistaken anthropomorphism in the interpretation of nature. But though we are now too well informed to fall into similar errors, there are still many beautiful lessons to be learned from these myths."'

It might almost be Madame de Rosier talking, just a century before. But Charlotte was too rational to be put off with rationalisations. '"But how", she persisted, "can you learn anything from what doesn't exist?" And she left the table defiant, howbeit depressed. "Don't you mind *her*", I said consolingly; "how can she know anything about it? Why, she can't even throw a stone properly."'

But though Miss Smedley might not be able to throw stones: though she might be a kill-joy at times and over-conscientious about imparting knowledge, she was also kind. This the children discovered for themselves, as we are told in the sad little story of her departure, significantly entitled *Exit Tyrannus*. When the children first heard that she was going they had 'blindly revelled in the contemplation and discussion of her past tyrannies, crimes, malignities; . . . and in mapping out the shining days to come'. Yet when the great day arrived everything went wrong, and the planned celebrations fizzled out. 'At breakfast, Miss Smedley behaved in a most mean and uncalled-for manner. The right divine of governesses to govern wrong includes no right to cry. In thus usurping the prerogative of their victims, . . . they hit below the belt. . . . There were no lessons that morning, naturally—another grievance. The fitness of things required that we should have struggled to the last in a confused medley of moods and tenses, and parted for ever, flushed with hatred, over the dismembered corpse of the multiplication table.'

It was the finality of this good-bye which worried our young philosopher. 'Did you come to love a pig, and he was taken from you, grief was quickly assuaged in the delight of selection from the new litter. But now, when it was no question of a peerless pig, but only of a governess, Nature seemed helpless, and the future held no litter of oblivion.'

The boys, who almost to the last had kept up a pretence of jubilation, began to remember things they liked about their governess. Harold, the youngest, started it: 'She wants me to write to her', he said. 'Says she doesn't mind the spelling, if I'll only write. Fancy her saying that!' 'She gave me a knife my last birthday', said Edward. 'It wasn't much of a knife—but I wish I hadn't lost it.' 'When my legs used to ache', I said, 'she sat up half the night, rubbing stuff on them. I forgot all about that till this morning.'

As with Edward's knife, so with the governess. She wasn't much of a governess, but they wished they hadn't lost her. Yet off she drove with her trunks in the station fly, leaving us no clue as to her relations with her employers, her salary, or the reasons for her leaving. All that remained of her was a gap in her charges' consciousness. They had planned a celebration: 'Yet no flag floated defiantly in the sun, no cannons proclaimed the passing of a dynasty. From out of the frosted cake of our existence Fate had cut an irreplaceable segment.'

During the 'nineties governesses were in their heyday. They were, moreover, as much in demand for small boys as for little girls: they moved not only amid a cloud of pinafores, but also upon a wave of sailor suits. Often, of course, schoolrooms were co-educational, but it was not by any means unheard of for a governess to be engaged for the teaching of boys alone. Hence it has come about that as many men as women writers seem to associate governesses with their memories of childhood.

Although our next two studies of governesses in the 'nineties were not written until about thirty years later, there is no reason to exclude either of them as a period piece. For both deal with the time in which their authors, Hugh Walpole and Mr. Harold Nicolson, were little boys. Both are written from the child's point of view, supplemented by the sympathy for grown-ups which comes with being oneself grown up. And as the details of daily life in childhood are apt to be imprinted with special sharpness on the memory, I think we may safely accept the pictures which they give us as true to two very different sorts of governess-environment.

The hero of Hugh Walpole's *Jeremy* (1919) was born in 1884, the same year as his creator. Both of them, therefore, were eight years old in 1892, when Miss Jones became governess to the Cole family in the cathedral town of Polchester. This family consisted of Mr. Cole, a clergyman; his placid wife; Helen, aged ten; Jeremy himself; and Mary —plain and clever—who was a year younger than the brother whom she idolised. The house also harboured a spinster sister and Bohemian brother of Mrs. Cole.

This is not one of Hugh Walpole's better books. The whimsical machinery creaks a little, and the characters are carefully assorted types who behave exactly as an experienced novel-reader would expect. One must not, therefore, be surprised if the governess behaves in a consistently governessy manner. Not that poor Miss Jones was what I have called the 'governessy' type, or dragon, for although she tried to be so when she arrived, she soon descended into the very depths of the bullied, baited class. But she was governessy in the sense of displaying few idiosyncrasies outside the characteristics of her calling.

When the children first heard that they were going to have a governess, they were a little apprehensive; for 'the word "governess" had an awful sound' to them. They need not have been afraid. 'Thirty years ago', observes the grown-up Hugh Walpole, 'governesses were an incapable race'; Mrs. Cole had to choose 'between idiotic young women and crabbed old maids, and she finally chose an old maid'. To us, as students of the History of Governesses, it is interesting to notice that Hugh Walpole (writing in 1919) assumed that governesses then must be an improvement on those of his childhood. I myself, a page or so back, said that the 'nineties were the heyday of the governess. Yet here is Hugh Walpole asserting with equal assurance that they were—at that time—incapable; with the unmistakable implication that their capabilities had improved in the intervening years. Perhaps our researches into later history will prove whether he was right; or whether governesses are (as is commonly supposed) a dying race.

Mrs. Cole certainly hit upon an unnecessarily incapable specimen, and solely on the recommendation of the Dean, who had once had Miss Jones's brother as his curate. Mrs. Cole could get no testimonial of Miss Jones's teaching powers, as she had never been a governess before. Up to the age of fifty she had kept house for a bad-tempered brother, and being stranded, on his death, without money or relations, she simply 'thought she would be a governess'. On the strength of occasional visits from nephews and nieces, she assured Mrs. Cole that she 'had had to do with children all her life'; and Mrs. Cole accepted this assurance and engaged her.

Miss Jones did not make an auspicious start. She arrived without an umbrella, but with an attack of the neuralgia to which she was a martyr. And though Mrs. Cole tactfully had tea with her and the children in the schoolroom, Miss Jones nullified any possibility of a good impression by kissing Jeremy. It must be remembered that neither Miss Jones nor the children knew the rules of the governess-game as well as you or I. Should I suddenly find myself a governess (as I have done in dreams) I should know by this time—from books, if not from practice—just what to expect, and how to behave at every move. But 'Miss Jones had never been a governess before, and the children had never had one'; and Miss Jones suffered from the further disabilities of being 'ignorant, nervous, over-anxious, and desperately afraid of losing her situation'. In her sense of insecurity she tried to barricade herself behind routine: regular lesson-hours were appointed, from nine till twelve, and from four till five; a time-table was pinned up on the wall; and she armed herself with sanctions in the shape of graduated punishments.

Jeremy was at first prepared to be co-operative. He was 'proud of his advance in life; the nursery was now a schoolroom; his whole social status had risen'. Here Hugh Walpole has detected a child's angle on the governess-question which has hitherto escaped our notice. I had always imagined that a small boy—probably tagged on to his elder sisters' lessons—would consider it *infra dig* to be subjected to a governess. But I accept with complete confidence Hugh Walpole's point that for some small boys the schoolroom forms a bridge over which he strides from the nursery towards school. To such a boy, lessons (even with sisters) are promotion; and a governess is a grander person to be seen on walks with than a Nannie.

With a more experienced woman, therefore, Jeremy might have developed and expanded, but unfortunately Miss Jones was not the one to draw him out. From the very start she gave way to him, and let him see that she dared not appeal to his parents; and once he had felt his power, her life became a misery. He watched her carefully, found her weak spots, and took delight in wounding them. And where he led, the girls followed. He was not a particularly cruel boy, as boys go; yet he devised for poor Miss Jones a variety of ingenious tortures. These included 'the Torture of Losing Things, the Torture of Not Hearing, the Torture of Many Noises, the Torture of Sudden Alarm, the Torture of Outright Defiance, and the Torture of Expressed Contempt'. Lesson hours became a horror of wasted time, arguments, dumb insolence and lost battles; until Miss Jones saw Jeremy 'as a real child of Evil', and her 'morning descent into the schoolroom was real hell'.

One day—left alone after a particularly disastrous session at the schoolroom table—Miss Jones broke down, and was discovered by Jeremy in floods of tears. Taken by surprise, she poured out to him all her terror of dismissal and her despair of ever finding work as a governess again. Jeremy was proud that she should talk to him as a grown-up instead of trying to shield him from life. He was touched, too, by her evident helplessness. So he offered her his handkerchief and said she must stay with them always. He promised that he would be good henceforth, and answered for the girls' being the same. Mrs. Cole should never dismiss Miss Jones on account of insubordination in the schoolroom. This touching scene (which, to my ears, does not ring quite true) had happened only just in time. The housemaid, who, with the other servants, despised Miss Jones, had told Mrs. Cole about the goings-on at lesson time. Jeremy overheard his mother telling his aunt that Miss Jones wouldn't do: 'I hear she can't keep order at all. I'm sorry, it's so difficult to get anyone.' Boldly Jeremy stepped forward like a knight-errant redressing wrongs, and protested that Miss Jones was 'all right', and that they would all be good if only she might stay with them.

And so she stayed—in spite of disagreeable Aunt Amy who (herself a poor relation) 'had always despised Miss Jones as a poor, unfortunate female who was forced to teach children in her old age because she must earn her living—a stupid, sentimental, cowed old woman at whom the children laughed'. But when Aunt Emily was left in charge for a short time, and tried to interfere in the schoolroom she found the tables turned. For Miss Jones and the children by this time understood each other perfectly. When it came to making common cause against Aunt Amy, Jeremy and his sisters could laugh *with,* and not *at* their governess.

I have felt some doubt about including Miss Plimsoll in my Chapter of Governesses, because Mr. Harold Nicolson's delightful book *Some People* (1927), in which she occurs, is written in autobiographical form and mood throughout. Miss Plimsoll is categorically described as having been governess for over seven years to his brothers and himself; and the list of embassies to which she accompanied the family provides an historic background which can be checked and verified. Surely, then, Miss Plimsoll was a real-life governess and not a character in fiction? On the other hand, Mr. Nicolson states in an 'Author's Note' that 'many of the following sketches are purely imaginary', and I believe that Miss Plimsoll is to be numbered among these. My belief is confirmed by the way in which he talks of her at one point as being still alive and giving tea-parties; whereas I am sure he is too kind a man to have run any risk of wounding her in her retirement. Miss Plimsoll, I persuade myself, is a composite character or else one specific governess so transformed as to be unrecognisable.

Aesthetically, however, Miss Plimsoll is real enough. If she is composite, then the component elements have been so skilfully welded that she is all of a piece and has the ring of pure metal. From the moment she descends from the train at Budapest in her red dress and peaked bonnet, until she goes ' bobbing out in a row-boat ' to join the steamer off Morocco, Miss Plimsoll never says a word out of character. And her character, though a little irritating, is a sterling one.

She is our first example of an ambassadorial governess. We have encountered other governesses abroad: for instance, Ethel Newcome's Miss Quigley at a German *spa,* and Mrs. General at an alpine *hospice.* But never one whose duties carried her into diplomatic circles in Budapest, Constantinople, Bulgaria, Gibraltar and Morocco. Yet such adventurous openings for governesses cannot have been uncommon. Diplomats who in England would have sent their children to day schools, needed someone to educate them in their own language while abroad; and ambassadors' wives are too busy entertaining to spend much time with their children. In such a life a governess was (and probably still is) essential to provide a regular life for the children, take them for walks, teach them, nurse them when ill, and look after them on journeys. She had to protect them from beggars, from sophisticated foreign children, from mad dogs, from train-sickness, from mosquito-bites and germs and bombs.

Miss Plimsoll, for instance, first exercised her authority by forbidding visits to the Panoptikon in Budapest, for fear her charges should pick up the germs of scarlet-fever; and at first she did not feel happy in Constantinople. 'She mistrusted the food, . . . and was always asking whether things were "really safe".' This insular caution grated on the nerves of the boys' father, but perhaps their mother felt that they were safer with a true-born English governess. Miss Plimsoll certainly acted with admirable *sang froid* in clapping her dogskin gloves ('which smelt faintly of ammonia') over little Harold's eyes when the Greek lady committed suicide on the Acropolis.

She felt more at home when they moved to the summer embassy at Therapia; for here, on the shores of the Bosphorus, was a patch of English earth on which, with 'brisk enthusiasm', she initiated the building of the Hut. Miss Plimsoll was evidently efficient, for she was the only person I have ever heard of who carried out almost to completion a design from *The Boys' Own Paper.* She even achieved accurate measurements with a tape measure which sprang back into the entrails of a bulldog with scarlet eyes. It is true that the Hut was finally finished by the gardeners. But Miss Plimsoll's failure was not with planks or nails: she broke down rather on the handling of her human material.

The Good French Governess would have approved of the Hut, for hut-building, like radish-seed, played an important part in Miss Edgeworth's theory of practical education. And I think that Madame de Rosier's matter-of-fact, utilitarian approach would have gone down better with the Nicolson boys than Miss Plimsoll's romantic breeziness. She kept telling them that they were pioneers in a virgin forest, but at the same time 'she had a fervent feeling for the British Navy, and her words of command tended to assume the nautical rather than the strictly pioneer dialect'. Under her stirring adjurations the boys became bored, sullen and deliberately clumsy. They let the roofing linoleum roll back on Miss Plimsoll, and released the bulldog on her knuckles. Finally they exclaimed in unison, 'We *hate* the Hut', and poor Miss Plimsoll began to cry.

Mr. Nicolson assures us that when he went back years afterwards and found the ruins of the Hut among the bilberries, he felt remorse. But at the time, he was unmoved by Miss Plimsoll's tears and offered no consolatory promise to be good. He reacted differently from Hugh Walpole's Jeremy to the phenomenon of a crying governess. And in so far as *Some People* and *Jeremy* may be assumed to be autobiographical, we can only deduce that Hugh Walpole was a nicer little boy than Master Nicolson, or (more probably) a much less truthful man.

During a winter at Sofia, Mr. Nicolson tells us, a permanent drop of moisture dangled at the tip of Miss Plimsoll's 'sharp and pointed' nose. His elder brothers were now at school, and he himself was to begin serious lessons. He describes Miss Plimsoll sketching out a 'plan of campaign' as she unpacked her belongings into strange suspect cupboards—'her zest for her own tidiness mingling with that vague sense of being put upon which is the brown aura in which all governesses have their being. "Sums first", she said, placing a celluloid box for hair-pins on the dressing table. "I always think it's a good thing to begin with sums; and then from ten till eleven we must do history. . . . At eleven we stand down."'

In Sofia, too, occurred the incident of the assassinated M. Stambuloff's severed fingers—preserved in spirits and displayed in a window for all to see. The horrid little boy lured his governess to contemplate this morbid sight, and was justly punished by being haunted by those fingers afterwards himself. Heaping coals of fire, she sat up with him night after night until he fell asleep; with the result that he succumbed to her, and promised (against his precocious better judgment) that he would try for the Navy.

Proud of her convert, she gave him a boatswain's whistle and told him 'what a *dear* little middy' he would make.

When they stayed in Government House in Gibraltar, however, Miss Plimsoll let him down, abandoning him to lonely terrors while she went out to inspect the Fleet lying at anchor in the harbour; for 'the call of the White Ensign was too much for her'. It was *his* turn to do the letting-down when they crossed in a cruiser to Morocco. While Miss Plimsoll was 'immersed in a religious trance', and trembled with emotion at the welcoming salute of guns, the little boy was sick into a canvas bucket. He said he thought he would not go into the Navy after all. 'Hush, dear', she said then; but the next day she added: 'Don't you think, dear, that we must be careful, we must be *very* careful, not to become a muff?' He was nine years old now, and resented this insinuation: he would show his governess which was the muff. So he terrified her by scrambling round the cornice outside the Legation, and frightened her mule into throwing her into the Moroccan dust. Finally, he locked her in her room and lost the key. 'I think', said his father on this occasion, 'that it is high time that boy went to school.'

The most heartrending of all Miss Plimsoll's humiliations at her pupil's hands was when he stood by and watched her write, in Old English characters, the word 'Dairy' instead of 'Diary' on the vellum cover of her cherished birthday present. He displayed her mistake to everyone. 'My triumph', he writes, 'became positively orgiac. . . . All my repressions were suddenly released. As usual, Miss Plimsoll dissolved into tears.' And as usual, he did not respond. He melted, however, when he saw her actually packing up to leave. 'Her possessions had become so familiar to me. . . . That blue dress which she wore for tea-parties, that dove-coloured silk which she wore when she came down to dinner.' (It would be fascinating to know how often this occurred: among diplomats it must, surely, be almost impossible for the governess to live 'as family'.) Remorseful, the little boy said, 'I'm sorry, I really am.' Then he locked himself in the water-closet and 'cried softly; soft enough to indicate manliness and restraint: just loud enough to make certain that people could hear'. Not such a nice little boy as Jeremy, certainly, but much more real!

So Miss Plimsoll passed on into another family, and attached herself to another little boy, to whom she enlarged continually on the romance—not of the Navy but of Diplomacy. Whether or not she actually drove in a cab through Sofia or wore a blue dress for tea-parties, Miss Plimsoll undoubtedly lives in our imaginations among the immortal governesses. And among these, she and Jane Eyre are the two whose acquaintance I (for one) value most highly and most frequently renew.

The Turn of the Screw, by Henry James (1898), contains the only known example of a ghostly governess. Some people may consider that the tragic seriousness of this story should set it beyond my pryings after sociological detail; and I can assure them at once that I do not propose to investigate the ghostly Miss Jessel's relations with her sometime pupils. Personally, my withers are unwrung by the alleged horror of this story. I can never quite believe in those two children—beautiful as gods and apparently as good as angels—yet corrupted by nameless vice. But however shocked I was by their corruption and suffering, I think I should still see no reason against searching the book for information about a governess's life.

And we are told quite a lot about the narrator, a governess whose name we are never given even in the third-person introduction. She was the youngest of several daughters of a country parson. In search of her first job she answered an advertisement, and went to London in some trepidation for an interview. At once she was dazzled by the charm of her prospective employer—a rich bachelor with a house in Harley Street and a country place in Essex. He explained that he wished her to be 'in supreme authority' at Bly, his country house, to take sole charge of an orphaned nephew and niece of whom he had been left the guardian. His idea of 'sole charge', moreover, comprised the condition that she should never refer anything to him or bother him in any way about the children. He was, indeed, the apotheosis of the irresponsible employer; and the measure of his irresponsibility is provided by his saying of Miss Jessel, the last governess, that she 'had done for them quite beautifully—she was a most respectable person'.

Later, when the live governess knew the dead one to be 'infamous', and 'the most horrible of women', she said of her employer that 'his indifference must have been awful'. But at that first interview she was so captivated as to feel that everything he did must have sufficient reason: her only misgiving was lest she herself should be unfitted for the task. Other applicants, he told her, had been afraid of the undertaking: 'It sounded dull, it sounded strange.' And she herself was 'young, untried, nervous: it was a vision of serious duties and little company, of really great loneliness. But the salary offered much exceeded her modest measure', and apparently her parents did not insist on further enquiry or references. So off she went to the unknown Bly and its mysterious inhabitants, as Jane Eyre went to Thornfield and Becky to Queen's Crawley.

Like Jane Eyre, she found a most sensible and sympathetic housekeeper in provisional charge, who greeted her with 'as decent a curtsey as if I had been the mistress or a distinguished visitor'. She was favourably impressed with the house, and had 'a sense of the liberality' with which she was treated. Straight from a crowded vicarage, she was delighted with 'the large, impressive room, one of the best in the house, the great state bed, the long glasses in which', she says, 'for the first time I could see myself from head to foot'. She was glad, too, to share this room with her lovely little charge: 'to watch, teach, "form" little Flora would too evidently be the making of a happy and useful life.'

Indeed, this unnamed governess undertook her duties in a spirit sadly lacking in most of her kind. When Miles returned from school, mysteriously expelled, she kept her promise not to consult his uncle, and felt sure that the school must have misjudged him; for to his sister's charm and gaiety he added a rare brilliance of mind. She entered into the children's imaginative games, and delighted in their company. 'My charming work', she said, 'was just my life with Miles and Flora, leading me to wonder afresh at the vanity of my original fears, the distaste I had begun by entertaining for the probable grey prose of my office. There was to be no grey prose and no long grind. It was all the romance of the nursery and the poetry of the schoolroom. Instead of growing deadly used to them—and it's a marvel for a governess: I call the sisterhood to witness!—I made constant fresh discoveries.'

She was wise enough to know her limitations—that Miles was 'too clever for a bad governess, a parson's daughter, to spoil'; and that he could in fact teach her things that she had not learned in her 'small, smothered life'. She encouraged him to treat her as an intellectual as well as a social equal. 'His "my dear" was constantly on his lips for me, and nothing could have expressed more the exact shade of the sentiment with which I desired to inspire my pupils than its fond familiarity. It was so respectfully easy.'

It is true, of course, that Miles and Flora, in this manifestation, were as much better than normal children, as they were worse when they came under the influence of Peter Quint the dead valet, and Miss Jessel the dead governess.

Yet we may be sure that their living governess was of the sort who would have done her best for even the dullest children. These two, she met more than half way in their brilliance and charm. She showed them that she loved them, and responded to all their moods. Had she not so won their trust she could not have saved Miles at the end.

Miles once told her that she was 'a jolly "perfect" lady'. We must agree with him in this opinion, and assert also that she was a 'jolly perfect governess'. For she possessed the supreme gift—denied, it appears, to most governesses—of enjoying herself with children. She was courageous, too. When the haunting horror of Peter Quint and Miss Jessel, and their perverted partnership, became gradually known to her, she fought tooth and nail for the children's souls. And of all the governesses whom we have considered, I believe that only Jane Eyre would have had intelligence and courage to do as much.

It seems that governesses never come singly in the works of Henry James. In *What Maisie Knew* (1898), as in *The Turn of the Screw,* there are two; and once again there is a struggle for a child's soul between the powers of good and evil, with a governess aligned on either side. This time, however, evil is not made manifest in ghosts, but in the selfishness and malice of human beings; and I, for my part, find the sufferings of its victim far more horrible.

The plot and the component characters of *What Maisie Knew* are so complicated, that it would be aesthetic sacrilege to subject 'the Master's' syntactic *pointillisme* to a crude three-colour process of analysis. It is enough to say that a small girl is tossed and torn throughout the book between her divorced and detestable parents; that her first governess marries her father, while her mother marries a weak but delightful man called Sir Claude—of unknown surname; and that Maisie finally chooses to cut her tender, sensitive little self free from the lot of them, and to live with her second governess, Mrs. Wix.

Of Miss Overmore, who later became Maisie's stepmother, we are told little in her capacity as governess, save that she was 'almost too pretty' for the job, 'a lady, and yet awfully poor'. Mrs. Wix, on the other hand, is described with loving detail. When Maisie first saw her, she presented a 'sad and strange appearance, the appearance as of a kind of greasy greyness', and her hair had turned to 'a turbid, sallow, unvenerable white. . . . She wore glasses which, in humble reference to a divergent obliquity of vision, she called her straighteners, and a little, ugly, snuff-coloured dress' which was 'glazed with antiquity. The straighteners, she explained to Maisie, were put on for the sake of others; . . . the rest of the melancholy garb could only have been put on for herself. . . . She was as droll as an animal towards the end of the "natural history".'

Poor Mrs. Wix, on her first emergence from her 'dingy decencies', was thus the very picture of an elderly, worn-out governess who has been downtrodden for many years. In all that time she had not even learned to make the most of her slender stock-in-trade as a teacher, but was continually betraying her lack of any qualifications. Yet she soon won Maisie's heart by telling her about her own little girl who, at Maisie's age, had been run over by a hansom-cab. 'It was comfortably established between them that Mrs. Wix's heart was broken'; and Maisie felt that her new governess 'had been, with passion and anguish, a mother, and that this was something Miss Overmore was not, something (strangely, confusingly) that Mamma was even less'. Maisie was as lonely as Mrs. Wix, and had already suffered from indifference and insecurity. What she needed more than anything was a sense of abiding love, and this she found at last in her new governess. Maisie felt that 'somehow, in her ugliness and her poverty, she was peculiarly and soothingly safe; safer than anyone in the world'—a person on whom one could rest with a 'tucked in and kissed-for-good-night feeling'.

Maisie was right. Mrs. Wix's soul, though it had been worn as threadbare as her snuff-coloured dress, was made of a stuff as stout and durable. Even when she and Maisie were separated through the selfish whims of Maisie's parents, they did not lose spiritual touch with one another. Mrs. Wix did not write to her pupil, but 'her very silence became one of the largest elements of Maisie's consciousness; it proved a warm and habitable air. . . . Somewhere in the depths of it the dim straighteners were fixed upon her; somewhere out of the troubled little current Mrs. Wix intensely waited.'

When governess and pupil were reunited under the roof of Maisie's mother and Sir Claude, Mrs. Wix's devotion to duty was subjected to a severer test than that of absence; for to her love of Maisie was added adoration of Maisie's stepfather. Sir Claude gave her 'a five-pound note and the history of France and an umbrella with a malachite knob'. But 'what dazzled most' was his 'perfect consideration. He shook hands with her, he recognised her. . . . Even to the hard heart of childhood there was something tragic in such elation at such humanities: it brought home to Maisie the way her humble companion had sidled and ducked through life.' More subtly still he won the old dear's allegiance by confiding in her; until she exclaimed in ecstasy: 'He leans on me—he leans on me!' And as Sir Claude was fundamentally kind and good, as well as debonair, it is small wonder that Mrs. Wix confessed herself to be 'over head and ears' in love with him.

It is no new thing that a governess should be in love with her employer; nor is it surprising, even though in this case she was old enough to be his mother. And so far she had

had to make no choice between love and principles. Could she have gone on as she was, her life with him and Maisie would have been very heaven. But Sir Claude, unfortunately, was as weak as he was well-meaning; and he was involved in an intrigue with (of all people!) the ex-Miss Overmore—Maisie's stepmother and sometime governess. He therefore left his wife for ever, and carried off Maisie and Mrs. Wix to Boulogne; and then he proposed that the three of them should set up house on the Riviera with Maisie's stepmother. But he had reckoned too certainly on Mrs. Wix's allegiance to himself, and its power to blind her to moral values; whereas Mrs. Wix could still tell right from wrong. As she said to Maisie: 'You know how I'm affected towards him, but you must also know that I see clear.' And she saw very clearly that the dubious ménage in which he asked her to participate would imperil Maisie's soul as well as his. She made, however, a final bid to snatch them both from destruction. 'I have nothing of my own, I know', she cried—'no money, no clothes, no appearance, no anything, nothing but my hold on this little one truth, which is all in the world I can bribe you with: that the pair of you are more to me than all besides, and that if you let me help you and save you . . . I'll work myself to the bone in your service.'

When this appeal failed, Mrs. Wix knew that her idol had feet of clay and was being snatched out of her reach into perdition. As far as he was concerned, the wicked governess had triumphed over the good one. Mrs. Wix might, of course, have compromised with evil, and lived with Sir Claude and his mistress as Maisie's governess. But this would have been to sacrifice Maisie too, by submitting her to the influence of her stepmother's corruption and her stepfather's degeneration. 'A certain greatness had now come over Mrs. Wix', and she determined to have no more truck with evil, either for Maisie or herself. So she cut her losses and concentrated all her strength on the salvation of the child alone. 'I've just done it all for *you,* precious', she said—'not to lose you, which would have been worst of all: so that I've had to pay with my own innocence . . . for clinging to you and keeping you. Don't let me pay for nothing: don't let me have been thrust for nothing into such horrors and such shames.'

And Maisie did not let her pay for nothing. Though she loved her stepfather, who had always treated her with grave sincerity, she knew (thanks to Mrs. Wix) that it would be wrong to live with him if her stepmother lived in the same house. So when Mrs. Wix left their Boulogne hotel to return to England, Maisie went too. In the last scene 'Mrs. Wix so dominated the situation that she had something sharp for everyone. . . . She was girded—positively harnessed—for departure, . . . and armed with a small, fat rusty reticule which, almost in the manner of a battle-axe, she brandished in support of her words.'

Somewhere in London Mrs. Wix had a lodging of her own with a 'shabby door' and 'squalid stair'; and there, I am sure, Maisie would have been very happy with her staunch old friend—the most unselfish and heroic of all our governesses. I hope, however, that Sir Claude secured for Maisie her own little fortune, as he promised, so that Mrs. Wix could hire a really efficient governess to teach her charge. For Mrs. Wix had never been an inspired teacher and her methods were sadly out of date. Although she could not be bettered as a friend and guardian, she was not a good governess; and there were still a great many things which a really good governess could teach, which Maisie did not know.

The turn of the century confronts us for the first time with a play that has a governess for heroine. *The Man from Blankley's* by F. Anstey first appeared in *Punch* in 1893. It was produced at the Prince of Wales's Theatre in

1901 with Charles Hawtrey in the leading part, and revived at the Haymarket Theatre in 1906. The main characters are Mr. and Mrs. Tidmarsh of Westbourne Grove, their small daughter Gwennie, their rich uncle and aunt the Gilwattles, Marjory Seaton the governess, and Lord Strathpeffer—who arrives at the wrong house and is mistaken for the man hired from Blankley's to avoid a party of thirteen.

Marjory Seaton combines all the ingredients of the downtrodden governess, with a dash of snob-value added. But her position as snob-exhibit in the Tidmarsh home is very different from that of previous governesses. Her employers are parvenus and vulgarians of the deepest dye, and use their power over the governess to enhance their own self-importance. But unlike Thackeray's snobs, for instance, their snobbishness is that of plutocrats rather than would-be aristocrats. They do not value Marjory because she has worked for titled people or numbered such among her friends, but because her father has lost a considerable fortune. Hence they do not fawn on her as the Pontos fawned on Miss Wirt, but relish their power to remind her constantly that she is a penniless dependant.

On the day of the Tidmarshes' dreary dinner-party, Marjory has been told that she will be wanted in the drawing-room after dinner. She has put on a gown which shows up the fussy dowdiness of Mrs. Tidmarsh's own 'creation'. Gwennie immediately draws attention to the dress, tactlessly remarking that it is 'smarter than Mummy's'. And when Marjory explains that it is the only one she has left, Mrs. Tidmarsh complains complacently: 'You needn't remind me *quite* so often that, before your father lost all his money, you were in very different circumstances—because I am perfectly aware of the fact. Otherwise I should not have felt justified in asking you to come down this evening. My friends are *most* particular.' Even the child has caught this offensive tone. 'I've got quite fond of you', she says to

Marjory, 'though you *are* only the governess. But then, you weren't a governess *always,* were you?'

Marjory is asked to correct the French on the menus and firmly told that she will, while doing this, be quieter in the schoolroom even though the fire has gone out. While she is out of the room Mr. Tidmarsh (a nonentity, like so many husbands of governess-bullying wives) is told that Miss Seaton may have to dine with them. 'What!' he exclaims, 'the governess? Oh, my dear, won't she look a little out of place among us?' (And so she does—like a pheasant in a poultry yard!) To which Mrs. Tidmarsh can only counter by way of comfort: 'Fortunately, most of our friends know that she was once well off.' At the close of the century, as at the beginning, employers are judged and damned by their behaviour to the governess. But never before, since the Williamsons in Lady Blessington's book, has their behaviour been so openly and unashamedly purse-proud. For we are verging on the Edwardian era, when it sometimes seemed as if the only equality recognised was the equality of wealth.

Although Mrs. Tidmarsh knows perfectly well that the dinner will be disastrous without a fourteenth to balance the uncountermandable man from Blankley's, she makes a favour of asking the governess to join them. 'I and Mr. Tidmarsh', she says, 'have been wondering whether we could manage to find a place for you. Of course you are too sensible to expect us to make a *precedent* of it—but—a—you seem a trifle run down and depressed' (no wonder, poor girl!) 'and we thought that—just for *once*—a little cheerful society—.' Marjory is quite touched by this unaccustomed consideration, until the *enfant terrible* enlightens her as to the real situation. When Marjory reproves Gwennie for her frankness, saying 'your mother would be very angry if she knew you had repeated it to *anybody*', the horrid innocent replies: 'Why, I only repeated it to you—and you're *nobody,* you know.'

Gradually the guests arrive, each more sepulchral and moronic than the last. Old Aunt Gilwattle immediately gives Marjory a bad mark for her dress: 'Black silk and a high neck used to be considered full dress for a governess in *my* young days.' And Mrs. Tidmarsh excuses her own over-indulgence of the governess by reminding her aunt that Miss Seaton 'was a lady once'. 'In my opinion', replies the old lady tartly, 'the sooner she forgets what she *was* and remembers what she *is*, the better.'

It is curious, I think, that neither 'lady' makes even a pretence of connoting gentility with gentle birth. A lady, they argue, is rich; and when her money goes, her status as a lady automatically goes too. In contrast we may remember how angry Emma Woodhouse was at the suggestion that *her* governess could possibly not have been a lady; and how Margaret Harrington, in *Amy Herbert,* said grudgingly that Emily Morton 'must be something like a lady, or Mama would not let her be with us'. But Mrs. Tidmarsh clearly had no qualms about allowing Gwennie to consort with an ex-lady. In this play there is manifested a really new and nasty quality of snobbishness—a fundamental change in the basis of social thought and feeling.

The guests are as bad as the Tidmarshes and their relations, though some of them make a feeble pretence of liberality. When Mr. Poffley, an inane young man, flirts with Marjory, the arch Miss Flinders asks him if he is aware that it is the *governess* to whom he was making himself so agreeable. 'Oh yes', he replies. 'I—er—flatter myself I'm above any petty social prejudice.' And Miss Flinders —hoping to win his admiration—agrees sycophanticly, while cattily commenting on her rival's dress.

When Lord Strathpeffer is announced, having mistaken the house in a fog, he is naturally mistaken by the Tidmarshes for the man from Blankley's. He and Marjory recognise each other, but even *she* thinks he has undertaken a degrading task in order to make money and consequently 'high-hats' him. The guests are surprised and pleased to find that the Tidmarshes have a titled friend; and the self-styled radical, Uncle Gilwattle, is secretly transported with elation. The stage is set for two acts of intricate misunderstandings. In all the subsequent social interplay, Marjory's position as governess proves an important factor. Uncle Gilwattle asks if his niece doesn't know better than to send a lord down with the governess: Mrs. Gilwattle says that 'that little minx of a governess is carrying on in a very forward manner with Lord Strathpeppermint': and Miss Flinders patronisingly assures Marjory that Mr. Poffley is 'not at *all* the sort of man to pay serious attention to a young lady in *your* position, dear Miss Seaton'. It is all according to tradition; and we might be at Thornfield during Mr. Rochester's house-party, or the brass-founder's villa in *Martin Chuzzlewit,* rather than in Westbourne Grove in 1901.

The only person who recognises the lady in the governess's disguise is the butler—and this marks a great departure from the manservant's contempt for Ruth Pinch. For menservants (as we have noticed) form a class which is apt to look down on governesses. Dawes is a visiting butler, who has come in for the evening to 'oblige'. He thinks very poorly of the Tidmarshes, and considers himself infinitely condescending to work for them at all. All his thwarted craving to abase himself in snobbish servitude is called out by the aloof and neglected governess; so that when the parlourmaid, handing coffee after dinner, offers none to Marjory, Dawes magnificently reproves her: 'Governess or not, she's the only lady here, and you'll be good enough to serve her.'

Traditionally—for these customs have by now assumed for us the ritual movements of a ballet—Marjory is asked to go into the inner drawing-room and play the piano to the ladies. When told who is playing, Mrs. Gilwattle comments: 'Ah, I felt certain no *lady* could play with so much expression. . . . You make too much of that girl, Maria; you encourage her to forget her place. She's undermining your authority with your own child. . . . She's evidently paramount in *this* house.' Thus challenged, Mrs. Tidmarsh insists that Gwennie should 'repeat' her piece, which (Gwennie declares) Miss Seaton had forbidden her to do. Unfortunately, Gwennie associates 'repeating' with the information about the man from Blankley's which (in the first Act) Marjory had told her she must not 'repeat' to anybody. Under duress, Gwennie explodes her bombshell, and pandemonium breaks loose. The guests depart in disorder, and Marjory is left alone with the now explained Lord Strathpeffer, to apologise to him for the trouble she has caused. When Mrs. Tidmarsh re-enters, swineherd-counterjumper and goosegirl-governess are revealed in their true nature as Prince and Princess; the curtain falls on them in each other's arms, preparing to live happily ever after.

How far may we accept *The Man from Blankley's* as serious evidence of the manners of the time? All comedy-farces must be exaggerated, of course. On the other hand, the very fact that they are topical and ephemeral is a guarantee that they did not seem outrageously false to their original audience. On this point we have an interesting comment by Anstey himself, who wrote an introduction to an edition of the play published in 1927. In an author's note he started out by drawing attention to the inevitable 'dating' of the play during the thirty years since it was written. For instance, Mrs. Tidmarsh would, in 1927, have been able to ring up Blankley's to cancel her hired guest at the last moment. Moreover, Anstey claimed, 'A girl like Marjory Seaton, suddenly reduced from wealth to poverty and obliged to earn her own living, would find many careers open to her which she would prefer to becoming a governess.' And even when the play was revived in 1906, he says, critics had protested that the Tidmarshes' snobbishness was already a thing of the past. But, he goes on, 'I do claim that *The Man from Blankley's*, after due allowances have been made for the exaggeration almost necessary in humorous dialogue, is by no means an unfaithful picture of a certain section of the middle-class of that time, and was accepted as such. Its chief claim to interest consists in being, as it were, an historical document, a record of conditions that are past and gone for ever.'

In its author's opinion, therefore, *The Man from Blankley's* was already a costume play when he wrote his introduction to a new edition thirty years after its first appearance in *Punch*. It should be much more so for us to-day—twenty years later again, and with another world war behind us, and a social revolution in full swing. And yet—and yet, all the evidence goes to show that Anstey's 'modern' attitude to snobbishness and governesses was premature. Neither of these phenomena is 'past and gone for ever'. There are still Marjory Seatons brought up as butterflies by foolish and financially unstable fathers; and they still become governesses both in fact and fiction. As for snobbishness—that is still with us, and probably always will be. Perhaps in the future we shall have the snobbishness of Commissars. It is the quality rather than the intensity of Mrs. Tidmarsh's snobbishness which has departed from the employers of governesses in more recent books. As we go on into the twentieth century we shall find governesses just as lonely in their position between employers and domestic staff as were Marjory Seaton or Agnes Grey. We shall find, too, governesses just as snobbish as Miss Wirt. But on both sides the snobbishness becomes subtler. Sometimes it is based on a plucky fight to maintain a dying social order. Sometimes, again, it is intellectual: the governess's education and background are as different from those of her employers as Metroland was (in the nineteen-twenties) remote from Bloomsbury. And in these cases friction and loneliness are the result of having no real interests in common. But never again in the course of my twentieth-century reading have I encountered an example of purse-proud, plutocratic arrogance so crass and barefaced as that of Mrs. Tidmarsh in *The Man from Blankley's.*

CHAPTER V

EDWARDIAN

The Edwardian Age; V. Sackville-West, *The Edwardians*; Rosamond Lehmann, *The Ballad and the Source*; Elizabeth Evelyn, *No Promise in Summer*; Marion Crawford, *The Undesirable Governess*; Saki, *The Schartz-Metterclume Method*; Schools versus Governesses Again.

GOING forward a few years, let us see what the governess's position was in the age of Maud Allen, bearing-reins, Post-Impressionism, aeroplanes, motoring-bonnets and Maeterlinck. Some of these things, of course, already existed in the 'nineties, and there can be no sharp demarcation between one age and another. Yet the human mind seems to crave temporal landmarks, and to invest past epochs with an atmosphere of which their inhabitants were not aware —their adult inhabitants, at any rate. On children—who live so much in a world that is common to children of all periods—the impact of a number of small things from the adult world imprints a vivid picture of the time. The age in which a child grows up is, for him, isolated. It has no past for comparison; and is apt to be cut off from the future by the iron curtain of school. It exists in itself, exempt from the detached criticism which comes with the growth of period sense. Our awareness, therefore, of the epoch of our own childhood is sharper than of any other, though probably distorted and inaccurate.

My own childhood was lived mainly in the Edwardian age; and it was then, too, that I had a governess. It is with her, therefore, that I associate the haphazard list of things with which this page is headed. It was with my governess that I saw Maud Allen dance at a charity matinée; and with her (as we came out) that I deplored the torturing bearing-reins on the waiting horses. Motoring-bonnets, it is true, I remember from an earlier, nursery age, but I think my mother still wore one sometimes after I was promoted to the schoolroom; and I used to make her hatpins out of polychrome sealing-wax, to fasten it more firmly on her lovely head. I was not taken to see the Post-Impressionists; but I can remember how my parents—reared in an atmosphere of Arundel prints and photographs of the Acropolis—were startled and shocked by their visit to the exhibition. Nor was I taken to see *The Blue Bird,* because my mother thought it morbid; but I read it eagerly (in English, I'm afraid) and revelled in its vague, unwholesome symbolism.

Other events stand out for me from the Edwardian age. The White City, with its invigorating Flip-flap and terrifying Japanese wrestlers; Hungarian bands at garden-parties; German bands and concert-parties at the seaside; the King's funeral; the Balkan wars, in the shape of a map pinned to the schoolroom wall; the Carthorse Parade on Whit Mondays, mingling the scents of dust and hawthorne; early films at the Polytechnic; and my first visit to the theatre to see *Henry VIII.*

If my memory has spilled over into the reign of George V, that is simply because my governess stayed with us until I and the century were aged thirteen. Personal landmarks are more striking than the historical, and I have already said that a child's impression of its epoch is inaccurate. Small, schoolroom happenings are jumbled now with world events, and all—from this distance—carry equal weight. But all—and this is the point I wish to emphasise—are inextricably tangled in memory with my governess, who was my beloved and inalienable companion through this period.

And just as this mental newsreel, scratched and blurred now from over-frequent showing, represents to me both the Edwardian age and the governess who dominated my daily life, so many other children must (in the same way) identify an epoch with its presiding spirit in the schoolroom. A governess coloured the 'nineties for Mr. Nicolson—colourful though his childhood would have been in any case; and someone like Miss Jones added a warmer tone of grey to the grisaille of Hugh Walpole's Polchester background.

I wish I had found more examples of Edwardian governesses to compare with my own experience: it is a period on which (as a general historian of governesses) I feel myself to be an especial expert. But alas! my researches have yielded little fruit. I have found only a handful of Edwardian governesses; and three of them occur in novels whose authors are looking back with a nostalgia like my own. These tempt me to linger in the past myself, and to recall my own happy relationship with 'Moley'. But I must make no exception in her favour. This is a history of governesses in fiction, and she was very much a governess in real life.

The novel with which we enter this new age is actually called *The Edwardians*; and although Miss Vita Sackville-West wrote it in 1930, the period of the book is a quarter of a century before, when its author was herself a child. It is the study of a great house and family at a certain period of their history. Chevron, which forms the central theme—almost the main character—is a house as old and noble as the one in which Miss Sackville-West herself grew up; and the book has the richness of a tapestry into which the turrets, chimneys, courts and gatehouses of Chevron are woven in equal proportion and prominence with the human figures.

These figures comprise an ancient and aristocratic family, with their smart week-end guests, their tenants, servants and hangers-on. We are shown their splendours and scandals; their dignity and vulgarity; their snobbishness; their conscientiousness, frivolities and self-distrust. Above all, we see how the human lives are interwoven with the house's longer life: how everyone, from duke to gamekeeper, from duchess to housemaid, is part of the web and woof of Chevron.

In this heraldic assemblage of lords and ladies, with their favourites, retainers, horses and dogs, the figure of the governess has its tiny place. Miss Watkins never, in fact, appears in person; but we know that she is there. And from the attitude of more important persons we can judge how small and unconsidered her position in the household really was.

At the beginning of the book, Chevron was presided over by a dowager Duchess—still a famous beauty and brilliant hostess, who entertained there for her son. She also had a daughter, Viola, who, though seventeen, and beautiful in her own way, was still kept partly in the schoolroom. For a schoolgirl daughter with a bow in her hair and frilly dresses fitted better into the Duchess's picture of Chevron and herself than would a silent, critical young woman. So although Viola was allowed to lunch with the house-party, she ate her supper in the schoolroom, after kissing her mother goodnight at her dressing-table. Evidently, the main use for a governess in the Duchess's complicated life was to keep Viola out of the way, and to keep her young.

Miss Watkins is only mentioned once, when the Duchess tracked down an elusive guest—an explorer invited because of his sudden fame—to a distant summer-house. The summer-house 'served as an outdoor schoolroom; the walls were scribbled over with sums and childish drawings, the table-edge carved into scallops by an idle penknife'. This was clearly one of those schoolrooms in which attention often wanders; but perhaps it had served many children as an ante-room to worlds undreamed of even in the history of Chevron. Here, at any rate, Viola had dreamed of liberation from the family tradition; and here, when the Duchess found them, she and the explorer were talking as one free spirit to another.

'I do hope, Viola', said the Duchess, 'you haven't been boring Mr. Anquetil. And what about your lessons, my dear child, surely you ought to have been doing those? Why, the table is littered with your books. What *will* Miss Watkins say?' Having thus adroitly put Viola back into the schoolroom—her proper place—by stressing her youth and state of pupillage, the Duchess hastened to identify Anquetil's viewpoint with her own. He was not unattractive, in an unusual way, and he was famous: it was intolerable that he should prefer Viola's company to her own.

'I must really take you away, Mr. Anquetil', she exclaimed, 'and let Viola go on with her lessons, or the poor child will get into trouble—I always wonder whether Miss Watkins isn't a little *too* strict with her, but one doesn't like to interfere too often; governesses have their own methods, haven't they? And it's scarcely fair to make them feel one doesn't trust them.' Not that she cared a pin about Miss Watkins's methods: she had handed Viola over without question, on the tacit understanding that she was not to be bothered with the child.

Even Anquetil—while laying the foundations of life-long friendship and love with Viola—had gained a much better idea of Miss Watkins's methods than her employer would ever do. 'That's quite all right, Duchess', he answered, playing up to the myth of Viola's age; 'I squared Miss Watkins, on condition that I might tell Viola stories till luncheon. I explained that it would be good for her geography. That's the way to learn geography—talk to somebody who's been there, instead of learning paragraphs out of a repulsive little primer like this.'

Even if the Duchess only wanted a governess for the sake of keeping a schoolroom in being, she might at least have employed one more educationally up-to-date. A good teacher might have reconciled Viola to her backwater: she would certainly have been a better money's worth. But

Miss Watkins evidently taught geography on the system of 'Northumberland; capital Newcastle-on-Tyne; noted for coal'. She probably taught history out of *Little Arthur*, and scripture from *Line upon Line*. I imagine that she was elderly, and had been handed on (like a globe or a blackboard) from some cousin's outgrown schoolroom.

This, as I said, is the only mention of Miss Watkins in *The Edwardians*. Anquetil stayed on at Chevron after the Duchess returned to town, and dined with the young Duke and Viola. On that evening, no doubt, the governess ate her supper alone upstairs. For in the meticulously ordered hierarchy that prevailed at Chevron, a governess must have been unusually lonely. After mid-day dinner the housemaids carried their pudding across the court to eat it sociably in their own sitting-room, while at night, in the steward's room, visiting valets and lady's-maids were becomingly entertained by the butler and the housekeeper. But there was no social equal, no natural companion, for the governess. It is true that the Duchess employed a secretary, whom she paid £150 a year and who also found herself stranded high and dry among superiors and inferiors. But Miss Watkins is never mentioned as a possible boon companion for her, though the lady's-maid and housekeeper are rejected as possible aspirants.

I hope Miss Watkins soon left Chevron, if only to be handed on (again like a globe or blackboard) to some other schoolroom. Even the Duchess could not postpone for ever the evil day of Viola's coming-out. But when the time came, Miss Watkins would easily find some other house (I hope a humbler one) in which to produce her 'repulsive little primers', and unpack her personal belongings. In the Duchess's set there was no lack of beauties who feared the rivalry of grown-up daughters; and to selfish mothers, such a governess—guaranteed old-fashioned and free of ideas—was a veritable treasure.

The Ballad and the Source (1944) by Miss Rosamond Lehmann, is a melodrama of subtleties, a horror glimpsed through the golden dream of retrospection. Childhood is delicately remembered, and there are light touches in it which stab my own memories into life. The phonograph, for instance, proclaiming an 'Edison Bell Record', and the Liberty scarf draped round Mrs. Jardine's hat, might well have been numbered among my personal collection of Edwardiana.

The first governess in the story is a familiar foreign type—a Belgian this time, but still called simply 'Mamselle'. Like most foreign governesses she dressed abominably, and took the children out to tea wearing an *ensemble* which included 'her best off-mustard flannel skirt', a 'hand-crocheted black bolero scalloped in violet . . . and a white felt tam-o'-shanter at a chic angle'.

She indulged in psychological explanations of her charges' characters. She told Mrs. Jardine, their tea-party hostess, that Jess, the eldest girl, was 'un esprit fier et intransigéant. . . . Le fond est ex-cel-lent'. While 'la cadette' was 'douce et sérieuse'. She assumed a 'fluting' voice for social occasions; and could command 'a gesture of indescribable delicacy—something between a bow, a shrug and a deferential *moue*'. But once out of the house and walking home with the children, she turned nasty and decreed that Jess should go supperless to bed. 'Off with their heads', muttered Jess in her sister's ear—'a code phrase arising out of our governess's marked physical resemblance to Tenniel's Queen in *Alice in Wonderland,* employed by us to convey warning and signalise defiance'.

Every summer Mademoiselle 'vanished unlamented to Belgium for her long annual holiday'. In the summer following the tea-party, the children went often to Mrs. Jardine's house, and made friends with the old lady and her grandchildren who were staying with her. They made the most of their freedom; for Mademoiselle, with her social manner and slick psychological judgments was not a propitious deity for presiding over friendships. On her return 'an era of stricter discipline' began. 'To pay us out for the general aroma of frayed moral fibre which she had sniffed on her return, Mademoiselle had persuaded my mother that it was in the interests of our health and education not to permit us to go out to tea during term-time.' But a farewell visit had to be paid to the house next door, and the children 'managed to leave Mademoiselle behind with her weekly migraine'. For Mademoiselle was prone to the occupational disease of governesses, who seem to carry their Achilles' heel in their heads. In the summer of 1914 Mademoiselle departed as usual for her holiday in Belgium, and this time she did not return. 'More than a year later a letter reached us, describing the horrors of occupation. . . . Jess said it was a judgment on her. We never saw or heard from her again.'

Meanwhile Mrs. Jardine, the mysterious Sybil whose personality pervades the whole book, had her grandchildren committed permanently to her charge. The two elder ones were sent to school. But she thought that Cherry, the youngest, needed 'the discipline of an intelligent, emotionally sane governess', and hoped it would not prove '*altogether* impossible to find such a woman'. The quarry whom she ultimately ran down is among the more unusual of our governesses. She is described in a letter which Mrs. Jardine wrote, containing 'an account of Cherry's general improvement under the care of a superlatively excellent young governess, Tanya Moore by name. . . . She was the daughter of a Russian dancer . . . and of an Irish father, a painter, of dissolute habits.' Tanya Moore's father had much in common with Rebecca Sharp's, but there the resemblance between the two girls ended. Tanya was no adventuress.

She was at first esteemed a treasure: 'Nothing could exceed the perfection of her touch with young children.'

And after Cherry's death from meningitis, Tanya stayed on as companion to the older children and their grandmother, who were now living in France. But she was not Mrs. Jardine's only protégée. There was also a young sculptor whom she had discovered and attached closely to herself; and with this sculptor Tanya unfortunately fell in love. Mrs. Jardine's letters at once took on a different tone, and she wrote that Tanya had 'attempted in the house a rôle to which neither birth nor quality gave her right. . . . *There is no getting away from* it . . . BREEDING DOES TELL.'

Mrs. Jardine was unconventional and had chosen an unconventional governess. She had lifted her out of poverty and insecurity, and idealised her into a princess. And when she felt herself emotionally betrayed, Mrs. Jardine had hidden her failure behind a screen of snobbishness. As for Tanya, turned neck and crop out of the house, the poor child felt lost and guilty. Not only was she thrown back into the harsh world without a penny, but also without a friend and without self-confidence. Not only was she hurt in spirit, she was also materially worse off than she had been before. Her relations with Mrs. Jardine had been too intimate to allow for any traffic in wages or references; and Tanya suffered from having been treated too much as a friend.

Perhaps, after all, there is something to be said for a due formality between employer and employed. A lack of it puts such a governess as Tanya too much at the mercy of her patroness. Her position was as insecure as that of a Tudor monarch's favourite. A cut-and-dried arrangement as to notice, references and hours of work may seem pusillanimous, but it provides a much better basis for mutual respect, and even mutual love, than some vague 'ladies' agreement' between friends.

Again we come to a novel in which much of the action that concerns us is laid in the reign of George V, and again I am unscrupulously calling it Edwardian. Eras do not end with royal funerals, especially when these are shortly followed by the outbreak of great wars. And I am convinced that the Edwardian aroma lingered until August 1914—albeit a little faded, a little musty, like neglected potpourri in a chintzy Edwardian drawing-room.

No Promise in Summer (1946) by Elizabeth Evelyn is the story of a woman told in the historic present by herself; and a large part of it is devoted to her childhood in Eton (where her father was a housemaster) before the first world war dealt the school so heartrending a blow. Like many little girls with elder brothers, Virginia is practically an only child during the term. She is a leader among her numerous friends, and eggs them on in dangerous games until 'nurses and governesses protest as noses bleed and shins are hacked'. Her parents therefore decide that she is becoming 'too much of a tomboy', and break it to her that she is to share a daily governess with her best friend, Violet Trefusis.

Miss Sateen, their first governess, 'has sandy hair, a long lumpy nose and no sense of humour. . . . Violet is determined to be popular; I am determined to be first; and we make straight for our goals, employing incessant tricks that drag Miss Sateen backwards and forwards in her efforts to be fair, and to imbue us with the qualities we lack.'

Miss Sateen is not as old-fashioned as Miss Watkins in *The Edwardians.* Instead of primers, she uses plasticine as a medium for teaching geography. But she is evidently not up-to-date enough for Virginia's father, and is succeeded by a young, go-ahead governess of a sort that is entirely new to us. Miss Hardcastle fits into none of our categories. It seems strange, indeed, that she should have been a governess at all, and not a mistress in a girls' school. But perhaps she wanted leisure for writing; for 'she has articles published in well known literary papers' and wins an occasional prize.

Miss Hardcastle is an 'eager-voiced young woman with an Oxford degree'. She 'has no fancies; she views us impartially as two girls to whom she must impart knowledge'. She reads poetry and prose to them, and inspires Virginia to write herself. She has an unrestrained enthusiasm for the French Impressionists; and plays tennis with the young Eton masters—volleying, serving overhand, and wearing white buckskin shoes. Eager to inspire Virginia with these enthusiasms, she takes her to the Tate Gallery and Wimbledon.

'As the months pass, Miss Hardcastle mounts higher and higher on her pedestal, to stand at last on the top, in her white piqué tennis dress, perfect in my eyes.' Virginia has, in fact, developed a 'crush' on Miss Hardcastle—what at my school we called (short for *grande passion*) a G.P. Our only previous hint of such a situation was in *The Daisy Chain,* and there (it may be remembered) the position was reversed: it was the governess, Miss Bracey, who adored Ethel with a jealous, touchy adoration. For the most part Victorian governesses were either too socially despised or too severe to be hero-worshipped by their pupils. And if such a psychological phenomenon did actually occur, its danger would probably have been unrecognised.

Not that there is anything unwholesome about Virginia's admiration for Miss Hardcastle. It is the most natural thing in the world. The governess is treated as a friend by Virginia's parents, and is probably a neighbour's daughter. Her youth, too, would seem to constitute her an elder sister to her pupils. This easy equality, combined with her competence, enthusiasm and dash, sets her up as an ideal to which Virginia herself can aspire, and spurs her to greater efforts both at tennis and English literature.

When the war breaks out Miss Hardcastle goes to work in London, and Virginia goes to school. Years afterwards they meet again. Virginia is now a young married woman, and all the attraction and dash are on her side. Miss Hardcastle has 'switched all her enthusiasm for tennis and the French Impressionists into the Young Women's Christian Association. . . . Her navy suit bags at the knees and creases across the shoulders, her shoes are low-heeled and brogued, a cloche hat covers her golden hair, and her voice alone remains to remind me of my far-off infatuation.'

The disillusionment will be familiar to all who have met their childhood's idols in after years. It is part of the changed perspective which makes old homes look cramped and old shockers quite unreadable. But in this case the change was not entirely subjective. Miss Hardcastle had really changed. That extra streak of masculinity in her composition which had made her so attractive to Virginia as a girl, had transformed her into an earnest spinster. Henceforth she held no glamour for her old pupil. Yet she interests *us* because of her uniqueness. She is the only boyish, comradely governess whom we shall meet: the only one to inspire 'crushes': and the only one to find her happiness in the espousal of good works.

After two retrospective books we come to two written in the Edwardian age itself. No rosy mist obscures the view in either of them, and in the first this view is a trifle crude and glaring. *The Undesirable Governess* by F. Marion Crawford (1910) is like those bold sketches drawn by lightning-artists on the music-hall stage; and like them, it is accompanied by topical and silly patter. The governess who gives her name to the book is not undesirable in her capacity as governess; on the contrary, her employer, Lady Jane Follitt, found her 'so thoroughly satisfactory' just because she was repellent in appearance and therefore undesirable in the eyes of Colonel Follitt and his sons. For Lady Jane had suffered so much from governesses with pretty faces and designing ways, that she was for a long time reluctant to replace the one whose photograph she had found in the Colonel's pocket.

Meanwhile Evelyn and Gwendoline, the teen-age girls, ran wild. They potted rooks and peppered horses with their father's gun; they rode steeplechases on their brother's favourite hunters; and they poached trout not only with worms, but in March, too! All this, Lady Jane could bear with equanimity. But when they locked up the chauffeur and gave the Mercedes an endurance test on the moors, even Lady Jane put her foot down. For she was a motor-maniac; and this outrage drove her to insert in the paper an advertisement which is unsurpassed in all our annals of vulgarity. It read thus: 'Governess wanted, to take charge of two girls of fourteen and fifteen respectively. Must have first-rate degree and references. Charm of manner, symmetry of form, and brilliancy of conversation especially not desirable, as husband and three grown-up sons much at home.'

It is true that Miss Pinkerton in *Vanity Fair* hinted that an attractive girl might prove unsuitable in Sir Huddlestone Fuddlestone's family; and that some of Lady Blessington's *nouveaux riches* could hardly bear their husbands to speak civilly to the governess. But never before have we met with an avowal so barefaced and shameless as this advertisement. Making every allowance for the fact that *The Undesirable Governess* is a burlesque—even a farce—its tone suggests that a certain section of Edwardian society was insensitive to *nuances* of good taste and good feeling. But perhaps I am taking too seriously a book which does not pretend to be anything more than an afternoon's light reading, and is certainly not a serious contribution to the history of manners.

In due course Lady Jane received an answer from an applicant, saying that she was aged twenty-three, had taken a first at a woman's college, and fulfilled only too well the physical requirements specified in the advertisement. Her unimpeachable references were taken up by telegram, and

Miss Ellen Scott arrived in Yorkshire for a fortnight's trial. The family's reactions to her humped shoulder, lame leg, blotchy face, red nose and scraped-back hair were various. The Colonel and his two younger sons ignored her; Lady Jane was delighted with this literal fulfilment of her needs; and the girls feared that Miss Scott's régime would mean an end to all their escapades. For they could not hope that she would—like all their previous governesses—spend her time flirting with the men until she should be ignominiously sacked. The domestic staff approved of her and pitied her; 'the housemaid brought her hot water as often as if she had been one of the family', and 'Lady Jane's own maid considered her "a perfect lady".' When Lionel, the scholarly eldest son, arrived home, he exhibited a very different reaction from the rest. He already knew Ellen in London, where he had studied Sanskrit with her father; and she had applied for the job with his consent, so that she might win his parents' heart before he announced his intention to marry her. He had not, however, known about the repellent aspect demanded by his mother; and he thought Ellen had had an accident until she explained to him the mystery of her padded shoulder, thickened sole, and rouge-blotched face.

This ingenious disguise was not the only mystery that surrounded Ellen Scott. She was also the only governess I know of who was a foundling. She had been left on her foster-father's doorstep as a baby; and hitherto no clue had been found that might lead to the discovery of her real parents. It happened, however, that the Follitts numbered among their fashionable friends a family of balloon-addicts named Trevelyan, who took Jocelyn Follitt with them on a flight. They made a forced landing in the grounds of a lunatic asylum; and while they were dining there an inmate (also called Trevelyan) had a heart attack and died. As the balloonists proved to be related to him, the doctor confided to them his belief that Sir Ralph Trevelyan's daughter was still living and was heiress to the dead baronet's estate.

Meanwhile the undesirable governess had been undergoing a transformation. Lady Jane liked her so well that she began to wish her a little more presentable. 'What made the governess look like a housemaid, though it was clear that she was a lady, was her red nose and the blotch'; so Lady Jane gave her bottles of potent Parisian lotion, which worked wonders. The governess's lameness and crooked shoulders also miraculously improved, until the younger sons began to notice her. At the same time, the hard-worked girls took heart. If she became any more attractive, she would be sent packing and their poaching days would begin again. They were right in their prophecy. Lady Jane caught the Colonel admiring Ellen in the library, and her ladyship's 'peace of mind faded away like a pleasant dream'. Yet it was Ellen herself who gave notice, and her employer was at first reluctant to accept it. 'I never', she said, 'had a governess I liked, till now. If you knew what I'd been through with them! But you! You're the ideal.' And she hinted that, instead of leaving, Ellen might scrape her hair back again and neglect the treatment of her complexion.

But when Lionel announced his engagement to Ellen, even the susceptible Colonel agreed that she must go. 'You'll be very fond of her some day', protested Lionel, 'when you get over the idea that she's been governess to the girls.' He added that she would go at once, and only asked that his mother should not be rude to her. 'As if one could be rude to a governess!' retorted this high-born English gentlewoman. During the scene of dismissal which followed, Lady Jane insisted that her eldest son could never marry a governess: 'There are laws to prevent such things —I'm sure there are.' Ellen, however, could now counter-attack with the bombshell of her birth and fortune. She 'produced a large envelope from the inside of her coat—for, being a governess, she possessed a pocket', and announced herself to be Diana Trevelyan, an heiress. When Lady Jane had sufficiently recovered from the agreeable shock, Diana explained the mechanism of her deformities and blotches. 'All I had to do', she said, 'was to make myself thoroughly undesirable; and I did!'

After the wedding, the girls ran wild again. 'It looked as if no one but the matron of a police-station could ever be satisfactory as a governess at King's Follitt.'

It is natural that Saki, that cold, cruel critic of society, should have included governesses within his survey; and there is an excellent example of his approach to our subject in a story called *The Schartz-Metterclume Method.* It occurs in the collection of short stories called *Beasts and Superbeasts,* published in 1914; but though the events described in it may possibly not have occurred during the reign of Edward VII, the atmosphere is unmistakably Edwardian.

The heroine, Lady Carlotta, is not really a governess at all: she is an involuntary impostor, a governess *malgré lui.* Her method, too, is so fantastic (as its name implies) that she ought, perhaps, to be held over to the end, and included in my appended menagerie of Grotesques. Yet her setting is in ordinary life, and all the occurrences in her brief tenure of office are—though unlikely—not impossible. I therefore include the story boldly in my serious case-list.

Lady Carlotta, then, a society young woman of downright character and ready wit, missed her train and was stranded at a wayside station. There, before she had time to collect herself, she was collected by an unknown Mrs. Quabarl with the words: 'You must be the new governess.' 'Well, if I must be, I must', thought Lady Carlotta to herself, as she submitted to being swept away in a motorcar.

And she wondered how best she could extract amusement from her new capacity. As they drove to the Quabarls' house, Mrs. Quabarl enlarged upon her children's characters. She said that 'Claude and Wilfred were delicate, sensitive, young people, that Irene had the artistic temperament highly developed, and that Viola was something or other else of a mould equally commonplace among children of that class and type in the nineteenth century.'

Here Saki hands us the clue to a fascinating social theory. For I believe that when he said 'class and type' he spoke specifically and with intent; and that he was not comparing the Quabarls with their social inferiors so much as with their betters. We have only to compare Mrs. Quabarl's attitude towards her children with that of the Duchess in *The Edwardians* to see how right he was. The Duchess's daughter was sensitive and artistic: yet the Duchess would never have admitted the fact—would never even have recognised it. The aristocracy and their smart friends did not indulge in psychological or educational theories. They were tough. They condemned their sons to the insanitary, barbaric discipline of Eton, and their daughters to the grim obscurity of schoolrooms. It was the middle-classes who thought their children highly-strung, and patronised schools based on bathrooms and the cult of '-isms'. As for educational theory, Miss Watkins with her 'repulsive little primers' was good enough for a duchess's daughter; but the little Quabarls were to have their lessons made interesting.

'In their history lessons', explained Mrs. Quabarl, 'you must try to make them feel that they are being introduced to the life-stories of men and women who really lived, not merely committing a mass of names and dates to memory.' Lady Carlotta, who belonged to the world of Chevron, and had no doubt been educated by just such a governess as Miss Watkins, pricked up her ears. She might have been badly taught, she might not have been considered sensitive; but her brains were unimpaired, and they worked quickly. She determined to give the little Quabarls the history lessons that their mother wished for them.

'French, of course', continued Mrs. Quabarl, 'I shall expect you to talk at meal times several days in the week.' To which Lady Carlotta replied decisively: 'I shall talk French four days of the week and Russian in the remaining three.' It was lucky for Mrs. Quabarl that the new governess was an impostor, for had she been genuine, the family would have had to endure Russian meekly in the future. Mrs. Quabarl, for all her dictatorial manner, was 'knocked off her perch' by this announcment, and could never have resisted its application.

That evening Lady Carlotta had dinner with her 'employers', who were evidently accustomed to have the governess living as one of the family. 'She helped herself well and truly to wine and held forth on various vintage matters. Previous governesses had limited their conversation on the wine topic to a respectful and doubtless sincere expression of a preference for water.'

Mrs. Quabarl was already shaken, but worse was still to come. Next morning she found her two little girls posed on the stair in unconvincing fancy-dress. 'We are having a history lesson', explained Irene; 'I'm supposed to be Rome, and Viola is the she-wolf. Claude and Wilfred have gone to fetch the shabby women.' The 'shabby' or Sabine women proved to be the lodge-keeper's little daughters, whom the boys were dragging to the house under the eye of their 'governess' and the threat of a 'number-nine spanking' from the fives-bat which she held menacingly in her hand. Mrs. Quabarl, even more afraid of the lodge-keeper's wife than of the 'governess', set the captive children free, and demanded to know what it was all about. She learned that her theory on the teaching of history was being put literally into practice.

'Early Roman history', explained Lady Carlotta brusquely: 'the Sabine women, don't you know? It's the Schartz-Metterclume Method to make children understand history by acting it themselves; fixes it in their memory, you know. Of course, if, thanks to your interference, your boys go through life thinking that the Sabine women ultimately escaped, I cannot really be held responsible.'

Summarily dismissed, Lady Carlotta left with a parting blow. When Mrs. Quabarl had first found the 'new governess' on the platform without luggage, she had patronisingly assured her that the maid—not herself—would lend her all she needed for the night. Now, Lady Carlotta was revenged. She asked Mrs. Quabarl to keep her luggage when it arrived, casually adding that it included a panther cub which would require a generous diet of chickens.

If Lady Carlotta was really (as I have assumed) a product of the haphazard educational methods of the aristocracy, who apparently took the governesses sent to them by friends with no questions asked, then her imaginative gifts spoke highly for these methods. Neglect stimulates resource; and a child brought up in a mental prison may (like Saki himself) fight its way to intellectual freedom. But it may *not*. The Duchess's was a hit-or-miss method; and whereas in the cases of Lady Viola and Lady Carlotta it scored notable hits, it must in a hundred others have fallen wide of its mark, and left the child dull and limited. So that we cannot sweepingly assert that the less intelligent a governess, the more intelligent her charges will become.

It is a tempting theory, but hardly one to be uncritically adopted. For in education—more, perhaps, than in any other sphere—the individual is all-important. Miss Smedley, whose priggishness thwarted the children in *The Golden Age,* would have delighted Jeremy's clever sister Mary; and I am sure that even an Edwardian edition of that paragon, the Good French Governess, would have driven Lady Carlotta to the bad. Every child responds to a different treatment, and it is even possible to imagine children for whom the Schartz-Metterclume Method would have worked wonders.

Before we leave the Edwardians, there is a word to be said about the question of schools as compared with governesses. Some forty years have passed since the publication in 1871 of *Middlemarch,* the book which last provoked me to a discussion of this subject; and in that time a vast change has occurred in their respective standings. In the last quarter of the nineteenth century, girls' schools multiplied rapidly and improved immensely; and by the end of the Edwardian era it was becoming more and more usual to send girls to school for a good education, and not merely to get them out of the way or 'finish' them. The first world war accelerated the change. In *The Ballad and the Source,* the Belgian governess was caught on her holiday by the outbreak of war, and her pupils were sent to boarding school. Miss Hardcastle, in *No Promise in Summer,* went to London to do war work, and her pupil was sent to the local High School.

As we go on, we shall find that the status of the school improves still more, while the governess tends to become either a nursery-governess—qualified to teach young children—or a crypto-mother's-help, qualified for nothing but to be generally useful. Even before 1914, one would have thought, the choice for an educated girl between the careers of governess or schoolmistress would have been an easy one. All the advantages in matters of friendship, variety, promotion, long holidays and scope for progressive teaching would seem to lie on the side of school; and yet we have two Edwardian governesses who preferred to bury their degrees under the bushel of private teaching.

The first of these, Ellen Scott in *The Undesirable Governess,* admittedly had no intention of sticking to her job.

Yet the insufferable advertisement inserted by Lady Jane demanded as a matter of course that any applicant 'must have first-rate degree'. And though Marion Crawford's book cannot be taken very seriously, he evidently did not imagine such a requirement to be preposterous. More puzzling, because so much more realistic, is the case of Miss Hardcastle in *No Promise in Summer*. She had an Oxford degree, and she was a good tennis player. She was an organiser, an enthusiast, an inspiring teacher and a born leader among women. Yet she chose to throw herself away as governess to the daughters of two Eton housemasters. I can only account for her odd behaviour by supposing that she wished to live at home for a time, and had not decided on teaching as her permanent life's work.

We shall meet a few more well-educated governesses before this book is ended, but no more university graduates. The culture of Miss Angela Thirkell's Miss Bunting, for instance, was of the old school and linked her with Lucy Morris, Jane Eyre, 'poor Miss Taylor' and even the Good French Governess, rather than with Miss Hardcastle. Such culture is immensely valuable and has not, I trust, been lost entirely from the education of English girls. But the future of this education lay, after 1914, with the Miss Hardcastles; and their field of activity was the school rather than the schoolroom. One woman cannot teach one child the quantum theory, hockey, comparative religion, chemistry, economics, bee-keeping, book-keeping, Russian, dietetics, psychology, eurhythmics and American history—nor any six of these. Even if she were equipped with a smattering of them all, the modern governess lacks the effrontery with which Miss Wirt imposed herself and her curriculum on her employers.

CHAPTER VI

THE FIRST WORLD WAR

Peter de Polnay, *Children, My Children!*

OUR only governesses who went on being governesses during the first world war occur in Mr. Peter de Polnay's *Children, My Children!* (1939). These governesses, Miss Davies and her French colleagues, are most unusual; yet they are much more normal human beings than the other characters in Mr. de Polnay's amusing but rather horrifying fantasia. Mr. and Lady Moira Nicholas, a rich millowner and his aristocratic wife, are *opera bouffe* figures: Don Giovanni married to Isolde. Mr. Nicholas's friends and mistresses provide a shady cosmopolitan chorus, while Ivor, Molly and Edith, the children, are pitiable, lovable and loathsome.

Miss Davies herself was the dragon type of governess, being strict to the point of cruelty. She whacked the children with her hand and beat them with a cane. As their father also lashed out indiscriminately, it is no wonder that they lied ingeniously and did unspeakable things to frogs. In the villa on Lake Como the schoolroom was decorated under the personal supervision of Mr. Nicholas, and to no one's satisfaction but his own. During meals Miss Davies read aloud. She deserves all our sympathy when Ivor guesses correctly which of the boys in *Misunderstood* was destined for an untimely death. 'For it is the chief merit of that book that practically till the last chapter the young reader expects the delicate Miles to die.' Miss Davies was justifiably annoyed. 'She'd read that book to many children. The father is a baronet, which is very comforting.'

This last sentence gives us a line on Miss Davies's snobbishness, which was prodigious. Mr. Nicholas was the only commoner for whom she had ever worked, and the culmination of her career had been a situation in a German Grand Duke's court. 'Miss Davies liked referring to the Grand Duke at the slightest provocation.' She still sent him a card every Christmas, and during the war she wrote and asked him to use his influence for peace. 'I can assure Your Highness', she wrote, 'that looking back on my long career as a governess, that of all the pupils I've ever had Your Highness was the best and cleverest. I can say that with a clear conscience.' And so, indeed, she could; for it had long ago become the truth for her.

But nowadays 'it was no joke being sixty-nine', even though she had the help of a French governess and a nursery-maid, to say nothing of Mr. Nicholas's innumerable staff. Mademoiselle Guyard, the first of the French governesses, had taught Lady Moira as a girl. Although nearly blind, she was kept on out of kindness. She and Miss Davies would drink tea together, talking in German of their past and present employers.

When Lady Moira shot herself, Mr. Nicholas sacked Mademoiselle Guyard, who went to live with Lady Moira's brother. She was succeeded by a French girl who shocked Miss Davies by wearing a silk blouse, and won Mr. Nicholas's attention by the same means. She is the first governess since Lady Blessington's to receive dishonourable proposals: unlike Clara Mordaunt, she did not spurn them. When Mr. Nicholas had tired of his *affaire* with her, he sacked her, and her place (in the schoolroom) was taken by Mademoiselle Beaune. 'She was old. Her chin was covered with wiry hairs. She was short-sighted, and spent her time darning. . . . If after the war was over her country would let her darn the cathedral of Rheims she'd be the happiest woman on earth.'

Miss Davies held her own through all these changes. She was forever interrupting her reading aloud of *Mis-*

understood or the war news in the *Morning Post* to correct the children's table manners. She would ask, 'How do you hold your fork, Edith?' or 'Ivor, where's your hand?' And once, when Molly in an unguarded moment asked her what a snob was, she delivered a lecture on her own interpretation of the word. 'Common people', she explained, 'call good-mannered people snobs. It is all jealousy. The one thing in life is perfect manners, especially perfect table manners. . . . If a young man of your own class wants to marry you, he won't look at your face to see whether it's beautiful or not, but to watch how you eat asparagus. . . . Manners are everything.' At the end of the discourse Molly asked: 'Will we have asparagus for lunch?' for 'that had been the only word that had interested her in the entire monologue'.

Many governesses have been sticklers for the correct use of knives and forks. Miss Davies is, I think, the only one to exalt the art into a philosophy of life. And it is a small star for youth to hitch its waggon to. Yet Miss Davies's homily, like her daily perfunctory injunctions, was powerless to hurt her pupils. As we have seen, her words ran off Molly's mind like water off a duck's back. Even had they taken effect, they would have proved far less pernicious than Mrs. General's attempt to harness her pupils with selfish mental blinkers.

Miss Davies meant well. Even her wallopings were not sadistic. The children were really very naughty, and she was old and tired. And although she secretly loved Mr. Nicholas, and admired Lady Moira, she was driven almost beyond endurance by their goings-on. They were continually quarrelling, committing suicide and getting murdered—all most reprehensible, and so unlike the dear Grand Duke.

CHAPTER VII

BETWEEN THE WARS

E. M. Delafield, *The Diary of a Provincial Lady*; M. J. Farrell, *Full House*; Ethel Lina White, *The Wheel Spins*.

APART from those in *Children, My Children!* there is a gap in my historical knowledge of governesses between the Edwardian Era and the Between-War Age. Governesses—witness Miss Plimsoll—are usually patriotic; they are also frequently efficient and sensible. I therefore feel sure that they served their country staunchly in the first world war. By the time it was over a change was already coming over the status of governess. Middle-class parents who lived in London sent their little girls as well as boys to a day-school, and either persuaded their old Nanny to stay on or let a maid look after the children's clothes and take them to and fro in buses. The Minivers, for instance (those in Miss Jan Struther's book, not those of the film!), who would in earlier days have had a governess, kept the children's Nanny as their maid and friend.

Such governesses as there were, were mainly nursery-governesses, and many of them were foreigners. Swiss girls, for instance, were trained in kindergarten methods, and were good needle-women. Their foreignness was also held to reduce social problems to a minimum. Furthermore, it was hoped (often vainly) that they would teach their charges French or German. They were more often to be found in the country than in London, because schools were less accessible there, and a governess was in every way more useful. I say 'in every way' advisedly, for governesses were by now approximating to superior 'mothers' helps'. The days were past when a governess's duties were confined to the schoolroom. Between the wars they were already expected to 'do' their own rooms, and help with the garden, dogs and ponies. It was an advantage if they could drive the car and make an omelet on the cook's day off. They were expected to turn their hands to anything and make themselves generally useful.

From the strictly educational point of view this change represented a lowering of status, though not necessarily of competence. Socially, too, it was perhaps a come-down: such governesses as Lady Blessington's Clara Mordaunt would have thought it *infra dig* to make their own beds; and it would have been demeaning themselves to the level of stable-boys to catch the pony or brush the dogs. Yet such jobs are really only a small part in the whole changed status of women and the changed standards of living; and what the governess of the nineteen-thirties had lost in dignity, she had gained in friendship and variety.

Two of my governesses from between the wars were country governesses, and the first of them was a foreigner. This was the unnamed Mademoiselle from the late Miss E. M. Delafield's entertaining *The Diary of a Provincial Lady*. Now, Mrs. Miniver and the Provincial Lady were of much the same social standing, and probably had friends in common. But as the Minivers were a great deal richer, and (I am afraid) more snobbish, we should expect, by earlier standards, that *they* would have been the ones to have a governess. The fact that it was instead the Provincial Lady who included one in her small household is therefore evidence that by this time a governess was definitely employed for use and not for show.

Mademoiselle is ubiquitous in the Provincial Lady's Devonshire home. She lunches with the family, and goes with them to meets and picnics. It is true that she does not help much outside the house, since she holds the view that 'fresh air gives pneumonia'. But she atones for this by constant help with Madame's clothes. On one occasion she 'removes and washes Honiton lace from old purple velvet', assuring Madame that it will be '*gentil à croquer* on new taffeta'. And then—on the rumour of a fancy-dress ball—is anxious to transform the taffeta 'into Dresden China Shepherdess *á ravir*'.

During a measles epidemic 'Mademoiselle is *devouée* in the extreme, and utterly refuses to let anyone but herself sleep in Vicky's room.' But the Provincial Lady finds it hard to determine 'exactly on what principle it is that she persists in wearing a *peignoir* and *pantoufles* day and night alike'.

I wonder, by the way, why it is that the French governess of fiction is always so badly dressed? The one in *Amy Herbert,* for instance, though she had a dress in Parisian fashion, wore a black wig, and a cap covered with ribbons and artificial flowers. Madame de la Rougierre also wore a wig and adorned herself with bits and pieces. Even Louise in *John Halifax, Gentleman* was at first 'sad-clothed'. Only the Good French Governess was perfect in this respect, as in all else. As for Mademoiselle, she returns from a holiday wearing 'a new black and white check skirt, white blouse with frills, black kid gloves embroidered with white on the backs, and a black straw hat almost entirely covered in purple violets'. And she dresses up to walk to the village in 'black kid gloves, buttoned boots with pointed tips and high heels, hat with little feather in it, black jacket, and several silk neckties'.

In spite of her town clothes, however, Mademoiselle does not fit too badly into the discomforts of English country life. It is true that when she suffers, it is not in silence; but her sufferings are rather in her spirits than in her flesh. She has a genius for throwing verbal wet-blankets over everything, and conjuring inspissated gloom with a single phrase. She calls the bulbs which the Provincial Lady has been cossetting in bowls '*ces malheureux petit brins de verdure*'; and when Vicky runs a mysterious temperature, tells a story of a whole family killed by smallpox; while a proposed holiday in Brittany provokes the comment that 'this year is one notable for *naufrages*'. Her most devastating statements start with *on dirait.* When someone comes home blue with cold, '*on dirait un cadavre*'. When they return to the house after seeing Robin off with a school friend, '*on dirait un tombeau*'. And when the Provincial Lady proudly exhibits a gay dress that she has brought back from the South of France, Mademoiselle's '*on dirait un bal masqué*' is so deflating that the dress is never worn again.

She is so untiringly temperamental and emotional that a large part of her employer's energy is spent in diverting threatened scenes. For in the new, inter-war way of middle-class life—all living as one big family in one small house—it is impossible to relegate the governess to the schoolroom until the children are in bed. Employers are by now as eager to please the governess as governesses in the bad old days were assiduous to please employers. Even the baiting is not always on one side.

Incidentally, *The Diary of a Provincial Lady* is the first book we have considered for some time which describes a governess from the employer's point of view, rather than from that of the pupils or the governess herself. Indeed, I think it is the first since *The Daisy Chain.* And it is worth remembering that E. M. Delafield was an admirer of Charlotte Mary Yonge; and that when the Provincial Lady went to the South of France, *The Daisy Chain* was among the books which she took with her for the journey. Perhaps as she read once again of Ethel May's wearing sessions with Miss Bracey, she nerved herself against future scenes with Mademoiselle.

And she has need for all her patience and sense of

humour when the time comes to think of sending Vicky to school. The proposal provokes in Mademoiselle a prolonged and catastrophic *crise de nerfs.* The resulting scenes sometimes take place in the schoolroom, where Mademoiselle has her supper of ' cheese, pickles and slice of jam roly-poly grouped on a single plate ', declaring that this is the supper that she likes: sometimes in the drawing-room, where ' Mademoiselle weeps on the sofa, and says that she will neither eat nor drink until this is decided. I suggest Horlick's Malted Milk, to which Mademoiselle replies, "*Ah, ça jamais!*" and we get no further.' For some time ' extreme tension prevails in the house, and Mademoiselle continues to refuse food '; but she finally reappears, having ' apparently decided that half-mourning is suitable for present crisis ', as she wears ' black dress from which original green accessories have been removed '.

After the worst of these encounters, the conclusions are ' (*a*) that Mademoiselle is *pas de tout susceptible, tout au contraire*; (*b*) that she is profoundly *blessée, froissée* and *agacée*; and (*c*) that she could endure every humiliation and privation heaped upon her, if at least her supper might be brought up punctually '. After which they both weep; and the Provincial Lady confides to her diary her opinion that the French are ' not only exhausting to themselves ', but also have a ' marked talent for transferring their own capacity for emotion '. When the matter is decided and the school chosen, Mademoiselle announces that she will *succomber* unless she leaves at once. At her departure, ' all ends in emotional crescendo, culminating in floods of tears ', and the children are ' unusually hilarious all the evening ' after she has gone.

Children have a disconcerting way of displaying indifference when they are expected to feel distress; and the Provincial Lady had often wondered whether Robin and Vicky were like the children in *High Wind in Jamaica.*

But on this occasion I do not think that they were heartless. They were simply less upset by the departure of a governess than Victorian children would have been, because it made less difference to their lives. When children spent all their time apart with the governess, seeing their parents only after tea, they were desperately dependent on her, and she could make or mar their happiness. But when the Provincial Lady wrote—and still more to-day—parents, children and governess did many things together; and there was no defensive barrier separating the schoolroom from the drawing-room.

This arrangement, as we have seen, presents many problems to the mother: she may be bored, irritated or even bullied by the governess. The father, too, may sometimes want his family to himself. But for the children it is no doubt far more wholesome. They are on easy terms with their parents, and neither fear nor adore their governess. Their loyalties are undivided, and they are not tempted to 'tell tales'. As for the governess herself, she surely gains by the new relationship. She enters more into the lives of her employers, and meets their friends and neighbours. And if more demands are made on her, they are made not as from an employer to a servant, but by one human being to another.

I ended my section on *The Diary of a Provincial Lady* with a panegyric on the happy new relationship existing after the first world war between parents, their children, and the governess; and, on the whole, I think I was right in generalising thus. And yet our next book shows that in 1935 many of the old, familiar disadvantages of a governess's life remained; that the odd jobs demanded of her in a country house could become a burden; and that the old, gnawing loneliness was unassuaged. While *The Diary of a Provincial Lady* was appearing in *Time and Tide*, a book was published in which a governess still played a bullied and pathetic part.

The Irish setting of *Full House* by Miss M. J. Farrell is certainly very different from the Provincial Lady's home. The house is stately, the garden exquisite; and the family is smart, aristocratic and intelligent. They talk the fashionable, clever jargon of the nineteen-thirties with an Irish brogue. They are most of them kind, and would certainly have thought themselves abreast of modern tolerance; and yet Miss Parker, 'the little bearded governess' is as helpless, as lonely, as 'out of it', as Agnes Grey.

Miss Farrell has rather unfairly loaded the dice against Miss Parker by investing her with a beard. Jane Eyre had no such disability to paint in her 'portrait of a governess, disconnected, poor and plain'. Miss Parker was also unlucky in her employer, for Lady Bird (Olivia) lives in an unreal world in which she herself is all-important, and everyone else exists to serve her vanity and self-conceit. Poor Miss Parker, with her indefinite duties and anomalous standing, is always at hand to subserve her ladyship's conception of herself.

When we first meet her, she picks the wrong tulips for Lady Bird; and immediately Olivia begins to wonder whether she should not look for a new governess. 'A Swiss girl would probably be cheaper, and certainly sew better, although she might not work so diligently in the garden or be so attentive to the dogs when they were sick.' We are told that Miss Parker had lunch in the schoolroom with her pupil Markie, except on Sundays, when they lunched with the others in the dining-room, but she ate alone in the schoolroom at night; and would often feel 'very flat and alone. A very sad little governess'. Though the grown-up daughter Sheena liked her, she and Miss Parker 'had no common ground whatsoever'. Nor could she find companionship elsewhere. 'Lady Bird's maid was quite a dear, but Miss Parker was terrified of any real intimacy with servants. She clung to her void with pathetic obstinacy.' At the same time she realised that she really had very little to complain of. She had 'plenty of food, a moderately soft bed, a fascinating child to teach, a beautiful if lonely part of Ireland to live in'.

Once again, the loneliness was the heaviest cross for a governess to bear. And in this case, geographical loneliness was added to the isolation of her job. She had 'no other governess to speak to, no cinema to go to in free time. No place at all where she could run or pop in or out. To pop in or out or run in for a chat seemed now to Miss Parker to be the sum total of bliss.' Like Jane Fairfax, Miss Parker did not really appreciate being with the rich: her mortifications were only the greater. She had never felt so forlorn in previous, less exciting families. 'With the Littles, for instance, Mrs. Little had been an invalid, and so Mr. Little had been obliged to consult her in many small matters. And with the Jervises, Mrs. Jervis had made quite a confidante of Miss Parker when matters were more than strained between Mr. Jervis and herself.' Even when Sheena sent Miss Parker to meet her lover with a letter, she did not much enjoy the adventure. 'For although it was comforting to meddle herself once more in the drama of current life, this affair of Sheena's had no note of cosy intrigue about it.' Like so many governesses, Miss Parker wanted to belong. 'Here, with the Birds, one had nothing. . . . Nothing to give. Nothing given. Miss Parker more than welcomed the hundred and one extraneous tasks fastened on her by Lady Bird. It gave her a feeling of being required, of having a little of their lives.'

And Olivia exploited this craving to belong quite shamelessly. She never conceived of a governess having emotions of her own, or anything to give that was not demanded of her as a matter of course. She found her invaluable as an

15

auxiliary gardener and kennel-maid, and would wonder during lunch 'how best to employ the hours of Miss Parker's afternoon. Whether she should help to fertilise the melons; dress the dogs in sulphur and train oil; wash the flower-vases; or pack up the books for the library.'

Poor Miss Parker was even seasick when the Birds were not. Sent in a boat with Mark to see that he did not catch a chill, she was so overcome that she had to be landed on an island. At first, her solitude was a relief: it was a new autonomous loneliness. 'Miss Parker was quite accustomed to the feeling of being the superfluous member of a party. . . . It was the loneliness of being with people that (she) knew about, not the divine aloneness of being by herself.' But when, for a long time, they forgot to pick her up, she began to think bitterly: 'I'm only the governess. I don't matter. It will be quite a good joke when it occurs to them that they've forgotten me.'

Miss Parker had a summer holiday, though we are not told whether it was the only one in the year, or how long it lasted. When she got back to Silverue, Lady Bird was away, and her pupil 'Markie was cold, unconfiding and swaggering'. Schoolroom tea was drearily familiar: 'The same bread and butter, the same little buns, the same last half of a chocolate cake, the same strawberry jam. It was really an incomparably nicer and better tea than any which Miss Parker had eaten throughout her holidays, but somehow coming back to it distressed her very much.'

The same round of chores was also waiting for her. At tea-time the housemaid gave her a piece of paper—'(not on a tray, Miss Parker could not help observing)'—on which was written a formidable list of tasks. These included:

'Worm doses. Cheerio. Chuggy. Mouse. *Watch Mouse.*

Cheerio—*Excema* dressing.

Try new purge (in rod-room) on Mouse. *Watch effect.*

Pick dahlias and Michaelmas daisies Wed. Evn.
Plant 1,000 crocus in Yew Square. Plant "Windy Morrow" daffodils in Cedar Tree bed.
Please weed rock-garden in spare time.'

There were fourteen imperious demands in all, and only three 'pleases' scattered among them! No wonder Miss Parker 'felt suddenly and sickeningly overwhelmed'. 'Oh', she thought later, 'if only I had something to call my own in the Autumn, something to make safe for the Winter, how wildly happy I should be.'

Miss Farrell has a sensitive understanding of the human heart, and she has here given us a poignant summary of the governess's barren lot. We have considered already how acutely a normal girl must have longed for a husband, home and family of her own. But it was not merely sexual starvation from which Miss Parker suffered. That, indeed, she would have felt whatever her work, because of her beard—for which she could not blame the Birds. Nor was she a grumbler: on the contrary, she was a sensible little thing, who counted her blessings like a miser. But she wanted something of her own—something to work for and look forward to. It might even have helped had Cheerio, Chuggy or Mouse been her own dog, to worm or not as she thought fit.

With the Birds, then, Miss Parker fell between two stools, or even three. She was not a retainer in a great house, like Miss Watkins in *The Edwardians*. Nor was she the friend and confidante of a humble family, as she had been in previous situations. Nor, again, was she of the temperament to make herself felt through 'scenes', like the Provincial Lady's Mademoiselle. Even had she wished to behave emotionally, she may have guessed that Olivia's bird-of-paradise mind was constantly pecking at the idea of a Swiss girl for Markie.

Unfortunately, the governess's economic status has not

improved during the years under our review. We are not told what Miss Parker's salary was. It must have been a great deal more than Jane Eyre's thirty guineas a year. Yet the decline in the value of money would have left her little better off; and a governess's salary had not increased in the same proportion as a cook's or housemaid's wages.

What was worse, the supply of governesses in 1934, when Miss Parker was at Silverue, far exceeded the demand. I myself was looking for a nursery-governess that very year; and although domestic staff were then very hard to come by, I still remember my horror at the numbers of pathetic women sent to me by an agency for governesses. In towns, as I have said, governesses were seldom needed for small children, and older girls were more often sent to boarding-school than in the past. Add to these trends, the competition from Switzerland—to say nothing of the slump—and you will see that governesses in the nineteen-thirties were no more in a position to make their own terms than in the eighteen-thirties when Lady Blessington's heroine embarked on her career.

The relatively low wages of governesses, and the number of them desperately in need of work, would account for their employment by lower income groups. The Littles and the Jervises, with whom Miss Parker had been so cosy, probably sent their children to school. They needed no schoolroom; nor did they snobbishly decide to 'live upon a fine governess', like Thackeray's Pontos. They had a governess simply and solely because they could not get a cook-general at their price—if at all. And whereas the Provincial Lady found Mademoiselle an incubus, and occasionally a fury, Mrs. Little and Mrs. Jervis probably welcomed Miss Parker's companionship. These ladies lived, I imagine, in the suburbs, whence husbands go to London every day, and wives, too superior to gossip with neighbours over the garden wall, and lacking a local centre for their lives, are left forlorn. To them, Miss Parker was a godsend.

She was their social equal, perhaps their educational superior. She not only changed the library books, but also read them and talked them over. She enjoyed the same films, and the same magazines. Above all, she would not mind sharing (with a friend and equal) the dreary round of making beds and washing-up. It is scarcely surprising, then, that Miss Parker should have felt more herself among these homely Surbiton sparrows than in her Irish aviary of exotic birds.

The last of our between-war governesses may possibly have contributed to England's preparations for the second world war, as she is the only governess I know who was a spy. That is to say, she was a spy in her film manifestation; for Miss Froy, the innocent victim of Miss Ethel Lina White's terrifying novel, *The Wheel Spins* (1936), is a very different person from Miss Froy the secret agent in Hitchcock's drama called *The Lady Vanishes* (1939). The only things which the two Miss Froys possess in common are their aged parents, their name, their oatmeal tweed suit and their position as English governess in a Ruritanian family.

Let us take first Miss Froy of *The Wheel Spins*, explaining by the way that the book is a thriller rather than a detective story, and therefore exempt from my ban on crime. Miss Froy was 'a negative type in every respect—middle-aged, with a huddle of small indefinite features', but 'not sufficiently a caricature to suggest a stage spinster'. She was a case of arrested development, due perhaps to years of juvenile company and an insular attitude to foreigners. She used schoolgirl slang, and still thought of herself as the pretty young thing to whom her father's curates were accustomed to propose. Her only passion was for mastering languages; and although this enthusiasm led her to take situations amid fantastic scenery, she could find no better words to describe it in her letters home than 'simply topping'.

Nor did she interest herself sufficiently in Central European politics to know that it was unwise to leave her situation with a very important person in the government, and arrange to return after her holiday and teach the children of the leader of the opposition. Finally she committed the *gaucherie* of waylaying her very important employer in the middle of the night to say good-bye to him, thereby imperilling the alibi he needed after 'bumping off' an opposition editor. Central Europe being what it was, it was natural that on the homebound express she should be kidnapped, and her unconscious body be disguised with bandages and plaster as a disfigured casualty on its way to a brain operation in Trieste. Miss Froy was only saved from being dumped into an eel-infested river by the persistence of a fellow-traveller; and I think her rescue was almost more than her stupidity deserved. She had had more opportunity for adventure than any governess we know; yet she was as parochial as a monthly nurse, and waited for adventure to be thrust upon her. The Miss Froy of *The Wheel Spins* did not, I am afraid, bring credit to the great fictional tradition of English governesses, during her sojourns abroad in *chateau, schloss* or *villa*.

The film version of Miss Froy, so delightfully impersonated by Dame May Whitty in *The Lady Vanishes,* was a very different proposition. She too had been English governess in a noble Central European home; in fact, she was more convincing as a governess than her prototype in the novel, since she actually mentioned the existence of some pupils. It is true, moreover, that she possessed some spinsterish characteristics such as knitting and an addiction to herbal tea. But behind the governess façade she was a special agent of the Foreign Office, and had turned her knowledge of local affairs to good account. Above all, she had memorised before she left for home a tune which contained a coded message of international importance. So that when—like the other Miss Froy—she was overcome by counter-agents, and was drugged, bound, gagged, and swaddled in bandages, she had become a heroine rather than a poor, silly Englishwoman travelling abroad. She went on being heroic after two young English people had rescued her from her mummied state. The thwarted brain specialist, finding that his victim had escaped him, had half the train uncoupled and run back into his own country, where it was halted in a lonely forest and attacked by troops. Caught like a rat in a trap, Miss Froy was still undaunted. She hastily hummed the vital tune to one of her compatriot rescuers, so that there should be two chances of its getting through instead of one. And then, clasping her hand-bag, she climbed out of the besieged train and ran off through a hail of bullets.

It is with immense relief that we see her again in the last shot, playing (on a Foreign Office piano to assembled secretaries, under-secretaries and cipher-clerks) the tune which she has carried in her head through so many hair-breadth escapes. This Miss Froy, we feel, may have swayed the destinies of nations; and she had certainly kept the flag of fictional English governesses flying in fictional foreign parts. Just as a governess's position might provide a most convenient screen for a criminal or a detective, so might a spy make her contacts and collect her information under the inoffensive guise of *la gouvernante anglaise* or *die englische Fraülein*.

CHAPTER VIII

THE SECOND WORLD WAR

Angela Thirkell, *Miss Bunting.*

I KNOW of only one governess who exercised her proper function—and died in harness—during the second world war. This is *Miss Bunting*, whose last days were chronicled by Mrs. Angela Thirkell, and published under that name in 1945. Miss Bunting was strictly an ex-governess at the beginning of the book. She was seventy years old, and was living as 'an honoured and very useful refugee' with a family of old friends and pupils in the neighbourhood of Barchester. But although she had retired, there was a war on. She therefore obliged the Fieldings, friends of her former employers, by going to look after Anne, their delicate daughter of sixteen. She was Anne's sole companion during the week, but helped to entertain her parents and their friends from Saturday till Monday.

Miss Bunting was very definitely not a Downtrodden Governess. Dukes, admirals, tradesmen and ironmasters alike deferred to her. Even the sullen Mixo-Lydian refugee, who cooked for her and Anne, respected her authority. For Miss Bunting had acquired a way with Slavs during a sojourn in Tsarist Russia. Nor was she a Governessy Governess. She soon won Anne's affection, and instilled in her both a love of Keats and social *savoir faire*. Least of all was she an Adventuress or Villainess.

She was, in fact, a classic example of the loved and trusted confidante. But before dismissing her as that, we must consider her snob value. It is true that Miss Bunting, like all Mrs. Thirkell's adult characters, was a snob of the deepest dye. Her eyes 'had quelled the heir to many a peerage or landed estate', and she had 'spent many years of her life avoiding being a nuisance to His Grace, or the Marquess, or his mere Lordship'. Yet she cannot, by any stretch of ingenuity, be herded with the Snob Exhibits. For her snobbery was dyed-in-the-wool, and was taken for granted like the quiet, authoritative colours of Harris tweed.

Miss Wirt would have appalled her, and she would very soon have taken 'Clare' Kirkpatrick's measure. She would never have considered—or needed to consider—a situation with the sort of people who acquire prestige by having a governess who talks titles. All her employers were known to one another: many of them were related. They all 'belonged' without a *nuance* of doubt or reservation, and Miss Bunting 'belonged' with them. She looked 'exactly like what a good ex-governess ought to look like'; and with 'her skirt unfashionably long, her hat unfashionably high on her head, her withered throat encircled by a black ribbon', was 'unmistakably a lady of birth, breeding and intellect'.

Moreover, her 'life as a highly-valued governess had made her very sensible to fine shades'. When Anne's mother protested that she didn't 'want to be too snobbish' about a girl from the local school, Miss Bunting 'took no notice at all of her employer's foolish and well-meant efforts towards democracy'. She declared roundly that 'the Hosiers' girls, though the school has an excellent record of scholarships, are not quite what one would wish'. On the other hand, she surprisingly added that 'We must move with the times. . . . When I first went out as a governess, no girl was allowed to walk out alone, not even round Belgrave Square.' She had indeed moved with the times a very long way; and as she coped courageously with wartime difficulties and makeshifts, she sometimes 'thought with regret of a more ordered life when well-trained servants announced the right people and the wheels of life ran easily'.

But it was not only for comforts and conventions that Miss Bunting felt nostalgic. She stood also for the many true and good values in the life that was so swiftly passing away. She had 'a very poor opinion of the whole system of women's education and the School Certificate Examination in particular', and thought it better to read aloud to Anne 'from the works of Dickens, Thackeray, Miss Austen and other English classics, besides a good deal of poetry'.

She had, indeed, read widely; and a pleasing aspect of her reading is that it had apparently made her as governess-conscious as I am myself. When her pupil said one day, 'Do you know who I think you are like?', Miss Bunting 'ran rapidly through, in her mind, a few famous governesses: Madame de Maintenon, Madame de Genlis, Madame de la Rougierre, Miss (sic) Weston, the Good French Governess, Jane Eyre: but to none of these characters could she flatter herself that she had the least resemblance.'

She was right in her estimate: she resembled none of the fictional governesses on her list. As we have seen, she was not villainous like Madame de la Rougierre, nor downtrodden like Jane Eyre, nor a doctrinaire like the Good French Governess. Perhaps she comes nearest to poor Miss Taylor. For she looked after Anne's health as sensibly as Miss Taylor cared for Emma's, and was in a fair way to make of her as sad a snob. But Miss Bunting was, I think, more devotedly and single-mindedly a governess. Though she could be as excellent a companion to Anne as Miss Taylor was to Emma, her favourite pupils had always been younger, and had been boys. As she lay dying in hospital after a stroke, she dreamed for the last time that she was confronting Hitler, and demanding that he should take her life instead of theirs. This time she managed to stay long enough asleep to have her will: 'Hitler swelled and swelled till the whole room and the whole world was full of him and burst, and all Miss Bunting's old pupils came running up to her. Her heart was so full of joy that it stopped beating.'

Having been a governess for fifty years, Miss Bunting must have met many of her kind. She would have considered Miss Parker a deplorable manifestation of modern life, and regarded her employers (including the Birds) with cool disapproval. She would have damned Margaret Seaton, of *The Man from Blankley's,* as a fool who could not hold her own as Miss Bunting (her contemporary) was doing: and she would have thought Miss Watkins, in *The Edwardians,* an old stick-in-the-mud. Perhaps she would have had most in common with Miss Plimsoll. They shared the widening influence of foreign travel, and a love of little boys. And Miss Plimsoll (as the elder) could have given her some hints as to how to make herself at home, yet unobtrusive, in the great world of admirals, diplomats and dukes.

Miss Bunting's snobbishness was of the best sort, which believed that breeding confers onerous obligations. She would have been shocked by a landlord who neglected his tenants, and spoken a piece of her mind to a younger son who did no work. I am sure that her motto was *noblesse oblige,* though she never needed to express the principle among those who lived by it. She was a relic of the past, both as a woman and a governess; but there were good things in that past, and she had lived and died in their service.

CHAPTER IX

POST-WAR

Post-War Speculations; Elizabeth Taylor, *Palladian, A Wreath of Roses*; I. Compton-Burnett, *Elders and Betters, Daughters and Sons.*

THE private governess, as an institution, survived the first world war, and still existed in the second. We have also seen how she flourished in the intermediate period. What, then, of governesses in the uneasy peace that has troubled the world since 1945?

Plenty of real governesses are still working. An even greater number, I suspect, are fulfilling similar duties under another name than 'governess', or no name at all. If you study the personal advertisements in *The Times,* you may indeed spot few overt advertisements for governesses. But you will see many happy country homes and good salaries offered to gentlewomen who are fond of animals and children, and willing to help in house and garden. From the other side, there are advertisements inserted by ex-Wrens or otherwise competent young women, who are fond of children and crave an outdoor life; and who are willing to work and to take responsibility. All these, I think, betoken a nebulous, undefined class of home-helps and children's companions, who are nursery-governesses in everything but name.

It is true, of course, that the governess's business was, in the past, essentially that of teaching; and advertisers who can prepare boys for Common Entrance and girls for School Certificate, will still call themselves governesses. But we have seen, in the case of Miss Parker, what multifarious duties were piled on governesses by the exigencies of modern life, even between the wars; and all these exigencies have been intensified since 1945. Domestic staff are even harder to find, and more impossible to pay or please; gardens run riot; and chickens scratch where no chickens scratched before. Surely it has occurred to many a housewife thus overwhelmed by work and the dread of illness that a governess would be an easier solution to her problem than some formidable Hungarian or Finn.

Even if the children go to boarding-school, they must be cared for in the holidays, and their maddening name-tapes sewn on their clothes. While during the term there are still the chickens, the garden and the house, which allow no holidays. If the children go to a day-school, they must be got off in the morning; and someone must see that they do their homework. If the woman who performs these miscellaneous tasks can also teach the toddlers their 'first lessons', or talk French to the eldest girl, so much the better. But even then she will probably not be called a governess.

I am convinced, then, that many governesses—both titular and disguised—are flourishing to-day in real life. It seems to me to stand to reason! But I can produce little evidence of their contemporary survival in books. Most of the post-war novels containing governesses are period pieces, and prove nothing—except that governesses are thought by the writers of these books to be exponents of some quaint old craft like thatching or hand-weaving. Governesses, it seems, have become a literary 'type' along with fauns, highwaymen, butlers, good-hearted trollops, and elder statesmen. I hope I have proved how profoundly I disagree with this archaic view of governesses, but having eschewed all dealings with historic reconstructions, I cannot pause to combat it.

I must, however, come boldly into the open and confess that I know no book at all that describes a governess living in an ordinary family since the war. Our four last books, published between 1937 and 1949, contain little period atmosphere. Miss Elizabeth Taylor's *Palladian,* for instance, has no 'dating' references to world events, though its action may have occurred some time during the war. The setting of *A Wreath of Roses* is definitely post-war; but then, its governess has long been living in retirement. As for Miss I. Compton-Burnett, her *Elders and Betters* and *Daughters and Sons* are, like all her work, timeless. So that although they have been kept until the end on account of their very modern idiom, neither can be cited in proof of my contention that the governess is still alive and kicking.

I have said that *Palladian,* by Elizabeth Taylor, is nowhere dated by internal evidence. But it belongs to the age of the cinema, glucose and Ryvita, and is modern in treatment and tone. It stands outside time only in the sense that the characters inhabit a world of their own; and in this self-contained quality it resembles the work of Miss Compton Burnett. But Miss Taylor documents her characters more fully; and does not (like Miss Compton-Burnett) leave us to learn about them for ourselves from the eddies and backwaters of their conversation.

Cassandra Dashwood, the heroine, establishes herself at the outset as a classic governess by being left an orphan. Soon after her father's death, she goes to spend a night at her old school, whose headmistress has found her a situation with the relations of another old-girl. 'What a corny sort of job', comments one of the prefects, when she hears what Cassandra is about to do, while Mrs. Turner, the headmistress, also feels in her vague, comfortable way that a governess is an anachronism and a pity. Telling Cassandra about her future pupil, she rambles on like this: 'Why she mayn't go to school like other children, I can't imagine . . . it is the forming of character, which contact with other girls would . . . so much more important than . . . no governess can give that . . . but it will fill in an awkward little time for you.' As for Cassandra herself, 'She was setting out with nothing to commend her to such a profession, beyond the fact of her school lessons being fresh still in her mind and, along with that, a very proper willingness to fall in love, the more despairingly the better, with her employer.' For Cassandra was a novel-reader, who knew what was expected of governesses in fiction—or some of the better known ones. And by great good luck, it seemed, Mrs. Turner had found her an employer built (equally with herself) on classic lines. For not only had he been irresponsible enough to engage a governess without an interview; he was also a widower and an eccentric.

The household in which Cassandra found herself consisted of her employer, Marion Vanbrugh; an aunt who kept house for him; her daughter Margaret, a woman doctor who was staying until her baby should be born; and his cousin Tom, once a medical student, and now a drunkard who carried on an affair with the local publican's wife, and made surrealist anatomical drawings. Sophy, Cassandra's pupil, was a polite and precocious little girl of nine.

Marion's house was an irregular Palladian collection of corridors, staircases, archways and alcoves, as mouldering and sinister in its own way as any Gothic abbey of a century before. Although the staff consisted only of a slightly cracked old Nanny and a daily woman, Cassandra was evidently not expected to do much house-work. She ate all her meals with the family; and soon Margaret and the two men were calling her by her Christian name. Neither Margaret nor her mother expected Cassandra to respect Marion, for he was an effeminate hypochondriac whom they despised. But as Cassandra realised later: 'Before she saw him or spoke to him, she had determined to love him, as if she were a governess in a book. Meeting him had merely confirmed her intention, made possible what she had hoped.' A martyr to neuralgia, he did not usually appear at meals. But he soon summoned Cassandra to his room to discuss Sophy's lessons; and it was not long before he had decided to teach Cassandra Greek, and she had decided that he would 'do to fall in love with'.

She also got on well with Marion's cousin Tom, though he disapproved of a governess for Sophy. 'Marion coddles her', he complained, 'wraps her in cotton wool. . . . When it comes to it, she hasn't anything real to help her. No experience. I don't believe in governesses, if you will excuse my saying so. . . . She wants to be rushing round with a hockey-stick, having crushes on other girls.' And he was not far wrong. Sophy's home was no place for an introspective child who made self-conscious resolutions not to be 'morebid'. She was also uncomfortably observant, and wrote in her diary: 'When my father came in, Miss D's hand trembled. He says I shall not begin Greek for the present, he is too busy teaching her!!?!! Fancy having to teach a governess.'

Nor was Sophy the only one to comment on the Greek lessons. Nanny, who disapproved of 'this so-call' governess' (for Nanny, too, was a classic type), thought to herself: 'Them Grecian lessons! Do they think I was born yesterday?' Even Cassandra herself, though she loved Marion, sometimes recoiled from his preciousness: 'Saw with clarity, for what it was, the titillation of Greek lessons, the cerebral intimacy, the impersonal taking up and dropping of hands.'

Cassandra was, of course, abnormally self-conscious and susceptible to atmosphere; and she had lived too much of her short life in books. She could not talk to Marion over a cup of coffee, without thinking that 'Jane Eyre had answered up better than that to her Mr. Rochester'. She constantly acted a part, and 'often dismayed herself' by the use of a 'schoolmistressy voice'. 'She was sometimes alarmed at the idea of this voice gaining on her in the years to come, until she had no other, until it was the scar her profession had left upon her.' Yet to others she did not appear to be hardening in the governess's mould. Tom, for instance, who once complained that she was insipid, and clasped her hands 'like a governess in a book', later thought to himself that she was getting to be more of a person.

Even in this family of introverts Cassandra's everyday life was normal enough, and presented many familiar strands in the governess-pattern. Although the schoolroom 'was no cosy, shabby place with fire-guard and cuckoo clock', and Cassandra 'could find nothing there more childish than an exercise book and Caesar's *Gallic War*', yet she taught Sophy her lessons there in the ordinary way. Nor were her duties confined to teaching; she plaited Sophy's hair before she went off to the pictures with Nanny, and took hot milk to her room when she could not sleep. After Sophy's afternoon rest, Cassandra would 'put on her look of a governess' (for there was a look as well as a voice) and take her to collect 'grasses in the park, to be brought back, classified and pressed'—an instructive but uninspiring hobby which takes us back to the Good French Governess and her tongue-grass.

When Cassandra was in and out of the kitchen, arranging flowers, Nanny did not offer her a cup of tea. For 'governesses are not quite servants in the usual sense of the word: their education puts them out of reach of the continual flow of tea which goes on in kitchens'. This distinction shows that conventions persist from age to age; and that governesses—hovering between two worlds—are still apt to miss the comforts of both. It is also interesting to notice that Cassandra was the first governess since Lady Blessington's Clara Mordaunt, who habitually read Shakespeare to herself before she went to sleep.

But although people did lessons, ate bread and dripping, and dusted stairs in this Palladian house, it belonged as much to the past—was as empty a shell—as its unsatisfactory master. And a day came when the rottenness of a mouldering garden ornament caused poor Sophy's death. After the funeral Cassandra left the house as precipitately as Jane Eyre left Thornfield, and sought refuge again at her old school with Mrs. Turner.

When the headmistress suggested vaguely that her leaving so suddenly was 'awkward', Cassandra retorted that 'one can hardly go on being a governess to a dead child'; and added to herself that 'one doesn't ask for references from those one loves'. Marion, however, was brisk to track her down and ask her to be his wife. As his aunt said, Cassandra made 'the change from governess to mistress of the house very charmingly. . . . It is like one of the fairy tales.' To which Margaret (who had neither respect nor pity for her cousin Marion) replied: 'But not a fairy tale in which I should want to be the heroine.'

And indeed, in this instance, the heroine was happier as a governess than she was likely to be after marrying her boss. The queer people among whom she was flung had been kind, and had treated her as an equal. Had she been a little older, a little less determined to fall in love, she might have found even their decadence and eccentricities interesting. And though Sophy's accident could not have been foreseen, she might have helped them before and after it with her freshness and young courage.

Cassandra Dashwood is indeed a sad example of the influence of governess-literature on a governess. We had cause to wonder, when considering *Dr. Deane's Governess,* by Jean Ingelow, whether girls about to become governesses derived a part of their prejudice from books. Was Agnes Grey's innocent enthusiasm for training young plants founded on the success of Madame de Rosier? Had Jane Eyre, on the other hand, read *The Governess,* by Lady Blessington, that she should have been so afraid of getting into scrapes? And had Miss Bracey in *The Daisy Chain* been piously brought up on *Amy Herbert?* Though we shall never know if they were influenced by books or not, Cassandra's story indicates that such an influence might be both possible and disastrous.

And while we can only guess at the novels read by governesses in novels, we can be pretty sure about their authors. Sometimes we are told specifically. Miss E. M. Delafield, for instance, read *The Daisy Chain*; Mrs. Thirkell not only knows *Emma, The Good French Governess* and *Uncle Silas,* but lets Miss Bunting know them too. As for Miss Elizabeth Taylor, it is obvious that she and Jane Eyre are well acquainted.

It is inevitable, I think, that an author's conception of a governess's life should be coloured by his reading. I am sure, for my part, that I could not write the story of a governess without dragging in most of the elements that I have labelled 'classic'.

Miss Elizabeth Taylor's most recent book, *A Wreath of Roses* (1949), has an unequivocally post-war setting, and is therefore strictly speaking our last example of a novel in which a governess occurs. Unfortunately for our researches, however, Frances Rutherford had stopped being a governess and become a painter some time before the war; so that, to us, this sensitive and subtle book is of special interest only as showing how life as a governess might affect the subsequent achievement of an artist, and her attitude towards her work. For though Frances is a good painter, after the manner of Bonnard or Vuillard, she is also (to all outward seeming) every inch the retired governess.

'She painted at set hours and did the washing-up first'; having, in fact, retained the regular habits and conventional manners of the schoolroom. Yet those who knew her best understood that she did so with deliberate intent and not because she had become set in her ways. When her old pupil Liz, and Liz's friend Camilla, came every year to stay in her cottage, she behaved to them almost as a governess to her pupils. She told Camilla that it was slovenly to walk about the house in her nightdress; she told Liz that she must do her duty as a vicar's wife. Yet her primness and precepts were not the result of unthinking habit, but were deliberately cultivated because she found in her status as retired governess a ready-made defence against the Bohemianism which she despised and even feared.

Although she was 'robust, physically and mentally', Frances was growing old. Rheumatism was rapidly putting her right arm out of action, and she knew that her next picture might be her last. She knew that she had wasted much of her artist's life 'teaching instead of painting. Teaching little girls like Liz, who do nothing better with their learning than read novels.' Yet she did not regret her governess's career, because it had given her an abiding friend in Liz, who hoped to persuade her old governess to end her days in the vicarage. Frances must, I am sure, have been a first-rate governess to have inspired such devotion; and a single-minded one, in spite of her creative urge. But though she had not attempted to paint seriously while she was teaching, it is hard to believe that she never experimented with her latent powers; and it is fascinating to speculate on the results.

Schoolroom portfolios and easels have, in their time, held artistic efforts in a variety of styles. Setting aside pictures contrived out of wool-work, seaweed or skeleton leaves, the output of brush and pencil is still formidable. Throughout our period, exercises in perspective have been achieved, with or without Miss Edgeworth's perspective machine. How many copies of engravings, begun under the sycophantic eye of a master, have been rubbed out and reshaded by the governess at night? How many sheaves of fuchsia, pansy and forget-me-not have been opaquely daubed with rose-madder, gamboge and Prussian blue? Christmas has annually produced a spate of cards adorned with 'original' designs—at first of posies, but later ringing the changes between Christmas trees, carol-singers, robins and holly-branches. (Snow is very difficult to paint; but the shadows may be brewed from cobalt and Indian red, while Chinese-white on dark paper gives a magical effect.) Little boys have been encouraged, in their leisure hours, to reduplicate hundreds of sailing-ships, paddle-steamers, railway engines, cars, tanks and ultimately aeroplanes. Young ladies have returned from holidays with ultramarine seascapes and fuzzy pencil-sketches of the picturesque. From the school-room, illuminated texts have started their weary journey to the housemaid's bedroom, and decorated programmes have fluttered forth to bazaars and fêtes.

Sometimes, perhaps, a real artist has emerged from this 'artistic' tutelage. Sometimes, too, a governess has nursed ambitions beyond the finishing of her pupils' daubs. Jane Eyre, for instance, would get out her colours, and carefully commit to paper those haunting, surrealist dreams of cormorants, bracelets, corpses, icebergs and bone-white brows. But never, I am sure, unless Frances Rutherford found time for an occasional experiment while she looked after little Liz, have those schoolroom easels displayed canvasses painted—and *well* painted—in the manner of Vuillard or Bonnard.

'What an elaborate conversation-piece! I feel I shall be quite lost in the midst of it', says one of the characters in *Elders and Betters*—thereby precisely expressing my own feeling when I embark on one of Miss I. Compton-Burnett's novels. Each one is woven from delicate threads, of different colours but identical texture; and the mind's eye must be adroit to follow them through the mazy interweavings which form the fabric and display the pattern.

Every character, from journalist to postmistress, from businessman to cook, has a great deal to say about every other character, and says it in the same language. They are all equally fluent—so fluent, indeed, that it takes careful reading to distinguish one from another. Yet if we bestow this care, we are rewarded by finding that each speaker has his own cast of thought and turn of phrase, so that we could almost follow the speakers' characteristic sallies, thrusts, reticences and concealments, without being told their names. Miss Compton-Burnett's children, moreover, are as subtly observant and as quick to wound as her adults. It might therefore seem a cruel fate to be a governess in any of her schoolrooms. But Miss Compton-Burnett, like Nature, leaves none of her creatures totally unarmed. If they lack teeth and claws, she endows them with tough carapaces or protective coloration; and though they may suffer under their skins, they can all hold their own in the conversational struggle for existence. We need not, therefore, fear to find a downtrodden governess in Miss Compton-Burnett's works.

Before, however, we tease out the governess-thread from the stuff of *Elders and Betters,* we must consider more fully its place in—or rather, outside—time. All negative clues thrust the story back into a period far behind its publication date of 1944. The fact, for instance, that a 'straitened' middle-class family thinks nothing of sitting down fourteen to lunch and eating chicken, places it before the second world war. While the allusions to station-flies and tradesmens' carts—coupled with the total absence of the internal-combustion engine—would seem to put it back into the last century.

But the truth is—as we have seen—that all Miss Compton-Burnett's books are outside time, and her characters exist in a self-contained world of their own. They are innocent of a period sense, of fashion, and of an interest in world affairs. They speak pure English, uncontaminated by slang or catch-phrases, alike in the drawing-room, the kitchen and the nursery. So that to have included *Elders and Betters* in the 'nineties or the Edwardian era, simply because it never mentions motors, would have been absurd.

Miss Lacy, 'a small, grey-haired lady of sixty', was daily governess to the two Calderon children—Julius aged eleven, and his younger sister Theodora; and had previously taught their grown-up brother and sister. She took her charges for a walk after their two hours of lessons, and on certain days she stayed for lunch and taught them again in the afternoon. Her pride in possessing private means was a source of amusement to her employers, and made her pupils wonder why she worked at all. 'Miss Lacy doesn't need any more money', said Julius, 'she inherited enough from her father. I mean, she doesn't need a little money, like she earns here. A lot, that would let her have a stable and horses, would be different.' While Terence, the grown-up brother, maintains that 'she has larger fires and better things to eat than anyone'.

She was treated as an old friend of the family. She called the Donnes—her ex-pupils' cousins—by their Christian names, 'as her natural prerogative', and regarded the family's affairs with 'privileged interest'. The children (so far as one can discover their real feelings) liked her, in a detached and speculative way. When she went walking with them, taking a hand of each, no one held 'that Julius was old for this treatment, or for an education confined to two hours a day', and the children did not seem to resent it. Dora, indeed, 'was aware that the usual training was different; but assumed that their family was a rule to itself'.

Miss Lacy talked to them as if they were adult: but so, in their various ways, did all their elders. I am sure they liked Miss Lacy's trick of quoting (or adapting) Scripture.

She had 'a regard unto' her umbrella, and held that 'of making many examinations there is no end, and much study is a weariness to the flesh'. Such language fell naturally on the ears of Julius and Dora. They had a private god called Chung, who was immanent in a rock in the garden, and to whom they prayed in times of crisis, which were abundant in their family. After their mother's suicide, for instance, they pleaded: 'Our governess, thy handmaid, does not see us with a mother's eye. But put kindness for us into her heart.'

She was certainly kind, and tried to allay Dora's fears as to her dead mother's whereabouts. Moreover, they were used to her, so that when their father got engaged, Dora stated simply that 'if Father had married Miss Lacy, there would not have had to be so much change'. The grown-ups, too, had become accustomed to her, and to her somewhat elaborate manner. A newcomer complained, for instance, of her method of making introductions—that she seemed 'to manage to make people look a little ridiculous. I should not like to be left to her tender mercies in the larger matters of life.' To which an aunt who had known her many years replied: 'You could depend on her in those. It is on the surface that she presents this front, and we have all got rather fond of it.'

Though she was keenly interested in all the farces and tragedies of the families with which she was involved, her principle was roughly (though Miss Compton-Burnett is never rough!) to live and let live. She disclaimed any wish to influence people's lives, and clung to her own privacy: 'One's own place, one's own room, one's own desk. They are all so superior to other people's.' A sentiment which many a governess would have echoed plaintively!

Miss Lacy was always conscious of being a governess, and was proud of her calling. 'I am', she said, 'that recognised product of my generation, an old-fashioned governess'; and the fact coloured and complicated her relations with her employers. 'She tended to veil her interest in people, lest it might imperil her equality with them, an attitude that came not from unsureness of herself, but from experience of them. That she esteemed her calling and pursued it of her own will, enhanced their opinion of her, but not of the calling; and she identified herself with the latter, and on the first score had never known uneasiness.' Which I take to mean that—unlike most governesses—she wanted to be liked and respected as a governess, and not for herself alone.

It is as impossible to compare Miss Lacy with any other governess, as to compare *Elders and Betters* with the work of any other novelist. Miss Lacy and her creator are unique each in her own realm, and so they would surely wish to be.

While we are in the mood of Miss Compton-Burnett and our ears attuned to her peculiar rhythm, it may be mentioned that Miss Lacy is not her only governess. *Daughters and Sons,* published in 1937, but set in Miss Compton-Burnett's timeless present, contains no less than three. And although the minds and actions of Miss Bunyan, Miss Hallam and Miss Blake are too intricate for summary, the book yields a handful of aphorisms on governesses which round off neatly our study of the subject.

> Governesses write so many letters before they come.
>
> It is just like a governess to begin by giving trouble.
>
> Governesses have that habit of ringing bells.
>
> I am the classic governess, driven by necessity. I hoped to be able to provide for my old age. I did not know at first that teaching was its own reward.
>
> Governesses are always concerned about what they eat. They find themselves where the food is better than in their homes, and they have no other interest in their lives.

It is held a success for the governess to marry the widower.

Governesses are touchy people. They are situated just where the touchiness is natural.

Spoken by various characters, these aphorisms are unvaryingly cynical, and might have been the work of some La Rochefoucauld of the schoolroom.

CHAPTER X

THE GROTESQUES

Maurice Baring, *An English Governess in the French Revolution*; Stephen Leacock, *Gertrude the Governess*; Oscar Wilde, *The Importance of Being Earnest*; T. H. White, *Mistress Masham's Repose*; W. M. Thackeray, *The Rose and the Ring*; Charles Kingsley, *The Water Babies*; Lewis Carroll, *Through the Looking-Glass.*

WHILE I deplore the tendency to degrade the governess into a literary 'type' and archaise her into a period-piece, and while maintaining that the supreme examples are always women first and governesses only incidentally, I have no wish to deny the existence of the Governess Idea.

Undoubtedly there are Platonic prototypes filed away in Heaven—patterns from which the Dragon, the Snob, the Villainess and the Victim are copied here on earth; and it is with these prototypes that I shall round off my study. We shall now soar far above the prosaic scrutiny of flesh-and-blood women with emotions, salaries and headaches, into the airy regions of disembodied Powers.

From one point of view, these archetypal governesses are frivolous. They are neither serious nor important enough to take their place in our sociological review. Some are caricatures, some are comics and some fairies; and I have tumbled them all together like clowns in a circus-ring, and collectively named them the Grotesques. Many of them, indeed, resemble clowns in embodying a popular lore. They are domesticated monsters, whose antics give release from childhood repressions and fears. They pull faces, and threaten knuckle-raps from harmless rulers, like the actors in a harlequinade with their sausages and red-hot-pokers. Others are literary cartoons or parodies, and I shall take this last class first, as it is, to my mind, the least significant. Let us glance, for instance, at the late Mr. Maurice Baring's *Diary of an English Governess Residing in Paris during the French Revolution*. This lady was engaged by a French Count and Countess of the *ancien régime*; but as she reached their Hôtel on October 7th, 1789, it is not surprising (to *us*) that she should have found the house deserted. As she had ' no command over even the elementary rudiments of the French language, and as the French never trouble to learn any language but their own ', she found it difficult to communicate with the *concierge*. But this did not trouble her, any more than her first supper, which she described as ' insufficient and badly cooked as all French meals ', or the mysterious emptiness of the house.

Year after year, all through the Revolution, she stayed on alone save for the *concierge* and his wife, until the family found it safe to return in the autumn of 1794. As she never took the trouble to learn French, she never knew what was going on about her. She mistook the fighting in the streets for fireworks, and the worship of Reason in Notre Dame for a ' display of Romish superstition '. When her employers finally returned from England, she showed neither surprise nor curiosity; and she ' respectfully declined ' the Countess's suggestion that she should learn French.

In this sketch of an English Governess, the emphasis lies, of course, on the adjective rather than on the noun. She is prejudiced against foreigners and against ' the sour wine of the country ' because she is English, not because she is a governess. Her indifference to danger is due to English phlegm, based more on English prejudice and ignorance than on English courage. Yet it was this aloofness—this tendency to regard even counts and countesses as ' natives ' —which made English governesses and nannies so popular abroad. It is easy for any foreign governess to impose on her employers, as we have seen in the case of Mrs. Newcome's Mademoiselle Lebrun, who claimed that her father had been one of Napoleon's generals. And an English governess did not even need embroideries of this sort to enhance her snob-value on the Continent. With her ugly clothes and stiff manner, she was patently a *mademoiselle bien élevée* to unaccustomed eyes; and rather than boast of her exalted origin, she could entrench herself behind the conventional English reserve.

Professor Stephen Leacock's Nonsense Novel, *Gertrude the Governess,* is a burlesque of the defenceless governess who marries her boss's son. She starts traditionally as an orphan: for 'Gertrude De Mongmorenci McFiggin had known neither father nor mother. They had both died years before she was born.' And of her father she only knew (like Dr. Watson's bride) that 'he was a high-born English gentleman, who had lived as a wanderer in many lands'.

Like Clara Mordaunt, Jane Eyre, and many another governess, Gertrude saw an advertisement beginning: 'Wanted a governess'. But the list of accomplishments demanded differed in quality (though not in quantity) from the usual run. They comprised 'a knowledge of French, Italian, Russian and Rumanian, Music and Mining Engineering', and exactly coincided with Gertrude's own attainments. She was interviewed by the Countess, who thus fails to qualify as one of our irresponsible employers. 'You are proficient in French?' the Countess asked. *'Oh, oui',* said Gertrude modestly. 'And Italian?' continued the Countess. '*Oh, si*', said Gertrude—and so on, through the rest of the required languages, to the Countess's growing delight.

At Knotacentinem Towers (pronounced Nosham Taws) Gertrude 'passed through a phalanx of liveried servants', and was welcomed by the Countess, who helped to carry her trunk upstairs. 'Her two little pupils became her slaves.

Even the servants loved her.' The gardeners brought her floral offerings ranging from roses to cauliflowers; and Lord Ronald, the Earl's son, was immediately enamoured of her. 'They played tennis and ping-pong in the day, and in the evening, in accordance with the stiff routine of the place, they sat down with the Earl and Countess to twenty-five cent poker.'

At the great Ball, 'Gertrude was the cynosure of all eyes', in the dress which she had contrived 'out of a few old newspapers'; and 'presented a picture of bright, girlish innocence that no one could see undisenraptured'. She turned out, of course, to be the missing heiress whom the Earl was trying to swindle out of her birthright, and whom the Earl had destined Lord Ronald to marry against his will. Again we are reminded of Clara Mordaunt and Jane Eyre, who both inherited fortunes before making their grand marriages; and I am altogether inclined to think that Professor Leacock has found time in his busy life to read a good many of our novels about governesses. Like all good parodies, *Gertrude the Governess* reveals its author's profound knowledge of its originals.

Miss Prism, immortalised in Oscar Wilde's comedy *The Importance of Being Earnest,* is a multiple monster with Dragon's eyes, the voice of a Loved Companion, the tail of a Villainess, the feet of the Downtrodden, and the undulating back of the Snob.

Her Dragon aspect is displayed by her governessy injunctions to Cecily, her pupil: 'You will read your Political Economy in my absence. The chapter on the Fall of the Rupee you may omit. It is somewhat too sensational.' The siren voice of a Loved Companion is audible mainly to Dr. Chasuble, the vicar, who described her as 'Miss Cardew's esteemed governess and valued companion'; and who said, 'Were I fortunate enough to be Miss Prism's pupil,

I would hang upon her lips', adding hastily, when the lady glared, 'I spoke metaphorically.'

The scaly tail of the Villainess is exposed by Lady Bracknell, who describes her as 'a female of repellent aspect, remotely connected with education', and accuses her of kidnapping a baby in her youth. Finally, the feet of the Downtrodden are betrayed when it becomes apparent that Miss Prism had not only mislaid the baby, but had done so while degraded to the humble position of pram-pusher or nursemaid; and the Snob is betrayed by the way she crumples up before Lady Bracknell's accusation.

Miss Prism, as one would expect of Oscar Wilde, is the most highly stylised of the Grotesques. I am afraid my fanciful portrayal of her as an heraldic creature or one of Ezekiel's beasts, has blurred her portrait. But it is her inner self that I was trying to express, her essence as a governess; and not her body, which (as we know) was clothed in a bustled dress and buttoned boots. As for her ideas on education and deportment—these, I think, are implicit in her implied descent from Mrs. General and her 'prunes and prism'.

I am exempting my Grotesques from the ban on period reconstructions, since they are all ideal figures existing outside time. For the same reason, I am not taking them chronologically in order of publication. My next example, for instance, is a modern one, drawn from Mr. T. H. White's ingenious fantasy, *Mistress Masham's Repose,* published in 1946. Maria, the heroine of this story, was twelve years old, the orphaned heir to a stately home set amid prospects, pleasaunces, temples, ruins, gazeboes and triumphal arches. Her guardian, the vicar, was in league with Miss Brown, the governess, to rob Maria of all she had. They were also greedy to catch and exploit the Lilliputians whom Maria discovered on an island in the lake. The villains, however (both 'so repulsive that it is difficult to write about them fairly'), were eventually routed and discomfited by Maria, helped by a professor, the cook, and the Lilliputians themselves.

Miss Brown—who is the prototype of all sadistic governesses and has much in common with Mr. White's witches—had been the vicar's matron when he was housemaster at a public school. 'When she sat down, she spread as a toad does on the hand', and she was 'cruel in a complicated way'. For instance, she made Maria wear football boots to church, and had 'a quick pounce of the ruler, like a toad's tongue catching flies'. Her personal belongings, in addition to various 'instruments for spying', included a collection of 'frills and fichus' which reminds us of Madame de la Rougierre. Though she was herself toad-like in texture, she was addicted to spiky accessories. She had 'thirty pairs of pointed shoes', and 'grey toque hats with pins in them'; and she knitted with 'long, sharp needles which clicked'. She wore 'hard rings, sunk in fat fingers', and her bedroom 'smelt of unused purses locked away in lavender and naphthalene'.

She was, moreover, a hypocrite, who read devotional books when laid low by one of her headaches. She professed a love of flowers and 'would tell anyone who chose to listen that the Dear Little Roses were her greatest joy'. She would spend a happy evening, eating chocolates 'with a kind of disdainful greed', and playing hymn tunes on the piano. Miss Brown was, in fact, a very wicked governess indeed, who shut up her pupil in the deepest dungeon, and even thought of murdering her. She is the personification of the powers that be and that abuse their power. Maria fought against her for the Lilliputian colony as a revolutionary fights for the Cause. Miss Brown is seen from the day-dream point of view of a child, and as a child's fantasies often have a masochistic tone—blending martyrdom with heroism—Maria naturally suffered torture at her hands. Quite as naturally, Maria endured imprisonment and starvation without flinching, and refused to betray her comrades. As in most normal day-dreams, right ultimately triumphs over wrong, and the wicked governess meets the same fate as witches, ogres, dragons and all devouring monsters.

From the most modern of our Grotesques we now return to the earliest—and also to Thackeray, who must, I think, have a special *penchant* for governesses. In the introduction to *The Rose and the Ring* (1854) he told his readers how he had spent Christmas 'in a foreign city where there were many English children', and of 'his friend Miss Bunch, who was governess to a large family that lived in the *piano nobile* of the house'. Miss Bunch begged him to 'draw a set of Twelfth Night characters' for the amusement of the young people. She was (he said) 'a lady of great fancy and droll imagination, and having looked at the characters, she and I composed a history about them, which was recited to the little folks at night, and served as our FIRE-SIDE PANTOMIME'. It almost looks as though, in the composition of this story, Thackeray had a dual personality consisting of an author and a governess—of Mr. Michael Angelo Titmarsh and Miss Bunch. Between them, they certainly cut out a most animated, tuppence-coloured pantomime figure of a governess in the person of the 'severe Countess Gruffanuff'.

Now, the Princess Angelica's 'accomplishments were announced to be even superior to her beauty; and governesses used to shame their idle pupils by telling them what the Princess Angelica could do'. But in reality, of course, she could only answer Mangnall's Questions if you asked her the right ones; and, though clever, she was '*as idle as possible*'. For Gruffanuff confined her duties to holding a sunshade over her charge's face, and telling her that she was 'a generous darling'. The Countess was, moreover, 'no better born than many other ladies who give themselves airs; and all sensible people laughed at her pretensions'. She was (as we all know, I hope) really Mrs. Jenkins Gruffanuff, wife to the palace porter whom the Fairy Blackstick had transformed into a knocker.

Gruffanuff was snobbish and spiteful. She took the waif Betsinda's little shoe and ragged mantle, and put them in a glass case 'in order that the little girl should not become too proud and conceited'. Gruffanuff was dishonest and designing. She had laid her hands on all the 'jewels, laces, snuff-boxes, rings and watches which belonged to the Queen, Giglio's mother'; and she therefore hated Giglio and did all she could to spite him, because she had done him a wrong. Only when she had become temporarily attractive, after picking up the magic ring, did she change her tactics and trick the Prince into a promise of marriage. She was a hypocrite who persuaded Giglio to sign this promise, under the pretence that it was an order 'for giving coals and blankets to the poor, this cold weather'.

She was also a bully and a tyrant. When Betsinda pleased her, she gave her an old ring, and told her graciously: 'You may unrip my green silk, and then you can just do me up a little cap for the morning, and then you can mend that hole in my silk stocking', speaking for all the world like old Miss Crawley to her sweet, useful Becky Sharp. And when Betsinda fell into disgrace, the cruel Countess called her a 'wicked beast' and a 'filthy hussy'; and after tearing the clothes off her back, drove her out into the cold street with a poker.

Gruffanuff was a hideous old hag. Yet she was vain, and always 'glad of an opportunity of decorating her old person with her finest things'. When she dressed herself up for her expected marriage to King Giglio, she wore 'a low white silk dress, with lace over, a wreath of white roses on her wig, a splendid lace veil, and her yellow old neck was covered with diamonds'. So that everyone said: 'What a figure of fun Gruffy is!'

But Gruffy was ruthless, as she showed on that same occasion of Giglio's wedding. 'I should like to know who else is going to be married if I am not?' shrieks out Gruffanuff. 'I should like to know if King Giglio is a gentleman, and if there is such a thing as justice in Paflagonia?' And she asked the Lord Chancellor and Lord Archbishop if they were going to 'sit by and see a poor, fond, confiding, tender creature put upon'. And she flourished Giglio's written promise in their faces. 'Phoo! the horrid old wretch!'

We all know (I hope) how she refused to be bought off, assuring her reluctant bridegroom that 'with thee and a cottage thy Barbara will be happy'; and how she was finally put down by the Fairy Blackstick's intervention. Her overthrow, as 'JENKINS GRUFFANUFF once more trod the threshold off which he had been lifted more than twenty years ago', is the uproarious overthrow that awaits all Pantomime Dames. Thackeray's stagecraft has once again achieved a quintessential governess, even though she is quintessentially Grotesque.

When I first read *The Water Babies* by Charles Kingsley, at the age of seven, it awoke in me dim yearnings after 'other worlds than this'; and I still fall an easy prey to its sentimental, wholesome and utterly Victorian mystery. I think its moral escaped me at the first reading: it did not make me want to be good, which is odd, as I was a sanctimonious child. Instead, it started me dreaming, and made me want to set out—like Tom—upon a quest.

Nor did I then think of Mrs. Bedonebyasyoudid as a governess, any more than I conceived of her as Conscience or Experience, or any other of the abstractions which she suggests to-day. Yet a governess she certainly was, in her 'black bonnet and . . . black shawl and no crinoline at all'; to say nothing of her 'pair of large green spectacles, and great hooked nose'. If any further symbol of office is required, it is afforded, surely, by the great birch rod which she carried under her arm.

Mrs. Bedonebyasyoudid is a mythical figure—a Norn, an Erinye, a Goddess of Justice. She is also mystical; being immanent in the subconscious mind and yet transcending space and time. 'Every one', she explains to Tom, 'tells me exactly what they have done wrong; and that without knowing it themselves. I am the best friend you ever had in all your life, but I cannot help punishing people when they do wrong. I am as old as Eternity and yet as young as Time.' She warns by example and punishes by retribution. But she cannot compel people to face facts or to make themselves whole men; and sometimes she cannot teach them 'save by the good old birch rod'.

Not only is Mrs. Bedonebyasyoudid a primitive goddess: she is a part—with the fairy Doasyouwouldbedoneby and Mother Carey—of a trinity of goddesses. And in their various manifestations all three preside over the Schoolroom of the Universe, evolving new species, effacing corrupt civilisations, and teaching the lessons of clean living and fair dealing. Like all good governesses, Mrs. Bedonebyasyoudid inspires her pupils to learn for themselves, and to face life bravely and kindly; but she is unique in teaching these lessons to the whole creation.

Both in *Wonderland* and *Through the Looking-Glass,* lessons provided Alice with an ever-lively theme for argument. She discussed them with the Mock Turtle, at the Mad Tea-party, with the two Queens, and endlessly with herself. In spite of this emphasis on lessons, it appears uncertain whether Alice had a governess. Her old nurse is mentioned several times. And as Alice's sister was grown-up, and her brothers (who collected sticks for the bonfire) probably learned about 'Oh mouse!' at school, it would appear unlikely that Alice had a governess as well as a nurse, all to herself.

We know that at one time she went to school. For when the Mock Turtle claimed to have had the best of educations, since he went to school every day, she retorted: '*I've* been to a day-school, too, you needn't be so proud as all that.' On the other hand, her discussion with the Gnat suggests that she may, after all, have had a governess. Expounding its thesis that it may be convenient not to have a name, the Gnat says: 'For instance, if the governess wanted to call you to your lessons, she would call out "Come here ——", and there she would have to leave off, because there wouldn't be any name for her to call, and of course you wouldn't have to go, you know.' 'That would never do, I'm sure', said Alice: 'The governess would never think of excusing me lessons for that. If she couldn't remember my name, she'd call me "Miss", as the servants do.'

It is certainly clear from this that Alice knew something about governesses. Perhaps one of her little friends had one—though I hope, for the honour of governesses, that it was not Mabel, who knew 'such a very little'. Or perhaps Alice had had one in the past herself. The point which makes me doubtful of this governess's real existence when Alice spoke, is that Alice refers to her as 'the' governess and not 'my' governess, as she surely would have done had such a person awaited her behind the looking-glass. Alice's choice of pronoun suggests to me that she—like the Gnat—is taking for argument's sake the case of a purely hypothetical governess; and that she talks of 'the Governess' as Socrates talked of 'the Good Man' or 'the Tyrant'.

Be that as it may, I am not proposing to include this

shadowy figure among my Grotesques, and no other governess is mentioned under that name in either of the books of Alice's adventures. There is, however, a character in *Through the Looking-Glass* of whom Lewis Carroll wrote himself that 'she must be formal and strict, yet not unkindly; pedantic to the tenth degree, the concentrated essence of all governesses'. And this character is, of course, the Red Queen.

Look at her picture, talking to Alice in the garden! As she says 'look up, speak nicely, and don't twiddle your fingers all the time', her right forefinger is shaken in admonition. (In passing, I wonder that neither Tenniel nor Carroll remembered the logical necessity for Looking-Glass characters to be left-handed.) Her skirts are folded orderly, her chignon is firmly netted, and her crown is fixed with uncompromising rectitude upon her head. She looks every inch the governess! She speaks like one, too, and is a stickler for clear enunciation and correct forms of address: 'Open your mouth a *little* wider when you speak, and always say "your Majesty".' The biscuit which she good-naturedly gives Alice to quench her thirst, is as dry as the information which old-fashioned governesses gave their pupils when they thirsted after knowledge. And all their narrow self-assurance is expressed in her brisk question, 'Thirst quenched, I hope?'—to which she fortunately did not expect an answer. There is something of a governess's complacent heartiness, too, in the assumption that in the Eighth Square it will be 'all feasting and fun'.

Yet when Alice finally arrives at the Eighth Square and they are 'all Queens together', the Red Queen is more of a governess than ever. 'Ridiculous', she cries to Alice's argument about no one speaking until spoken to; '"Why, don't you see, child—" here she broke off with a frown, and after thinking for a minute, suddenly changed the subject of the conversation.' Is this not the unmistakable technique of a governess who sees that a child's logic is unanswerable, yet will not admit her own fallibility? She evens treats the White Queen as if she were a backward pupil: 'She never was really well brought up, but it's amazing how good-tempered she is! . . . A little kindness—and putting her hair in papers—would do wonders with her.'

The Red Queen 'takes up' Alice's remarks even more than the other inhabitants of Looking-Glass Land—which is saying a lot. She contradicts automatically and on principle. She exploits her position as Queen and crypto-governess to the full, exacting the respect which no one thinks of paying her White compeer or even her Consort—unless he is asleep. She is as unyielding as her own crown, and as dry as her own biscuit. She measures, directs and encourages like Miss Plimsoll on the site of the Hut. And like so many of Lewis Carroll's adorable creations, she is strictly logical—with a logic which is based on false premises.

In every word and gesture, the Red Queen is indeed 'the concentrated essence of all governesses' of the governessy type. It is therefore fitting that her 'formal and strict, yet not unkindly' figure should stand as tail-piece, not only to the Grotesques, but also to the whole CHAPTER OF GOVERNESSES.

of a [illegible] who [illegible] [illegible] [illegible]
ver will [illegible] [illegible] [illegible] [illegible] the
White Queen [illegible] [illegible] [illegible] [illegible]
was really [illegible] [illegible] [illegible] [illegible]
[illegible] [illegible] [illegible] [illegible]
but in [illegible] [illegible]

The Red Queen [illegible] [illegible] [illegible]
than the [illegible] [illegible] [illegible] [illegible] [illegible]
[illegible] [illegible] [illegible] [illegible] [illegible]
principles [illegible] [illegible] [illegible]
purposes [illegible] [illegible] [illegible] [illegible]
think of [illegible] the White [illegible] [illegible]
unless [illegible] [illegible] [illegible] [illegible]
out at any [illegible] [illegible] [illegible]
[illegible] [illegible] [illegible] [illegible]
[illegible] [illegible] [illegible] [illegible]
[illegible] [illegible] [illegible] [illegible]
[illegible]

In [illegible] and [illegible] the White Queen [illegible]
the [illegible] [illegible] [illegible]
[illegible]. It is [illegible] [illegible] [illegible]
[illegible] [illegible] [illegible] [illegible] [illegible]
only to the [illegible] [illegible] [illegible] [illegible]
[illegible].